Sin, Shame, and Secrets

Sin, Shame, and Secrets

The Murder of a Nun,
the Conviction of a Priest, and
Cover-up in the Catholic Church

David Yonke

continuum
NEW YORK • LONDON
www.continuumbooks.com

The Continuum International Publishing Group,
80 Maiden Lane, New York, NY 10038

The Continuum International Publishing Group Ltd,
The Tower Building, 11 York Road, London SE1 7NX

Cover art: Father Gerald Robinson conducts the funeral Mass of Sister Margaret Ann Pahl on April 8, 1980. Twenty-six years later the priest was convicted of murdering the nun. The funeral was held April 8, 1980, in St. Bernardine's Chapel, Fremont, Ohio. Sister Margaret Ann's casket, draped with a pall, is visible in the foreground. The *Toledo Blade* Photo by Lee Merkle. Reprinted with permission.

Photo insert: All photos are the copyright of the *Toledo Blade*, used with permission, except #16, photo by Oblates of St. Francis de Sales religious order.

Cover design: Lee Singer

Library of Congress Cataloging-in-Publication Data

Yonke, David.
  Sin, shame, and secrets : the murder of a nun, the conviction of a priest, and cover-up in the Catholic Church / David Yonke.
    p. cm.
  Includes bibliographical references and index.
  ISBN-13: 978-0-8264-1755-8 (hardcover)
  ISBN-10: 0-8264-1755-8 (hardcover)
  1. Murder—Investigation—Ohio—Toledo. 2. Catholic Church—Ohio—Todedo—Clergy—Sexual behavior. I. Title.

HV8079.H6Y66 2006
364.152'3092—dc22

                                    2006024393

Printed in the United States of America

06 07 08 09 10 11   10 9 8 7 6 5 4 3 2

"Be sure your sin will find you out."

Numbers 32:23

Foreword

For more than a decade, I've been reporting on criminal trials across the United States for Court TV. Many of the murder cases have recurrent motives, greed and revenge, being the most common. Defendants and victims also fall into general categories, husband kills wife, mother kills child, pedophile sexually abuses then kills a child, to name just a few.

I traveled to Toledo, Ohio, in April 2006 to cover a remarkable murder trial that may or may not fit into the common categories for motive and certainly does not fit into the more common category of defendant/victim (except perhaps the most general, as prosecutor Dean Mandros said: "an angry man kills a woman"). A Roman Catholic priest was arrested in April 2004, for the murder, twenty-four years earlier of a nun in what many believe was the first such arrest and prosecution in the United States. That trial ended in May 2006 with the conviction of the sixty-eight-year-old priest, Father Gerald Robinson, who was sentenced immediately to fifteen years to life in Ohio's State Corrections prison system.

In the book you are about to read, David Yonke, the *Toledo Blade* religion reporter who attended the trial every day and had access to people and files far beyond the evidence introduced at trial, describes the 1980 crime, the initial investigation, and its rebirth in late 2003 from the Toledo police department's cold case files, and finally the trial. You will learn more than the jurors did about the Toledo diocese's response to the murder investigation in what some characterized as a cover-up or, at a minimum, a lack of total cooperation. Yonke describes extraordinary, unrelated allegations of sexual abuse by Father Robinson and other priests in the diocese. You will also learn about the decisions prosecutors made as to whether to charge Father Robinson, when to charge him and what motive, if any, to present to the jury.

I call this a remarkable trial simply because it was a priest accused of the vicious murder of a nun—a most unlikely scenario—which, were it not true, would be hard to imagine even in a work of fiction. Adding to the compelling nature of the case are the details of the crime: Sister Margaret Ann Pahl was strangled and stabbed thirty-one times with a letter opener (nine times through the chest in the shape of an inverted cross), apparently anointed with her own blood, and positioned and assaulted in such a way as to humiliate the virginal nun. All this took place on Holy Saturday in the sacristy of a chapel and in the presence of the Holy Eucharist. Why that day, that place, that victim, that weapon and in that manner?

Yonke answers those questions when he describes the motive that the prosecutors chose not to present. Every detail of the murder—from choice of the victim, the location, the date, the weapon, the shape and placement of the stab wounds to the position of her body—convinced more than a few people intimately familiar with this case that Father Robinson performed a classic satanic ritual murder. Yet the prosecutors did not try this case as a ritual murder or Black Mass. Why not? Mandros says, and rightly so, that they needed to present a case that twelve people could agree on; to suggest that a priest performed a satanic ritual murder on a nun may have been too difficult for all of them to comprehend. And so, the twelve jurors who sat in judgment of Father Gerald Robinson did not have to grapple with satanism, ritual, or Black Mass. But questions remain about whether this murder was as simple as an angry man killing a woman—or something much more sinister.

Beth Karas
Court TV

Acknowledgments

There is an army of people who have helped me along the way and I am grateful to all of them.

In regard to the task of getting this book into print, I must thank my agent extraordinaire, Sorche Fairbank of Fairbank Literary Representation in Cambridge, Massachusetts, and my editors at Continuum International Publishing Group, Henry Carrigan and Amy Wagner.

I am thankful to Diane Higgins for the initial inspiration and encouragement to undertake this project.

My editors at the *Blade* have been supportive and enthusiastic from the start and I thank them: John Robinson Block, Roy Royhab, Kurt Franck, Luann Sharp, Jim Wilhelm, Nate Parsons, and Wes Booher, and I appreciate my colleagues who graciously shared their resources and expertise, including Mark Reiter, Robin Erb, Christina Hall, Andy Morrison, and Allan Detrich, and my former Blade compadres Mike Sallah and Mitch Weiss. I would also like to thank Dawn Perlmutter, John Connors, White Knannlien, and Bill Gray.

Thanks to Beth Karas of Court TV for her outstanding coverage of the trial and for her willingness to write the foreword.

I want to thank the many people who took time out from their busy schedules to answer my questions and provide information for the book and for related work as religion editor, including Prosecutor Julia Bates, Sergeant Steve Forrester, Dean Mandros, Brad Smith, Dave Davison, Deputy Police Chief Ray Vetter, Dr. Henry C. Lee, Claudia Vercellotti, Jeff Anderson, Father Thomas Doyle, Sally Oberski, Father Jim Bacik, Catherine Flegel, Lee Pahl, Linda Waters, J. Christopher Anderson, Tony Comes, Barbara Blaine, David Clohessy, Teresa Bombrys, Barry Hudgin, Father Michael Billian, Father Stephen Stanbery, Father Patrick Rohen, Catherine Hoolahan, and Sister Jane Doe (Mary Curtiss) and Survivor Jane Doe. I greatly appreciate Fritz Byers' expert legal advice.

On a personal note, I want to thank my Lord, Jesus Christ, from whom all blessings flow; my patient and supportive wife, Janet; "the Fabulous Yonke Girls"— Dana, Lisa, and Cara; my loving siblings Rick, Paul, Elaine, and John; and my pastor, the Reverend Chad Gilligan, and all the "prayer warriors" at Calvary.

I am grateful to my parents, Ferdy and Lil, my godfather Artie Lauer, my brother Roy, and my lifelong friend, Tom Donovan—five special people who shaped my life beyond measure and who have gone on to glory.

Introduction

On the afternoon of Friday, April 23, 2004, as I was sitting in my cubicle winding up another week as religion editor of the *Blade*, the daily newspaper in Toledo, Ohio, police reporter Christina Hall stopped in.

"What do you know about a Father Gerald Robinson?" she asked me.

"Not much," I responded. "He's kind of a quiet guy. You don't see him around much. I've heard rumors about him but nothing recently. Why do you ask?"

"Because I think he's about to be arrested—for murder," Chris said.

That conversation marked the start of an amazing journey, one that had more twists and turns than a thriller by Dan Brown or John Grisham.

But this was not fiction.

Father Robinson was arrested that Friday and charged in the Holy Saturday, 1980, murder of Sister Margaret Ann Pahl.

It was, as far as we can tell, the only time a Roman Catholic priest in the United States had been charged in the murder of a Roman Catholic nun. Perhaps the only time, anywhere.

The murder was one of the most sensational cases to ever hit Toledo, but to have an arrest more than two decades later, and to have the suspect be an active Catholic priest made it the kind of news story that comes along once in a lifetime.

The next day, I met with cold-case investigators Tom Ross and Steve Forrester, who said the slaying appeared to be part of a ritual.

When I reported that allegation, I began receiving emails and phone calls from journalists and readers literally around the world.

I have spent the last two and a half years researching this story, though hampered by a gag order imposed by the judge that barred everyone involved in the case from speaking to the media.

I dug up as much background as possible, but the bulk of the information came out during and after the trial, which started April 17, 2006.

Today, sixty-eight-year-old Father Robinson is serving a life sentence inside a dank, maximum-security prison in Lebanon, Ohio, and plans to appeal the conviction.

This book chronicles the bizarre and disturbing story that includes allegations of satanic rituals, human sacrifices, and child sexual abuse, as well as evidence of a cover-up by church and law-enforcement officials.

At the same time, I am quick to remind readers that the vast majority of Roman Catholic priests are unselfish, dedicated servants of God who devote their lives to providing spiritual guidance and help to their parishioners and working for social justice.

Sin, Shame and Secrets is not a blanket condemnation of the Catholic Church, but a factual account of the horrific deeds of a few lone wolves who hid among the sheep.

These are the worst perpetrators in society because they abuse their position of authority as representatives of Jesus Christ, and their abuse can destroy people's souls as well as their minds and bodies.

The struggles that the Catholic Church has endured at the dawn of this millennium have provided an opportunity for growth and change. I hope and pray that church leaders' promises of openness and transparency will come to pass and lead to a new era of healing and spiritual power.

The more than 1 billion Catholics would not be the only ones to benefit. The changes would make this world a better place for all.

David Yonke
Sylvania, Ohio
August 6, 2006

Chapter 1

At precisely 5:00 a.m., the buzz of Sister Margaret Ann Pahl's alarm clock punctured the cool predawn stillness. It was Holy Saturday, the day before Easter and her seventy-second birthday. On Holy Saturday, unlike most days, there was no early morning Mass at Mercy Hospital, just a late afternoon service. Sister Margaret Ann reached for her alarm clock, switched it off, and rested her head on the pillow.

Were it any other day, the petite nun with the gray-rimmed glasses would have been up at the first buzz of the alarm clock, preparing for her day's duties as the sacristan—in charge of preparing the chapel for services—at Mercy, a Catholic-run hospital with a convent on the top floor and two chapels. Most days, Sister Margaret Ann was at work before dawn preparing the chapels for religious services—checking supplies, making sure there were plenty of consecrated Communion hosts and sufficient amounts of wine, incense, and candles. As part of her morning duties, she cleaned the chapels and the rooms next door—the sacristies—where she laid out the priests' vestments, polished the gold chalices and crucifixes, smoothed the linen altar cloths, and trimmed the candlewicks.

But Holy Saturday was always so different. On this morning, the only task Sister had ahead of her was to strip the altars of all religious decorations, a symbol of the somberness of the day and a reflection of Christians' mourning over the death of their Savior.

At 5:30 a.m., a second, hand-wound alarm clock clanged to life in the nun's spartan seventh-floor room. Her extra thirty minutes of rest had ended.

Rising quietly, the diminutive sister walked down the hall to the shower room, washed quickly, and slipped into the Sisters of Mercy uniform she had worn nearly all her life—a blue sleeveless jumper over a white blouse, with a black veil tucked over her white hair.

The first-floor wing of the hospital, where the main chapel was located, was unusually quiet that morning. Most of the nuns and the student nurses were either sleeping late or gone for the weekend, visiting relatives for Easter, and the hospital workers were at minimal staffing for the holiday.

Sister Margaret Ann walked to the nuns' dining area down the hall, picked up an empty green food tray, and carried it to the sacristy next to St. Joseph's Chapel, the last room in the hospital's west wing.

In the small sacristy—the preparation room lined with dark wooden cabinets and cupboards—she placed cleaning cloths, incense, a metal Paschal candle cover, a box of waxed paper, and a brown paper bag on the green tray, then carried it to a wooden pew in the chapel's front row for the work she had ahead of her.

With the sun climbing above Toledo's boxy skyline, Sister Margaret Ann made a quick trip back into the dining room and ordered breakfast from the only other person in the room, Audrey Garroway, an always-smiling cafeteria worker who had emigrated from Jamaica. The nun ate her usual breakfast—grapefruit, raisin bran, and coffee—quickly and in silence.

At approximately 6:45, Sister Margaret Ann finished her meal and rose from the table.

"It's time to go fix up the chapel," she said to Audrey, flashing a bright smile as she headed out the dining room doors.

Back inside the familiar confines of the chapel, the elderly nun slid a wooden chair next to the altar. She put a footstool in front of the chair, placed a sheet of newspaper on top of the seat so as not to scratch it with her shoes, and stepped up on the chair so that she could reach the drapes behind the altar.

First she took the gold crucifix and chalice off the altar, carefully carrying them into the sacristy and placing them in a small cabinet. Then, reaching as high as she could, she began pulling straight pins and peeling masking tape off the cloths and the wall to take the drapery down from behind the altar.

Sister Margaret Ann, approaching retirement, had become increasingly hard of hearing in recent years. She kept putting off retirement, however, because her work as the hospital's sacristan was fulfilling. It kept her busy and it was much less stressful than her previous jobs as a nurse, teacher, and hospital administrator.

The hearing problem was a concern, however. She was having more and more difficulty carrying on a normal conversation.

On this Holy Saturday morning, she walked into the sacristy to put away the candles and genuflected before the Blessed Sacrament, which was being kept in the sacristy until Easter.

The nun did not hear the sound of another person behind her, someone walking quietly, carefully, through the door from the chapel into the sacristy.

As Sister Margaret Ann stood on her tiptoes to reach a shelf in one of the cabinets, she felt the faint brush of a piece of cloth whisk over the top of her head. Startled, she instinctively dropped her chin as a defense mechanism, but the cloth had already closed around her neck.

She tried to turn around, but she could not move her head. The attacker snapped the cloth tight, so tight that the two small bones in the nun's neck broke in half. Caught under the cloth was a silver necklace and cross the nun always wore, and when the assailant pulled the cloth even tighter, the necklace pressed into her flesh, leaving an impression all the way around.

The small, elderly woman flailed her arms weakly, trying to reach around behind her, but it was impossible. In a matter of seconds, her body went limp.

Her assailant gave a final, mighty squeeze, then lowered the nun onto the sacristy's cold terrazzo floor. She was still alive, but just barely.

Kneeling over her body, his mind a dull roar, like a freight train was roaring through it, the assailant removed the cloth from around Sister's neck and unfolded it. It was a large, white linen altar cloth. He carefully laid it out, folded it over once, and draped it over Sister Margaret Ann's motionless torso.

He took a crucifix from the cabinet and, whispering in Latin, placed the cross directly over Sister Margaret Ann's heart—upside down.

As the attacker leaned over the nun's body, he reached into one of his pockets and took out a sword-shaped letter opener. It glinted silver in the dim glow of a streetlight.

Holding the dagger in both hands, he raised his arms up, looked heavenward, spoke again in Latin, and brought the knife down with a sick thud, piercing the altar cloth and the nun's chest. When he pulled the blade out, a small spot of blood seeped through the altar cloth.

Again, the killer lifted the blade high and brought it down with a snap, stabbing the nun just above the collarbone. Again he lifted the weapon and plunged it into her chest, repeating the motion until he had stabbed Sister Margaret Ann nine times.

The nine wounds made a specific shape along the outside of the inverted crucifix that had been placed over her heart.

The murderer then pulled the altar cloth back and stared at the nun's familiar face. He reached into a small duffel bag he had brought with him and took out a gold chalice, pressing it against her chest. He wanted to collect some of the blood in his golden cup, but the nun's heart had been barely pumping.

There was hardly any blood to be seen.

Enraged, the killer raised the knife again and stabbed Sister Margaret Ann in the left side of the chest. Again, he reached up and slammed the letter opener down into her chest. And again, but this time in her neck. The infuriated assailant kept lifting the blade and stabbing the comatose woman in left side of her chest, neck, and face—a total of twenty-two stabbings after the altar cloth was removed.

The killer then took the letter opener and pressed its handle and the side of its curved blade against the nun's bloodstained dress, covering it with blood. Then he pressed the handle against Sister Margaret Ann's forehead and said a prayer— anointing his victim to his dark lord.

He stood up. A surge of spiritual power rose through his veins. The lamb has been slain. The perfect sacrifice. This would give him great strength.

He looked down at the lifeless body and felt a sense of rage seeping into his brain. No, he was not yet finished.

He knelt down at his victim's side and carefully rolled the hem of her dress up onto her chest, folding it up neatly, little by little, until it was up to her bra. Then he reached down, grabbed her girdle and pantyhose, and yanked them down toward her knees.

He was surprised at how difficult it was. Her motionless body was heavier than it looked. Her girdle clung tightly to her body. But he pulled her undergarments down, the rage still pouring through his brain. He pulled the girdle and underwear all the way down to her ankles and then off of her left leg, until they were dangling around her right ankle.

Now his victim, this virginal nun, this servant of God, this perfect sacrifice whom he killed on Holy Saturday, right in front of the Holy Eucharist, was lying there, exposed.

He took the crucifix, gripped it tightly, and slipped it inside her.

"Here!" he said. "Here! This is your God. Hanging lifeless on the cross. See what good he did for you? You spent your life serving him. Here's what I think of you and your God. Here's what I think of your church."

The killer took the crucifix and placed it in his duffel bag. He picked up the altar cloth and tucked it under his arm. Then he walked through the sacristy door, hearing it lock behind him, into the chapel, past the rows of pews, and through the wooden doors into the dimly lighted hospital corridor.

In the weeks and months following the murder, detectives checked hundreds of leads, interviewed more than six hundred people, and investigated dozens of suspects, including the nun's colleagues and the hospital chaplains.

Many disturbing questions surfaced.

Why was a frail, elderly nun so brutally murdered on Holy Saturday? Who could have committed such a heinous crime? Was it someone she knew, someone who hated her so much he went into a frenzy and stabbed her thirty-one times? Was this actually a ritual killing, performed as a sacrifice to Satan?

Despite the numerous leads, within a week, police said they had only one suspect: Father Gerald Robinson, Mercy Hospital's chaplain. But there was no eyewitness to the murder. Police and prosecutors felt they did not have enough evidence to make an arrest.

The case grew cold. The altar cloth, the letter opener, the victim's clothes—they were all placed in storage in the basement of the Safety Building.

Rumors surfaced every now and then that a suspect was being investigated. Eventually, the detectives who investigated the case all retired. The murder that had made front-page news was now a faded memory.

Then, twenty-four years later, on April 23, 2004, two investigators with the Lucas County cold-case squad knocked on the front door of Father Gerald Robinson's house in West Toledo and charged the Toledo Roman Catholic priest with murder in the 1980 slaying of Sister Margaret Ann Pahl.

Chapter 2

Mercy Hospital, an imposing, seven-story beige brick-and-stone building, looms high over the low-slung homes and scattered businesses along tree-lined streets on the edge of downtown Toledo.

Operated by the Sisters of Mercy, a Roman Catholic religious order whose mission is to help the sick and the underprivileged, the hospital was built in 1914. Although it was just a mile from the city center, in those days it was considered to be in the suburbs.

Today, Toledo's suburbs start fifteen miles from downtown and the wood-frame homes and tiny yards around Mercy are part of an inner-city neighborhood, complete with the usual urban crime and violence.

Families in need of low-priced housing and senior citizens clinging to their childhood homes live side by side with crack dealers and gang members. At night, prostitutes strut along the sidewalks and teens wearing their gang colors go to war to protect their turf.

In 1980, the top floor of Mercy Hospital was a convent that served as the secluded, tranquil home for seventeen Sisters of Mercy nuns. All trained nurses, the sisters lived and worked amid the sick, wounded, dying, and grieving people who came to Mercy Hospital for medical—and spiritual—help.

The sprawling seventh floor of the hospital was the nuns' little oasis. Each sister had her own room—small and simple, with a bed, a nightstand, a dresser, and a closet. On the pale green walls of each room hung a wooden crucifix.

The nuns had their own small chapel for daily prayers, and the convent included two kitchens, a commons area, a large bathroom with tile floors, multiple sinks and showers, and a row of stalls.

In the bright, window-laden commons area, the nuns would watch television, listen to the radio or records, and read the Bible or other books while sitting in their own personal rockers or recliners.

Shirley Ann Lucas, who worked as a housekeeper at Mercy Hospital, used to come to the convent every Monday, Wednesday, and Friday afternoon to clean.

After lunch, the short, stocky worker would push her cart full of cleaning supplies into the elevator and ride to the seventh floor, where she walked down the hallway to the convent door and rang a buzzer.

"Whoever was up there would look through a little peephole," recalled Lucas, a tender-hearted woman who took great pride in her work. "If you were a good person, she would let you in. If you weren't, I guess they would leave you stay out there."

Now in retirement, Lucas fondly recalled the many hours she had spent scrubbing and dusting the convent.

"It was real quiet. It made you feel good to be up there," she said.

The one who supervised her work was Sister Margaret Ann Pahl, a retired hospital administrator, teacher, and nurse—and a stern taskmaster.

"She was very, very strict," Lucas said. "Very firm. Things had to be done a certain way."

Lucas learned quickly that Sister Margaret Ann was not about to overlook work that failed to meet her standards.

"She would come and tell you if you didn't do things right," Lucas said.

"When I first started up there, they had little sample bars of soap, I call them. And there was very little on some of them and I threw them away and put fresh on. And some of the toilet tissue that had maybe only a couple of sheets on it, I threw those away and put fresh on."

Two days later, when Lucas rang the buzzer at the convent door, Sister Margaret Ann let her in.

"She was waiting for me," Lucas recalled. "She took me into the bathroom, showed me how to take those old soaps and press them together. And not to empty the toilet paper rolls when there was one sheet on it," Lucas recalled, feeling both embarrassed and surprised by the nun's frugality.

Three decades earlier, Sister Margaret Ann—known at the time as Sister Mary Annunciata until changing back to her given name in 1968—had held the top position at Mercy Hospital in Tiffin, Ohio, as its supervisor and administrator. She later served as supervisor and administrator of a larger hospital, St. Charles in Toledo.

When she was in her sixties, Sister Margaret Ann stepped down from the high-powered hospital administrator posts and began easing into retirement.

Starting in 1971, she served in the pastoral care department at Mercy Hospital and was given the important role of sacristan, making sure that everything was in order for Mass and for all other religious services held in the hospital's St. Joseph's Chapel.

Sister Margaret Ann approached her role as sacristan with the same zeal and strictness with which she had run two hospitals.

It didn't take long for Shirley Ann Lucas to adjust to Sister Margaret Ann's critical eye. Of all the Mercy nuns at the hospital, Sister Margaret Ann seemed the most devout and serious. Lucas felt like the nun sometimes treated her coldly, but it was just the way she was. It was not mean-spirited.

The other nuns showed more compassion and interest in her life, Lucas said. She felt comfortable talking to most of them about her personal problems, and the nuns would offer advice and prayers.

Sister Margaret Ann, however, would just give orders on what needed to be done that day when she cleaned. She was all business and rarely had time for idle chitchat.

One spring afternoon, however, while Lucas was cleaning one of the bathtubs in the convent, Sister Margaret Ann turned on the stereo and began playing a Verdi opera.

Sister Margaret Ann, walking down the hallway, peeked her head inside the bathroom door.

"Do you like opera music?" she asked Lucas.

"Yes, I like some opera music," the housekeeper replied. "Not all of it."

"Who is your favorite opera singer?" the nun asked.

"I like Elvis Presley when he sings 'How Great Thou Art,'" Lucas responded.

Sister Margaret Ann's eyebrows arched. She looked hurt and angry.

"Catholics should not listen to that rock and roll singer!" she said, frowning.

The nun was from the old school, believing that the loud music and singer's gyrations were evil.

"I made a big mistake," Lucas said in retrospect. "I think the sister felt he was a little too wiggly."

Chapter 3

Like all the Sisters of Mercy living in the convent at Mercy Hospital, Sister Madeline Marie Gordon normally would get up before dawn to prepare for the 6:00 a.m. Mass.

There were only a few days of the year when the nuns did not have to rise at 5:00 in order to say their daily office, or prayer routine, before Mass.

One such exception was Holy Saturday. The only chapel service that day would be held later in the afternoon.

One of the holiest days on the Christian calendar, Holy Saturday falls between Good Friday, when Christians around the world reflect on Jesus' death on the cross, and Easter Sunday, the day they celebrate his resurrection.

On the chilly morning of April 5, 1980, Sister Madeline Marie was glad for the the luxury of an extra hour's sleep.

When her alarm clock went off at 6:00, she was in no hurry to get ready. She reflected on the significance of Holy Saturday as she got dressed, donning her blue habit with the black veil and pinning a gold crucifix on her lapel. When she walked through the sanctuary of the quiet convent into the main hospital, she glanced at her watch. It was a little after 7:00 a.m.

A soft-spoken and thoughtful woman with a round face and cat's-eye glasses, she rode the elevator down to the first floor and, as she stepped out, she noticed a stranger walking past. Odd, she thought. She had never seen this man before. She couldn't tell if he was a light-skinned black man or a dark-skinned Latino. The stranger was neatly dressed and had short black hair, but what she noticed most was his thin lips.

For some reason, she told herself to make a mental note of the strange-looking man, then continued to the nun's dining room, where she ordered grapefruit, coffee, eggs, and toast. The stack of plates on the counter was already down low, she noticed. Some of the Sisters had already been here, keeping their early-morning routine even on Holy Saturday.

Sister Madeline Marie walked to a table and sat down, thinking it might be nice to eat breakfast alone today. She didn't have many moments of solitude and she was feeling in a prayerful mood.

But her quiet breakfast ended abruptly as soon as Father Jerome Swiatecki entered the room.

"Hello, Sister!" the big priest boomed. "Hang on, I'll be right with you."

One of two Roman Catholic chaplains at Mercy, Father Swiatecki was impossible to ignore. For starters, he was a very large man, about six feet tall and well over 250 pounds, with an oversized belly that gave his black priest's robe an oval shape.

The priest, with a high forehead and short, dark hair slicked straight back, loved being around people and loved to talk. The jovial father could hold a conversation with anyone, on just about any subject.

Sister Madeline Marie thought it was good to have a priest like Father Swiatecki around the hospital. Unlike Mercy's other chaplain, Father Robinson, a small and quiet man who was often aloof and cold to coworkers and patients alike, Father Swiatecki was easygoing and always eager to talk with ailing patients and their worried families.

When he wasn't comforting and counseling patients, he was talking about sports or current events. Father Swiatecki had a way of getting people's minds off their troubles, which, in a busy city hospital, was a trait that came in handy.

Now the priest was pouring himself a large cup of coffee and heading over to the nun's table with three frosted doughnuts on his tray.

"Good morning, Sister Madeline Marie! How are you this fine Holy Saturday morning?" Father Swiatecki asked, a big smile stretching across his face. "I'll bet you enjoyed that extra hour of sleep today— I know I sure did."

"Yes, Father, it truly was a blessing to be able to sleep in today," she replied politely.

"You work too hard, Sister," he said. "You deserve a break. Probably should take a vacation, don't you think? But not today, of course. Not Easter weekend!"

He laughed at his observation.

"You're sure going to be busy tonight and tomorrow," he said. "What are you planning to play on the organ for the Holy Saturday service?"

"As a matter of fact, Father Swiatecki, I need to get down to the chapel and make sure the sheet music is all ready for the service. That's exactly where I'm going after breakfast."

Father Swiatecki took a huge gulp of coffee from the white ceramic mug, sighed loudly, and took a bite from a doughnut.

Suddenly, he waved an arm in the air.

"Hey, Sister Madeline, what do you think about that Mount St. Helens? That volcano really is making a lot of noise lately. Think it's going to blow soon? Today, maybe?"

"I don't know, father, I'm afraid I haven't been keeping up with it."

"Well, it's a scary thing, Sister. That volcano keeps spitting out more and more smoke and more and more ash. It's rumbling and shaking like it's about to blow sky high. I'd sure hate to be anywhere near it when it finally flips its lid. Aren't you glad we don't have volcanoes here in Holy Toledo?"

"Yes, that I am, thank the Lord," she said, nodding her head. "No volcanoes. Just tornados and floods and icy roads and blizzards. But nothing like a volcano. Wouldn't that be awful! Those poor folks in Washington State."

Sister Madeline Marie took her last bite of toast and a sip of coffee, and then stood up from the table.

"Well, if you will excuse me, Father, I'd better get down to the chapel. I'll see you at the service later," she said.

Sister Madeline Marie picked up her tray and placed it on the conveyer belt that rolled it back into the kitchen. Then she headed to the chapel.

The nun could see that the chapel doors were open and the lights were on.

As she walked down the hall toward the brightly lighted room, Sister Madeline Marie noticed a white cloth lying on the floor, just outside the wooden doors.

Strange, she thought, housekeeping must have dropped a pillowcase. She bent down and picked it up, folded it over, and tucked it under her arm.

As she entered the chapel, Sister Madeline Marie was struck with an eerie feeling, one that she could not explain.

She saw Sister Phillip sitting in one of the front pews, praying silently, and as she walked through the chapel doors she placed the pillowcase on one of the back pews.

Sister Madeline Marie looked around the chapel and noticed that the St. Joseph statute on the side altar to the right was partially draped with white cloth. It was a Holy Saturday tradition to strip the altars bare and take down the chapel decorations, a way of mourning Christ's death on the cross.

Good Friday is a day of incomparable grief for Christians, recalling how the Lord, Jesus Christ, the Son of God, was nailed to a cross, spat upon, crowned with flesh-piercing thorns, and willingly went to his death to bring forgiveness and salvation to humanity.

On the day after Good Friday, Holy Saturday, Jesus' body remained wrapped in burial cloths in the tomb while his mother and his followers mourned his death.

Today, Catholics strip the altars in churches around the world, temporarily removing all symbols of joy or triumph, until the Blessed Sacrament—the very body of Christ—is returned to the tabernacle during the evening vigil, awaiting Jesus' resurrection.

Sister Madeline Marie spotted a green cafeteria tray in the front pew, filled with pins and candles, tape and cloths, and other small items used in preparing the altars. Sister Margaret Ann must have been here and used the tray to carry the items in and out of the sacristy as she prepared for the services, she thought.

But the decorations were only half done, and Sister Madeline Marie saw no sign of Sister Margaret Ann. It was not like the hard-working nun to stop in the middle of a job. She must have been interrupted. Maybe there was an emergency. Or maybe she left to get some tools or materials.

Sister Madeline Marie knelt down in the first pew.

She pulled out a small rosary made from wooden beads from a dress pocket and began reciting her morning prayers, speaking softer than a whisper. She was speaking to God alone.

"Hail Mary, full of grace, the Lord is with thee, blessed art thou amongst women and blessed is the fruit of thy womb, Jesus. . . ."

When she finished the set of prayers to complete the rosary, Sister Madeline Marie went over to the organ to check on the sheet music for the upcoming service. Going over the list of hymns, she saw that there was nothing written down about the closing song. Father Robinson, who selected the music, must have forgotten to write it down, she thought.

She felt she'd better give the priest a call and find out now, in case it was a song she didn't know and needed to practice.

It was 8:15. She looked for a phone to call his residence, just a short walk down a few hallways and through a covered walkway.

Sister Madeline Marie walked over to one of the two wooden doors that opened into the sacristy, the closest room that had a telephone. But the door was closed and locked. Why would Sister Margaret Ann close the door if she was going back and forth between the sacristy and the chapel to get ready for a service? It didn't make sense to lock the door unless she had gone up to the convent on the seventh floor and didn't want to leave the room open while she was not around.

Sister Madeline Marie reached into her pocket for her keychain, found the one to the sacristy, and slipped it into the keyhole. She gave the key a turn and pushed the door open.

The room was dark; as she stepped inside, she noticed something on the floor. The hospital had been conducting CPR classes and it looked like somebody had left one of the CPR practice dummies in the sacristy.

With the window shades down and the lights turned off, the only light coming into the room was from the chapel behind her. Sister Madeline Marie bent down to take a closer look at the dummy, lying with its arms straight by its side and its legs straight out.

Suddenly, the nun jumped back in horror.

She turned and raced into the chapel, screaming hysterically.

Sister Phillip, an elderly nun who had been praying in the front pew, jumped up, startled, and looked wide-eyed at the screaming nun.

"What's wrong, Sister Madeline Marie?"

The hysterical nun motioned toward the sacristy door, wildly waving an arm as she struggled for words.

"Sister Margaret Ann—has been raped!" she yelled, then resumed screaming.

Sister Phillip grabbed the nun by the shoulders and looked in her eyes and saw sheer panic. She gave Sister Madeline Marie a gentle nudge, sitting her down in the front pew, then turned and ran into the sacristy.

Sister Phillip looked down and gasped in horror. Sister Margaret Ann, wearing her dark blue habit, was lying, motionless, on the terrazzo floor. It was dark but the nun could see, shockingly, that Sister Margaret Ann was lying there exposed—her dress was pulled up around her chest and her girdle and underwear were down around an ankle.

As the sacristy door clicked shut behind her, she reached over and flipped up a light switch. Sister Margaret Ann's arms were lying straight by her sides. Her legs were flat on the ground, pointed straight out from her body. Her thin face was badly swollen. She saw many small red marks on her face—stab wounds, she thought—and blood, a dark red stain, spreading in a semicircle around the neck of her dress.

Sister Madeline Marie, meanwhile, was still screaming uncontrollably in the chapel, her voice echoing throughout the west wing of the hospital's first floor.

Most of the hospital offices on the floor were empty, it being the Saturday morning of Easter weekend, but a small group of nuns and Father Swiatecki had heard the desperate shrieks and came running from the dining room down the hall.

"I heard this terrible screaming," Sister Phyllis Ann Gerold recalled later. "We ran to the chapel. I didn't know what had happened. I kept asking Sister Madeline Marie what happened. Finally, she said Sister Margaret Ann was on the floor of the sacristy."

Sister Phyllis Ann, the administrator and CEO of Mercy Hospital, looked at the sacristy door and noticed that it was shut. She raced over just as Sister Phillip popped open the door from within and emerged, screaming.

There on the marble floor was Sister Margaret Ann's body, lying stretched eerily out in the center of the sacristy.

Sister Phyllis Ann's first instinct was to try to save the nun's life, she said, but almost immediately she realized that Sister Margaret Ann was beyond any earthly help.

The realization that it was too late to save her friend and colleague gave way to a sick feeling in the pit of her stomach. Sister Phyllis Ann was shocked and disgusted by the scene in front of her. She had worked as a nurse for decades and had seen hundreds of dead patients, but this scene in the sacristy was unlike anything she had ever witnessed.

"The horror, the horror. It was just the weirdness of it," she recalled. "The first afterthought was, 'Why?' There was a ritualistic kind of layout of the dead body. It was so neat and so different."

The way that Sister Phyllis Ann's arms and legs were so straight, it just seemed unnatural to her.

"People don't usually die very straight," Sister Phyllis Ann said.

And it was strange that there was so little blood, she thought, especially with all the stab wounds in the nun's upper body.

Sister Margaret Ann's blue dress, with her gold cross on its lapel, had been neatly folded up around her chest. Her girdle, underwear, and stockings had been rolled down and were wrapped around her right ankle, exposing her pubic area.

Sister Phyllis Ann turned and left the sacristy to get help. She saw Sister Mary Flora standing in the chapel by Sister Phillip and told her to have the operator announce a "Mr. Swift" call on the public address system—a hospital code that a person is in dire need of emergency medical help. When a Mr. Swift call comes over the air, all medical personnel know they are to drop everything and rush to the victim's aid.

At about the same time, in a hospital cafeteria downstairs that was open to the public, two Toledo police officers were finishing their breakfast at the end of a midnight-to-8:00 a.m. shift.

The telephone rang loudly in the mostly deserted room and a cafeteria worker picked it up. Waving the receiver in the air, she called to the police officers: "It's for you."

Officer Dan Deeter looked over at his partner, Officer Dave Davison, and said, "Don't answer it. You know it's going to be something screwy—a fight in the emergency room or something."

It was after 8:00, and the two cops were done for the day. The last thing they needed was to have to step in and break up a fight between a couple of beggars or drunks, then have to stick around a few more hours to fill out the paperwork.

Davison, however, felt a sense of duty, as usual, and walked over to the phone, shaking his head at Deeter.

"Sorry, partner, I just have to."

It was a call that caught him completely by surprise.

"Someone said a nun died in the chapel," he recalled years later. "And right when I hung up, a nurse came running into the cafeteria and said, 'We've got a dead nun in the sacristy.' We're thinking it must have been a heart attack or a stroke, because a lot of the nuns were old ladies."

The two policemen and the nurse ran out of the cafeteria and raced up a flight of stairs, then down the hall to the chapel. They saw Sister Madeline Marie sitting in a pew, sobbing, her tear-streaked face buried in her ands.

The sacristy door was open, and they could see a woman's legs stretched out on the floor.

They hurried through the door into the small side room.

"I knew right away it wasn't a heart attack or a stroke," Davison said. "There was blood and you could see stab wounds and the nun's panties were pulled down around her ankle."

By the time the two officers got there, one of the Sisters of Mercy had pulled the victim's dress back down to cover her genitals, but the undergarments were still around an ankle.

Davison reached down to check for a pulse and was surprised that the body was already cold and clammy.

Just then, the first medical doctor arrived, out of breath, and knelt beside Sister Margaret Ann's body.

He touched her wrist and, without a word, shook his head sadly.

Too late.

A dozen more doctors and nurses began hurrying into the chapel, carrying their medical bags and equipment. Someone had pushed a cart into the chapel laden with needles, smelling salts, gauze, and all kinds of emergency supplies.

Davison waved them all away from the sacristy.

There was nothing they could do for the woman now, he told them. The police officer ordered them to wait in the hallway, outside the chapel doors, while Deeter went to call 212—the code for the detectives' bureau—at the switchboard.

"Tell 'em we have a murdered nun," Davison said.

Just then, Father Jerome Swiatecki, the assistant chaplain, ran into the chapel, gasping for breath.

One of the nuns took his arm and told him that Sister Margaret Ann had just been murdered—and maybe raped.

The big bear of a priest, usually so joyful and loud, turned white as a sheet. Sister Phyllis Ann, half his size, grabbed his left arm, afraid he might fall backward.

Father Swiatecki's perpetual smile had turned into a frightened scowl. His shoulders slouched, his knees wobbled.

"Where—where is she?" he asked, and gulped.

"In the sacristy," Sister Phyllis Ann replied, pointing.

The priest turned and looked at the sacristy. A policeman was standing by its open door. Behind the officer, stretched out on the floor, he could see the thin legs of an elderly woman. He took a step, paused, then walked into the room.

Officer Davison nodded at the priest, stepping aside.

Like most clergy who serve in hospitals, Father Swiatecki had seen many deaths during his time as a chaplain. He had never become callous or immune, but over the years he had developed a sense of acceptance. It was part of life. The last part.

But this time, the burly priest found himself fighting back tears as he knelt beside Sister Margaret Ann's body.

He reached into a pocket and took out a small vial of anointing oil, twisted the cap open, and put a dab on his index finger.

The priest reached over and touched Sister Margaret Ann's forehead, making the sign of the cross with the oil on his finger.

"Through this holy anointing, may the Lord in his love and mercy help you with the grace of the Holy Spirit," Father Swiatecki said, his voice trembling as he recited the sacrament of the sick and dying. "May the Lord who frees you from sin save you and raise you up."

The priest bowed his head reverently, and continued in prayer.

Officer Davison, waiting for detectives to arrive, had stepped outside of the chapel and began chatting "off the record" with some of the nuns and hospital workers he had told to wait around to be interviewed.

"I asked everyone who did this, and they all said, 'Robinson' or 'the priest,'" Davison recalled.

He was worried that in the chaos of the moment—discovering a nun was dead, calling for medical help, and finding out she had been murdered—the nuns and hospital workers might have erased some clues.

"We sealed off the room as soon as we could to try to keep the crime scene from being contaminated. But by then a bunch of the nuns and all the doctors and nurses had already been in the room," he said years later, recalling the events.

The killer's fingerprints could have been smeared or footprints blurred by the stampede of nuns and medical workers trying to help.

Chapter 4

About ten minutes after the Mr. Swift call, five Toledo police detectives walked briskly into the chapel. Sergeant Arthur Marx, an athletic cop with a thick wave of black hair, was the lead detective. Assisting were Tom Staff and Larry Przeslawski, detectives with the crimes against persons unit, Detective Dan Foster of the sexual assault unit, and evidence technician Ed Marok.

Sergeant Marx told Sister Phyllis Ann that the police department would be setting up a command post, and she suggested they use the hospital's first floor boardroom, just a few doors from the chapel.

A veteran detective regarded by many colleagues as a "cop's cop," Sergeant Marx had investigated hundreds of homicides and had a reputation for being a bulldog when it came to investigating a murder. He also was one of the few officers in the department who had used deadly force, fatally shooting a naked, drug-crazed kidnapper who had surprised him in a dark hotel room, and wounding a burglar who picked up a gun and, despite Marx's stern warnings, pointed it at him.

Marx also moonlighted in a men's clothing store and got his tailored suits at discount prices. There was never any doubt that he was the best-dressed detective on the force.

One thing Marx never did was play games with the honchos in the front office. He resented it when the pencil-pushers tried to tell him how to do his job in the real world. His attitude could rub some bosses and colleagues the wrong way—they'd say he was arrogant. But Marx was a straight cop who worked hard and got the job done.

Marx asked Davison and Deeter for a rundown on what they had seen when they arrived at the chapel.

Davison was a veteran and a tough policeman, but when he was telling Marx about the nun's murder, he felt a wave of emotion. The nun's brutal murder bothered him in a way unlike any other crime he had handled.

"That poor woman, she deserved a better fate than this," he told Marx.

As he looked at the nun's bloody corpse, Davison vowed to himself that he would do everything he could to catch the sick person responsible for such a senseless crime.

Just then, the police radio crackled to life. A black man was acting suspiciously down at the Greyhound bus station, less than a mile away.

Marx pointed at Davison and Deeter.

"Check it out," he said. "Hurry. And don't take any chances. The killer is still on the loose, you know."

Davison opened his mouth to protest, but Deeter cut him short with a look. The two cops headed to their patrol car and drove to the downtown bus station.

No one at the Greyhound station knew anything about a suspicious character. No one acknowledged calling the police.

After wasting about twenty minutes talking to people who knew nothing about anything, Davison and Deeter headed back to the police station to sign out.

Years later, Davison said he had doubts about the police investigation right from the start.

"My partner and I basically found the nun, and then they pulled us off within half an hour to go down at the Greyhound station to look for a black man?" he said with disbelief. "We were the first ones on the scene. You'd think the detectives would have wanted us to stay. They could have sent any crew to the bus station."

Ten years after the murder, when Davison had retired on disability and did not have to fear harassment from his bosses, he launched a one-man crusade to reopen the investigation into Sister Margaret Ann's murder.

Davison wrote letters to the police chief, the mayor, the Ohio governor, the state attorney general, the U.S. attorney general, the President, and even Pope John Paul II, asking them to intervene and reopen the investigation into the nun's slaying.

He told everyone who would listen that the police and the Toledo diocese conspired to protect Father Robinson, trying to spare the Catholic diocese from the scandal of having one of its priests charged with murder.

"After the murder, we continued to work the night shift in that district and the only place to go for meals was Mercy Hospital," Davison said. "Everybody was talking about it. Everybody said the priest did it. The people at Mercy, they hated him. They just hated him."

He was convinced that the Toledo police department had tried to do whatever it could to keep the priest out of jail and to protect the reputation of Catholic Diocese of Toledo, one of the area's most influential institutions with connections to all levels of power in all walks of life.

Most of the top-ranking police officers were Catholic. So was the Lucas County prosecutor in 1980. And many of the judges.

The Catholic Church had the City of Toledo wrapped around its little finger, Davison said.

They certainly didn't want to arrest a priest for such a brutal crime. It would have been the biggest embarrassment in the history of the Toledo diocese, which was founded in 1911. Police never really looked hard for the nun's killer because they were afraid their investigation would lead them to someone they did not want to arrest—Father Gerald Robinson, Davison said.

While Davison and Deeter were out on their wild goose chase at the bus station, Sergeant Marx ordered Foster, Staff, and Przeslawski to begin interviewing all the nuns, doctors, nurses, and hospital workers who may have seen anything unusual.

Marx and Marok headed for the sacristy to begin looking for clues, analyzing evidence, and preserving the crime scene.

"Christ, look at this," Marx said, shaking his head. "The poor old lady."

He knelt beside the body and gently lifted her right arm. It was cold to the touch, but there was no sign of rigor mortis. He looked at his watch—8:45.

Marok opened his tool bag and took out a large Horseman camera, loaded a roll of black-and-white film, and started snapping photos of the nun and the surroundings.

"I don't know why they don't let me use color film," he griped to Marx, leaning over to take a picture of Sister Margaret Ann's blood-smeared face. "You can't capture all this stuff in black and white. Look at that dress—it's gonna look gray, not blue, in the photos."

"Yeah, I know you're right, Ed, but don't let it get to you," Marx replied. "Just take the photos. You know what headquarters says—they think color photos are too graphic for juries. Yeah, right! Just another genius decision from on high. I think the real reason is that Chief Bosch has a weak stomach."

Marok continued taking photographs from every possible angle, each flash of the camera going off with a loud pop.

After taking a series of photos of Sister Margaret Ann's face, he began to step back, photographing the body from different angles and distances.

Marok then took photos of the sacristy's furniture, windows, cabinets—everything in the small room he could capture on film

Not knowing exactly what to look for, Marok was aware that his photos might somehow, someday, provide important evidence. Since the clues were not apparent to him at the moment, he figured he'd better take pictures of everything.

Marx, meanwhile, was walking around the nun's body with a pad and pen in hand, taking down detailed notes.

The sacristy was approximately eleven feet wide and seventeen feet long. A small porcelain sink was on the south wall. There were dark wooden cabinets and drawers on most of the walls. A wooden crucifix hung above the sink. A shade had been pulled down over one window, the one on the north side of the room overlooking the parking lot. There were three small tables and one chair in the room.

The only thing out of place in the room was a telephone sitting on the floor, in front of the window. Marx wasn't sure why at the time, but eventually concluded that Sister Margaret Ann moved the phone so she could use the table to hold items she needed for the chapel as she removed them from the sacristy's cabinets and drawers.

Marx noted that Sister Margaret Ann's body was lying completely straight, in the very center of the floor. The only sizable amount of blood was an oval-shaped pool, about nine inches around, beneath her head. Not much blood for a multiple stabbing. Her gray-framed eyeglasses were lying on the floor, eight inches from her right hand, with smudges of blood on the right lens.

The victim's dress was heavily stained with blood in the upper left side of her chest. He touched the bloodstains with the tip of his finger—they were still moist.

He noted numerous puncture-type wounds on the left side of the nun's face and neck, and that there appeared to be traces of blood on her forehead and on the bridge and tip of her nose.

A long white linen cloth, which later was determined to be an altar cloth, was wrapped around the sister's right forearm. The cloth had puncture-type marks and bloodstains.

Sergeant Marx noted the victim's clothing: a blue jumper-type knit dress, a white long-sleeved blouse, a blue slip, and a white bra. Her gray pantyhose and a white elastic girdle had been pulled down and were wrapped around her right ankle. The nun's blue oxford shoes were still on her feet, laced and tied.

There were no visible signs of a struggle in the sacristy and no defensive wounds on the nun's body, Marx wrote.

When Marok was finished taking photographs, he opened his case and took out an evidence kit. The lab technician began checking the sacristy for latent, or hidden, fingerprints.

He was able to detect a few partial prints on the chapel side of one of the two wooden doors to the sacristy. He also found a partial print on a plastic box that the nun had used while preparing the altars.

When Sister Madeline Marie told Marx that she had seen a strange man walking down the hallway from the chapel toward the Madison Avenue exit, the detective sent Marok down the hall to check the exit doors for fingerprints.

Another hospital worker said she had seen a black man in the hallway attempt to walk into the planning office, and Marok checked its door for prints.

About scouring for prints, hairs, and any other trace evidence, Marok returned to the chapel to brief Sergeant Marx.

"I found eight prints on the glass exit doors," he said. "They're not good enough to make a positive identification with, but we can use them to eliminate suspects. And I found one hair on the planning office door. I'll send it to the crime lab for tests."

Sergeant Marx told Marok to start packing up his gear. That was the end of the search for physical and trace evidence. The police would now focus on interviewing people who may have seen something or someone of interest.

About 10:30 a.m., the coroner's office sent a crew to the hospital to remove the nun's body.

Valerie Berning, a 23-year-old Mercy housekeeping aide, was working in a different wing of the hospital when her pager went off. It was her boss, Vern Boeke. She found a phone and dialed his number, and he told her to get a bucket and mop and some cleaning solution and meet him in the chapel, pronto.

The nun's body had been removed, but there was cleaning to be done. Boeke told her to get to work and not to say a word.

"There was a lot of blood," Berning recalled. "It was pooled in the middle of the floor. There was some blood in the sink. Vern told me to just do my job and keep my mouth shut."

A few days later, Berning was assigned to clean the two-room hospital residence of Father Robinson. Her supervisor had signed out a key from the maintenance department and opened the priest's apartment door for her.

It was mid-afternoon and the priest was gone—the residence was empty. Berning began walking around the small apartment, picking up dirty towels and dropping them into her laundry cart.

She made the priest's bed and fluffed the pillows.

When she turned around, she spotted a silver, nine-inch-long, sword-shaped letter opener sitting on top of Father Robinson's desk.

Berning gasped and stepped back, bringing a hand to her mouth in horror.

"When I seen that letter opener, I just had bad feelings and I walked out of the room," Berning said. "I never went back."

Chapter 5

In the first few hours after the murder, Sergeant Marx and his team of detectives interviewed two dozen people. They wanted to quickly sift through the obvious, and not so obvious, questions: Who could have brutally killed a 71-year-old nun? Why? And why did the killer leave the sister lying there, half naked, exposed to God and the angels and whatever poor soul would walk in and find her?

In his experience investigating homicides, Marx felt it was safe to assume that the perpetrator was someone who knew Sister Margaret Ann Pahl.

Either that, or the killer was someone with severe mental problems.

Most murderers use just enough force to kill their victims. A bullet or two, a few jabs with a knife, a couple of blows to the head with a blunt instrument, or enough squeezing around the victim's neck to take his or her life.

This case was different. Bizarrely so.

The nun was elderly, frail, and small—only about five feet two and 135 pounds. He guessed the killer's first move was to grab Sister Margaret Ann from behind, around the neck, and choke her with extreme force. There were severe bruises on the sides of her neck, small red marks on her face that usually come from asphyxiation, and broken blood vessels in her eyes—all signs of strangulation.

The choking itself was probably enough to kill the old lady. And if he strangled her first, before the stabbings, it would explain why there wasn't much blood at the scene. Her heart was not pumping, or just barely, when the attacker stabbed her over and over and over.

But then, even more bizarrely, he pulled her girdle down and neatly folded her dress up over her chest, leaving this godly woman in a death pose that was humiliating and degrading.

He really must have hated her.

If it was a stranger who killed her, his guess was it was an escapee from the psych ward or a guy freaked out on smack or PCP, someone so out of touch with reality that he had no idea what it would take to kill the nun. He kept stabbing and stabbing until he was certain, beyond any doubt in his twisted mind, that she was dead.

Maybe he had some kind sexual problem, some kind of arrested development, the psycho-sexual maturity of a child, and pulled her underwear down for a forbidden look.

If the killer was some random mental case, he could have wandered into the chapel while Sister was working. The hospital was a magnet for weirdos. And it was in the middle of a decaying neighborhood. Security was tight, for the most part, but there were too many doors and stairs and elevators to keep it completely sealed.

Maybe the killer had wandered into the chapel looking to steal some gold chalices or other valuables. Maybe he had a drug habit and needed a fix. The nun might have given him a dollar or two and thought he was gone, or threatened to call security. He started to leave, then turned around and snuck up on her, grabbing her from behind.

There were a lot of possible scenarios. Marx walked out of the sacristy, through the chapel doors, and over to Sister Phyllis Ann Gerold's office across from the chapel.

The administrator of the three hundred-bed hospital, Sister Phyllis Ann was one of the few nuns who had kept calm during the emotional chaos after the murder. She had tried to comfort Sister Madeline Marie, who had found her friend's body, and after it was clear that Sister Margaret Ann could not be revived, she immediately went to her office and began making phone calls.

First, she called Sister Margaret Ann's sisters and relatives in Edgerton, Ohio, her hometown about an hour and a half west of Toledo. Then she called her superiors in the Sisters of Mercy religious order, whose U.S. headquarters are in California and international offices in Dublin, Ireland.

When she realized that the hospital's chaplain, Father Gerald Robinson, was nowhere to be seen, she called his residence on the first floor.

The 41-year-old priest, a Toledo native who had been assigned to Mercy for six years, answered the phone and said he had just gotten out of the shower and was drying off.

When Sister Phyllis Ann told him that Sister Margaret Ann had been murdered and possibly raped in the sacristy, Father Robinson said he would get dressed and hurry down to the chapel.

He never did arrive.

Sergeant Marx knocked on Sister Phyllis Ann's door.

"Come in," said the nun, putting down the phone.

"Hello, Sister," Marx said. "I know this is a difficult time for you and everyone at the hospital, but the killer is still on the loose and I need to get right down to business."

"Yes, of course, how can we be of help?" Sister Phyllis Ann replied.

"First of all, I am drawing up a list of people we want to interview. We're looking for doctors, nurses, nuns, priests, janitors, anybody who may have been working this morning and who may have seen something unusual. Also, I'm looking for anyone who may have seen Sister Pahl alive this morning—I want to know when and where they saw her and who she was with, if anybody.

"I'd also like to retrace Sister Pahl's steps, from her room on the seventh floor to the sacristy, and everywhere in between, as best as we possibly can."

"Certainly, Sergeant Marx. We have personnel files on everybody who works at the hospital. I'll get the books for you."

The sergeant and the sister started by going down the list of the Sisters of Mercy who lived in the convent and worked in the hospital. Without thinking, Sister Phyllis Ann included Sister Margaret Ann's name in the list. Awkwardly, she stared at the name, then lifted the pen and went to cross it out.

"It's okay, sister. Just keep her name there," Marx said, lifting his hand.

There were seventeen nuns on the list.

"How many priests work at the hospital?"

"Just two," Sister Phyllis Ann replied. "Father Swiatecki—Jerome Swiatecki—and Father Gerald Robinson."

"Do they live here, or in a rectory somewhere?" Marx asked.

"Yes, they do live here. They both have their own apartments. Father Swiatecki's is on the second floor, above the chapel. Father Robinson's is on the first floor, in the professional building."

After listing all the nuns and priests, Marx put the paper aside.

"Okay, that's a start. And that was the easy part, I'm afraid to say. Now, how can we get a list of the hospital workers who were in the building today? I need all the employees, including the doctors and nurses, plus all the nursing students."

Sister Phyllis Ann put her pen to her lips and paused.

"Here are the names of the people who I, personally, saw in the hospital today, not counting the sisters and the priests," she said, then started writing swiftly. Within a few minutes she had compiled more than thirty names.

Sister Phyllis Ann then began browsing through a file drawer full of manila folders, found the one she wanted, and flipped it open. It contained personnel files for Mercy's nursing students—thirty-two girls in all. They lived in the dormitory on the hospital's fifth floor, although most of them were home for the holiday weekend.

It was going to take a lot of time to talk to all these people, Marx thought.

He took a piece of paper and made four columns: one for each of the detectives. Then he wrote the names down underneath each detective, dividing them up as evenly as possible. These were the people he considered a priority to interview.

"We'll start with these and see what we find," Marx told Sister Phyllis Ann. "Now, can you fill me in on Sister Margaret Ann? Where is she from? What is she like? Who were her closest friends? Did she have any enemies?"

Chapter 6

Margaret Ann Pahl was born April 6, 1908, in a wood-framed farmhouse near the village of Edgerton, Ohio.

The fertile farmland, alongside the St. Joseph River and not far from the Indiana border, is subject to the severe swings of northern Ohio's climate.

From the searing heat of summer to the stinging cold of winter, weather is always a challenge for Ohio farmers.

When Margaret Ann Pahl was a child, horses and mules were used to plow the land in the spring, and horse-drawn reapers harvested the crops in autumn.

"We grew up a lot like the Amish live now," said Catherine Flegel, Sister Margaret Ann's younger sister and one of nine Pahl children.

Their parents, Frank and Catherine Pahl, owned two hundred acres of farmland, on which they grew wheat and corn and raised chickens, cows, and horses.

When Margaret Ann and her eight siblings were growing up, the farm had no electricity.

Kerosene lamps provided light at night, and heat came from an iron pot-bellied stove, stoked with wood.

The wood-frame farmhouse did not have indoor plumbing, and the family used an outhouse in back, near the barn.

Margaret Ann was a lot like all the other Pahl children. Sturdy. Quiet. Resolute.

On schooldays, the children would rise before daybreak to take care of their chores. The boys tended the horses; the girls milked the cows.

"I used to milk three cows every morning before school and in the evening when I got home from school," Flegel recalled.

At harvest time, the Pahl children also helped to shuck the grain.

After their morning chores, the youngsters would walk a mile and half to a red, one-room schoolhouse, where they learned to read and write, solve math problems, and memorize Bible verses.

Some of the Pahls' cousins were priests and nuns, and the family members were regular attenders at church.

"Our parents were very sincere," Flegel recalled. "I don't think they missed many services."

While Margaret Ann was a devout Roman Catholic, during childhood she never seemed outwardly zealous about her faith, according to her sister. Hers was a deep-seated belief in God, and she knew from early childhood that someday she would be a nun, Flegel said.

"She was just an ordinary girl. She had friends at school. She had a sense of humor. She liked to play. But she always knew what she wanted to do. She'd been called to be a nun," said Flegel, who was six years younger than Margaret Ann.

On September 24, 1927, when Margaret Ann was 19, her parents and younger sisters climbed into their Buick touring car—a boxy black vehicle with flared fenders, wide spoke wheels, and a canvas top—and drove ninety miles east.

Their destination: Our Lady of the Pines, a convent and retreat center on sixty-three wooded acres high atop a hill just south of Fremont, Ohio.

That's where Margaret Ann professed her vows to join the Sisters of Mercy, a religious order founded in Dublin, Ireland, in 1831, by Sister Catherine McAuley.

When the family returned to Edgerton, her sisters were surprised to find that Margaret Ann had left all of her belongings to them, neatly arranged and labeled in her room.

"She was always neat like that, everything just so," said another sister, Mary Casebere, to whom Margaret Ann left a bright red jewelry box.

The mission of the Sisters of Mercy was to help the economically poor of the world, especially women and children, and one of the ways they followed that vision was by founding hospitals. Women who joined the order found that nursing was the perfect way to put their spiritual and professional training to use.

Sister Margaret Ann spent two years as a novice, then three more years in the convent before professing her final vows.

Like all Sisters of Mercy, she took a vow of poverty, chastity, obedience, and service of persons who are poor, sick, and uneducated.

At first going by the name Sister Annunciata, she wore a ring to symbolize that she was betrothed to Jesus Christ.

Her student nursing experience was at St. Rita Hospital in Lima, Ohio, a Sisters of Mercy facility that rushed to open in 1918 so that it could treat victims of the influenza epidemic in Ohio—a global disaster that killed more than twenty million people worldwide.

Sister Margaret Ann's stoic, dependable personality, her intelligence, and her leadership qualities led to quick advancements.

She was promoted to floor supervisor at St. Rita's in 1933, and two years later was transferred to Toledo's Mercy Hospital, where she was appointed assistant superintendent of nurses.

By 1937, after teaching science for one year at Our Lady of Mercy High School in Cincinnati, the 29-year-old nun was named superintendent of nurses at Mercy Hospital, Toledo.

She had also served as nurses' superintendent in Lansing, Michigan, for a year before returning to St. Rita's, Lima, in 1940. Then, two years later, as America was caught up in World War II, Sister Margaret Ann was sent to Tiffin, Ohio, where she worked as floor supervisor at Mercy Hospital in that city about forty miles southeast of Toledo.

In 1948, Sister Margaret Ann was promoted to the top position at Mercy Hospital in Tiffin, serving as supervisor and administrator.

In 1959, she was transferred to Toledo to run St. Charles, one of the city's largest hospitals.

Known for being strict and businesslike but with a heart, Sister Margaret Ann was a woman who got the job done. Setting high standards for herself and those around her, she was quick to let her staff know if they were not meeting her expectations.

"She was from the 'old school' and was a perfectionist," one of her colleagues said. "She demanded that everything be done exactly as she wanted it done—and on time. If persons she dealt with did not do things as she expected, then she would vocally display her displeasure."

Sister Phyllis Ann, the Mercy Hospital administrator, described Sister Margaret Ann as "a devout person" and one who prayed diligently. But she also spoke her mind.

"She was a direct person in other areas. She stated her opinion," Sister Phyllis Ann recalled. "She had been in positions of power, so she stated her opinion."

Sister Margaret Ann was not much for idle hobbies. She devoted her life to serving God, according to her sister, Catherine Flegel, and besides visiting family members in Edgerton—and driving her nephew's Chevrolet Corvette around town—and taking a memorable vacation to Niagara Falls, her only real hobby was opera music.

In 1971, at age 63, Sister Margaret Ann returned to Mercy Hospital in Toledo, this time ready to leave the pressure and stress of hospital administration work behind her, taking a less-demanding but still important job working in pastoral care and as sacristan—the person responsible for keeping the chapel ready for Mass.

As the 1970s progressed, Sister Margaret Ann began to steadily lose her hearing, but she put the same effort and diligence into keeping the chapel clean and ready that she put into running a hospital with hundreds of patients and a multi-million-dollar annual budget.

Serving as sacristan was one more role she could devote to the Lord, to whom she had given her life.

Every day, she made sure that the supplies of Communion wafers and wine, the anointing oil, holy water, candles, and chalices were ready to meet the needs for daily Mass and for the sacraments.

She found it rewarding to rise early each day to clean and decorate the chapel in preparation for the day's services. She knew she was taking care of God's house, and that it was important to God and to his people.

Chapter 7

Sister Phyllis Ann Gerold picked up a thick three-ring binder containing personnel data for 1,400 hospital employees, and pushed it across the desk to Detective Sergeant Arthur Marx.

The notebook was thick and heavy, with the names, addresses, phone numbers, Social Security numbers, and other information for every worker.

Thank God there's no need to interview all these people, Marx thought.

Since Sister Margaret Ann had been killed in the early morning hours on a weekend, his detectives would start out with the employees who worked the night shift, weekends, and holidays. That would trim the list down significantly.

Marx thanked Sister Phyllis Ann for being so helpful and picked up the binder and took it with him to the police command post in the boardroom down the hall.

He called downtown and asked for Deputy Chief Ray Vetter.

A tall, stocky man with a military crew cut, Vetter was in charge of the investigation. That caused some concern for Sergeant Marx, knowing that Vetter was a strong Catholic—which the deputy chief had made clear to every member of the Toledo Police Department over the years.

With a nun being the murder victim, Marx worried that Vetter was really going to take an interest in this case.

Vetter told Marx that he was going to put four detectives on the case full time, starting Monday. He said he was planning to assign Detectives Dan Foster, Dave Weinbrecht, Dale Vaughn, and Lieutenant William Kina to the case.

The investigation would go on as long as necessary, Vetter said, but it sure would be nice to end it today—with an arrest.

Then the deputy chief gave Marx an order that startled him.

"Sergeant, I want all three copies of the police reports from this investigation to be sent directly to my office. Don't separate them. Don't tear them apart—keep the white, pink, and yellow sheets together, and send them right to me," Vetter said.

Marx was silent. Dumbfounded.

"You got that?" Vetter asked.

"Yeah, I got that," Marx said, slowly and deliberately. "Any particular reason for that, Chief?"

"No," Vetter snapped. "No particular reason. Just send me all the copies of all your reports."

"Well then, yes, sir, whatever you say. You're the boss," Marx said.

The forms used by police for their reports came printed in three color-coded pages. The officer who filed the report would keep the pink copy; the department that he worked for would get the yellow copy, and the deputy chief received the white copy.

The standard procedure was that once Vetter finished reading the reports, he would personally hand them to a clerk in the records division, where they would then go into the permanent file.

For Vetter to request all three copies. . . . Well, that was highly unusual. Unprecedented, Marx thought. And highly suspicious.

But time was ticking. He had a murderer loose somewhere in the city. He looked at his watch. It was 10:15.

He needed to take care of one unpleasant item of business that he had promised the Lucas County coroner's office.

Sergeant Marx called Sister Phyllis Ann and asked her to meet him in the sacristy.

When she arrived, he introduced the nun to Tim Fish, coroner's investigator, who said he needed a positive identification of the victim before having the body removed from the sacristy.

Sister Phyllis Ann nodded her head. "Yes, I understand."

"I'm sorry to have to put you through this," Fish said, then slowly pulled back the sheet that had been covering the nun's body

Sister Phyllis Ann raised a hand to her mouth and gasped. It was still beyond belief.

"Yes, that's Sister Margaret Ann—Sister Margaret Ann Pahl," she said softly.

"You have no doubt?" Fish asked.

"No. None at all," Sister Phyllis Ann responded. "That is definitely her."

Fish slid the sheet back over the body.

Sergeant Marx put his hand on Sister Phyllis Ann's arm and gently walked her out of the room.

"Sister, do you have a few more minutes? I'd like to ask you a few questions," he said.

The detective and the nun went across the hall into Sister Phyllis Ann's office, where they were joined by Sister Kathleen Mary Moross, coordinator of the Sisters of Mercy in Toledo.

Sergeant Marx told the nuns that one of the most common motives in murder is robbery or theft—and that perhaps the killer had gone into the chapel looking to steal something valuable, and the crime somehow escalated into murder.

Sister Kathleen Mary said she and several other nuns had talked about that possibility, too. Right after the murder, they looked around for Sister Margaret

Ann's purse and keys but couldn't find them. An hour or so later, one of the sisters found them in a cabinet in the sacristy.

Marx said he had asked Father Swiatecki to conduct a quick inventory of the sacristy, and to try to note anything of value that may be missing. The priest went through the cabinets and drawers and found two gold chalices, a gold crucifix, several gold plates, and a pair of silver candlesticks, all where they belonged.

Sergeant Marx felt confident in ruling out robbery as a motive.

Sister Phyllis Ann told him the only other unusual thing that she was aware of, and maybe it wasn't even worth mentioning, was that Sister Madeline Marie had noticed a clean-cut, dark-skinned stranger walking down the hall, away from the chapel, around 7:30.

But she added that people were always coming and going in the busy hospital, and she wasn't sure if the stranger was even worth mentioning to police.

Sister Madeline Marie, the nun who had discovered Sister Margaret Ann's body, also had found the altar cloth lying on the floor outside the chapel doors. She had picked it up instinctively, as any nun would do when they saw something out of place in the hospital, and set it down on a back pew of the chapel while she prayed.

When she found the altar cloth, it was folded over, and Sister Madeline Marie did not notice any blood at first. She thought the linen cloth was a pillowcase that had fallen from a housekeeper's cart.

About an hour after Sister Margaret Ann's body had been discovered, Sister Madeline Marie picked up the altar cloth from the pew, opened it, and saw all the bloodstains on the white linen. She assumed that it had been used in the emergency room or in surgery, and that it had been dropped by a hospital orderly.

She gave the altar cloth to Robert Shaw, Mercy's security manager, who realized that it might be related to the murder, and promptly turned it over to detectives.

Sister Kathleen, a husky woman with short-cropped brown hair, told Sergeant Marx that she was struggling with the thought that Sister Margaret Ann may have been raped.

"It could have been me, it could have been me lying there in the sacristy," she told him, tearfully.

She said she was feeling guilty that it was such an elderly, devout nun who was raped and killed, and that she was still in shock over the horrifying news.

Sergeant Marx told her that it was only natural to feel that way.

"Sister, do you remember what you did when you first heard the news?" he asked her.

"Yes, I certainly do. I said, 'Damn it!'" Sister Kathleen said, her cheeks turning crimson red.

Two days later, on April 7, 1980, Sergeant Marx picked up the bloody altar cloth that was on a table in the boardroom, folded it and tagged it, slipped it inside a large brown paper bag, and took it downtown with him to the Safety Building. He went to the basement and checked it into the property room, where it would sit untouched for more than twenty-three years.

Chapter 8

The team of five Toledo police detectives conducted more than six hundred interviews over the next three weeks, most of them leading nowhere, but they did scrape together a few clues.

An ambulance driver, Jerry Tressler, told them that he saw Sister Margaret Ann in a ground-floor hallway below the chapel about 6:50 a.m., and that they exchanged greetings. As far as the police could tell, Tressler was the last person—besides the killer—to see Sister Margaret Ann Alive.

A hospital security guard, Robert Wodarski, said he walked past the chapel around 7:00 a.m. and noticed that the doors were open and the lights were on.

An EKG technician, Leslie Kerr, said she punched in at the time clock around 7:00 a.m., walked to her first-floor office, glanced down the hallway toward the chapel, and saw that the doors were open.

When police asked her if she had seen anything or anyone unusual, she said no. It wasn't until years later that she told investigators she had seen Father Robinson standing by the chapel doors a little after 7:00 that morning, but at the time, police asked only if she had seen anyone or anything unusual. Seeing a priest by the hospital chapel was not unusual—she had seen Father Robinson there more than a hundred times. Nervous during the 1980 interview, Kerr said she tried to answer the police's questions, without elaboration, giving them nothing more and nothing less than what they asked for.

Doctor Jack Baron, one of the doctors who had rushed to the chapel for the Mr. Swift emergency call, told officers that he had come down the stairs and made a right turn, by mistake, and started heading away from the chapel.

When he realized that he was going in the wrong direction, he spun around and began toward the chapel. That's when he passed a priest, who was walking in the opposite direction.

"He looked back at me over his left shoulder and gave me a stare that went right through me," Dr. Baron told Detective Dan Foster.

The doctor said he didn't know the priest by name, but described him to police as wearing black clerical garb, about 35 to 45 years of age, five feet six or seven in height, weight around 160 pounds, with brown hair.

The description was a match for Father Robinson. But when he was telling the detective about seeing the priest in the hallway, he noticed that the officer didn't write anything down. Dr. Baron asked him why, but the detective just started asking other questions, about what he had seen in the sacristy.

"The policeman seemed more concerned with the next question, about whether the window shade was up or down. That always bothered me," Dr. Baron said years later.

A janitor and a receptionist who were working in the ground-floor lobby told police that they heard "frantic footsteps" about 7:30 the morning of the murder, running along a hallway on the open balcony above. They said the steps came from the direction of a covered walkway that led from the chapel and went down the hallway where Father Robinson was the only resident.

The janitor, Wardell Langston Jr., told detectives that the steps sounded as if "something was terribly wrong."

He said he stepped back to see if he could see anything over the balcony, but his view was blocked by a metal railing.

He thought for a moment about going up to the next floor to get a better look, but decided against it.

"Why didn't you go?" Lieutenant Kina asked him.

"I'm no hero," he replied.

Langston and the receptionist, Margaret Warren, said when the footsteps went down the hallway, they listened for the clang of a metal fire door. It was at the end of the hall and its push-bar door usually made a loud noise when the door opened, but they never heard the clang. They said the footsteps stopped just short of the fire door—and right near the door to Father Robinson's residence.

A Toledo policeman, Ulysses Howard, called Sergeant Marx to tell him that one of his neighbors, a lab technician named Grace Jones, had been working that morning and said she saw a priest walking out of the chapel carrying a duffel bag. She wasn't sure what time it was, only that it had to be after 7:00 a.m.

Father Robinson, meanwhile, had told police that he had been in his two-room residence the entire morning. He said he was drying off after a shower when he received a phone call from Sister Phyllis Ann telling him that Sister Margaret Ann had been murdered in the sacristy.

He said he never left his room until he got that call. Then he put on his clerical collar and his long black cassock and ran down to the chapel.

It was obvious to Sergeant Marx and his team that something didn't quite add up.

Chapter 9

Tim Fish, the coroner's office investigator, and Ed Marok, evidence technician, accompanied Sister Margaret Ann's body to the morgue located in the Lucas County Coroner's office.

Marok went about making a record of all possible evidence from the nun's corpse. He clipped her fingernails and put the 10 clippings in a marked envelope. He took a blood specimen, and oral, rectal and vaginal swabs, and hair samples from her head and pubic areas.

He typed a list of her clothing items that he had secured: blue shoes, white girdle, pantyhose, white bra, blue slip, white blouse, blue sleeveless dress, black veil, and necklace.

He then wrote down which tests needed to be done in the crime lab.

"On 4-5-80, Sister Margaret Pahl was found in the chapel sacristy of Mercy Hospital. She had been stabbed, strangled, and raped. As of this time there are no firm suspects.

"Clothing to be examined for presence of sperm. Also, group and type the blood on each item and compare it to specimen from the victim. Try to determine other foreign substances on the articles such as hair, blood, and/or fibers of the suspect. Attempt to determine the presence of sperm on oral, rectal, and vaginal swabs. Attempt to determine if there is any flesh or blood under the nails of the victim so that it can later be compared to the suspect."

Doctor Renate Fazekas, a deputy Lucas County coroner, examined Sister Margaret Ann's body and concluded that the puncture wounds in her chest, neck, and face were made by an instrument with a blade at least three inches long and half an inch wide. The weapon had an unusual shape to its blade, she noted. It was not just a flat blade, but one that had four sides, its cross section something like a diamond or a kite shape.

Sister Kathleen Mary had told Detective Dave Weinbrecht that a pair of sewing scissors that Sister Margaret Ann kept in the sacristy, mostly for trimming candle wicks, was missing, and police began looking at the possibility that scissors could have been the murder weapon.

Detective Weinbrecht asked Sister Kathleen to describe the missing scissors and asked if she had another pair like them. The sister gave him a pair that she said was similar to the missing scissors, although she guessed the missing pair was an inch or so longer.

The detective took the sample scissors to the police crime laboratory, where criminalist Josh Franks compared the shape of the blades to the holes in Sister Margaret Ann's clothing.

"It is the opinion of criminalist Franks and this officer that the holes in the dress were made by a similar instrument [to the scissors]," Detective Weinbrecht wrote.

The next day, Franks and Weinbrecht went to the county morgue and showed the scissors to Dr. Fazekas, who had conducted the autopsy on Sister Margaret Ann and who had preserved sample pieces of the victim's flesh.

The deputy coroner also had studied the crime-scene photographs of the puncture wounds that had been taken by Marok.

Doctor Fazekas conducted a series of tests, with Weinbrecht and Marok looking on, making punctures in the nun's preserved flesh and then comparing the shape of the wounds to the photographs taken at the crime scene. She concluded that scissors "very well could have been the weapon, but she could not say with 100 percent certainty," Detective Weinbrecht wrote in his police report.

The deputy coroner added, however, that the wounds to Sister Margaret Ann's face "appeared to have been made with an instrument sharper than scissors."

Chapter 10

In Fremont, Ohio, on the shade-covered grounds of Our Lady of the Pines Retreat Center, more than two hundred people crowded into the tiny St. Bernadine Chapel on April 8, 1980, to pay their respects to Sister Margaret Ann Pahl.

The funeral service was held three days after her murder, and two days after what would have been the nun's seventy-second birthday.

Her coffin, closed and draped in a white pall embroidered with an ornate cross, was in the center of the aisle as ten priests stood at the altar to pray for the repose of her soul.

The chief celebrant that afternoon was Father Gerald Robinson, wearing white vestments with the words "Peace" and "Love" stitched into them. The Toledo priest had worked with Sister Margaret Ann for six years as chaplain of Mercy Hospital.

"Into your hands, Father of mercies," Father Robinson said, reciting the liturgy, "we commend our sister in the sure and certain hope that, together with all who have died in Christ, she will rise with him on the last day."

Outside, massive storm clouds were roiling low overhead.

Suddenly, a blast of wind blew the chapel doors wide open. A flurry of dead leaves skittered into the room, blowing across the red flower-print carpet. The heavens erupted with a fierce downpour, rattling the metal cross on the chapel's roof and knocking out the power to twenty thousand homes.

"It wouldn't have surprised me one bit if that roof had come off the church," said Paul Casebere, Sister Margaret Ann's brother-in-law.

Father Jerome Swiatecki, Mercy's assistant chaplain, said in his homily that Sister Margaret Ann suffered "a violent, tragic, traumatic death, a death not only blasphemous but patently absurd. It stirs up within us a deep repugnance at death. What does it all really mean?"

Sister Margaret Ann was buried in St. Bernadine Cemetery, at the far end of the property that houses the Sisters of Mercy's chapel, retreat center, and former convent. All the Sisters of Mercy from the Midwest region are interred at the cemetery, surrounded by pine trees and a life-size statue of Jesus, his eyes and one hand raised heavenward, his other hand grasping a spear.

Chapter 11

Marx and Vetter met every morning in the Safety Building before the sergeant would head to his command post at Mercy Hospital. Each day, the list of suspects in the nun's murder continued to shrink as detectives eliminated more and more people—hospital workers who were off that day, nursing students who were away for the weekend, doctors and nurses with verified alibis.

The police were confident that the murderer knew the victim, and as the investigation progressed, they kept coming across signs indicating that the killer was someone trained in religious rituals.

The murder occurred in the sacristy on one of the only days in the year when the Holy Eucharist was placed in that small room.

Roman Catholic doctrine teaches that the consecration of the bread and wine by a priest literally transforms those elements into the body and blood of Jesus Christ—not symbolically, but into Christ's actual body and blood.

Throughout the year, the Holy Eucharist is kept in a tabernacle in the chapel. But on Good Friday, the day that Christians observe Jesus' death, the Eucharist is removed from the chapel and placed in the sacristy, where it stays until the Easter vigil and Christ's resurrection. It is then returned in a procession to the chapel, where it is kept the rest of the year.

Sister Phyllis Ann told Detective Weinbrecht that she was sure Sister Margaret Ann was killed in a ritual. The detective at first just brushed that suggestion aside, but the nun was insistent.

She had seen many deaths, she told him, and this one was unique. The way the nun's body was posed, with her legs straight, her arms straight at her sides, her genitals exposed . . . it all seemed part of a ritualistic killing, Sister Phyllis Ann said.

Doctor Fazekas concluded, after thorough testing of the swabs and other physical evidence, that Sister Margaret Ann had not been raped. There were, however, abrasions on the inside of her vagina. Although the nun was not raped, the killer had definitely molested her with something.

Sergeant Marx and Deputy Chief Vetter believed the murderer tried to pose the victim's body to make it look like a sexual attack in hopes of leading investigators down the wrong track while he got further away.

Vetter held a press conference a day after the murder, telling the media that police had not turned up anything "startling" and that they had few solid leads or evidence in the case.

A few days later, Police Chief Walter Scoble told the media that police were still not coming up with much. "We need a lucky break, coupled with diligent police work," he said.

The Lucas County Commission and Mercy Hospital together offered a $15,000 reward for anyone providing clues that would lead to the capture of Sister Margaret Ann's killer. The fund was later boosted to $24,000 with money contributed by medical doctors.

Still, police said they got fewer calls than they expected; and none of them was helpful.

Police checked into a number of bogus leads.

One anonymous letter to the police, for example, claimed that a student at the University of Toledo had "a perverse hate for the Catholic Church and especially nuns," that he is a psychopath and devil worshipper with "a great potential for violence." When police checked it out, the anonymous letter turned out to be written by the suspect's spurned gay lover.

One woman at the local welfare office called to say that her boss might be the nun's killer because he once twisted her arm, frequently threatened her coworkers, and had marks on his body that appeared to be scars from a knife wound.

A Mercy Hospital clerk reported a suspicious patient who told her that his mother went into the hospital for surgery in 1973, and he was told by the staff that she was dead. "But he feels his mother in fact did not die but is being held hostage by hospital employees, and his search for her is still very intense," police reported.

Mrs. Beverly Holmes, from the Toledo suburb of Maumee, called police to offer her services as a psychic and said she had helped the FBI solve a previous local murder case.

Mrs. Holmes said she saw Sister Margaret Ann's killer in her dreams. Detective Weinbrecht took notes, writing in his report that the woman described the murderer as "a white male from Delaware, unknown if state or street. The victim knew him. He was carrying a grocery sack and at times flowers, which means he is a delivery boy. This person knows music and plays a string instrument. He has a mental history, caused by the way he was treated by his parents. He is a negative person."

Detective Weinbrecht added a succinct conclusion: "This person appears to have no knowledge of the case whatsoever."

One lead that detectives took very seriously involved a trio of inmates at several different Ohio prisons. One prisoner wrote a letter on behalf of another, and mailed it to a Toledo judge claiming responsibility for the nun's death. Sergeant Marx and other detectives traveled around the state interviewing the prisoners.

They arranged for one of the inmates, Toledoan Archester Neal, to be transferred to Toledo so that he could take a lie-detector test about his claims that another inmate had confessed to the killing.

Neal passed the polygraph.

According to Neal, the killer and a friend were dressed in drag and hustling on the Toledo city streets the night of the murder when they decided to go inside Mercy Hospital.

Sister Margaret Ann confronted the two men in drag, asking them what they were doing, and one of them began stabbing her repeatedly, Neal told Sergeant Marx.

Neal said the killer told him that he buried his dress, wig, and the knife he used to kill the nun in his backyard of his inner-city Toledo home.

Sergeant Marx and Lieutenant William Kina got a search warrant and spent three futile hours on a hot afternoon digging up the yard with hand tools, looking for the evidence.

Nothing ever came from the prison connection, although Marx and his team continued to follow the lead off and on for more than a year after Sister Margaret Ann's slaying.

Chapter 12

As the days passed, the detectives found the trail getting steadily colder. The $24,000 reward had brought all kinds of strange characters out of the woodwork, but so far it proved to be more of a nuisance than a help.

"The lack of substantial evidence is frustrating," Chief Water Scoble told reporters. "After scores of interviews, we are still lacking the kind of evidence we need to solve this crime."

Police said they had found no useful fingerprints, no footprints, no pieces of clothing or fiber, and no weapon. They called on the public to keep their eyes out for anything that could help the investigation and to contact police if they had anything to report.

Police officials acknowledged that some evidence may have been destroyed when nurses and doctors and hospital workers rushed into the sacristy to try to save Sister Margaret Ann Pahl's life, but even if they contaminated evidence in the process, they were doing what they were trained to do by trying to provide emergency aid.

"I am not criticizing hospital personnel who may have moved her body or compromised evidence at the scene," Deputy Police Chief Ray Vetter told the press. "We're not blaming them in the least. The first priority is to try to save a person's life. Preserving evidence is secondary. And we don't even know if there was any evidence to be destroyed."

Ten days after the murder, police were still lacking evidence but had narrowed their search down to just a few suspects.

They felt the killer had to be someone who knew Sister Margaret Ann, someone with extensive knowledge of religious ritual, and someone with the opportunity and a motive.

After accounting for the whereabouts of Father Jerome Swiatecki and all the Sisters of Mercy nuns at the hospital, the detectives began focusing on one individual.

"There was only one suspect—Father Robinson," Vetter said years later.

The deputy chief said the police had considered the priest their prime suspect from day one, but it was against department policy to let that information get out, because it could jeopardize their case.

The suspect could flee or destroy evidence if he knew he was under investigation.

Eleven days after the murder, with virtually all suspects except one being eliminated from their list, detectives decided it was time to bring Father Robinson downtown for questioning.

On April 16, Sergeant Marx dialed the priest's room at the hospital and got Father Robinson on the line. The priest agreed to undergo an interview and a polygraph test at the Safety Building.

On the afternoon of Friday, April 18, Marx drove to Mercy Hospital and knocked on Father Robinson's door. The priest invited the detective to come in while he finished getting ready, slipping an arm into his black clerical jacket.

But aside from a curt hello and a few brief words, the priest didn't say a thing.

His residence was tiny, just two adjoining rooms about ten by twelve each, painted an institutional pale green, with a cubicle-sized pink-tiled bathroom. A crucifix with a wooden cross and a gold metal corpus was the only decoration on the walls. Several large windows, their Venetian blinds raised, overlooked a small green courtyard, with more brick hospital buildings on the other side.

A depressing place to live, Marx thought to himself.

The sergeant drove Father Robinson to the Safety Building in silence, and was grateful it was only a mile and a half. He led the priest to a small interrogation room on the second floor in 212, the detective's bureau.

Lieutenant William Kina, a jut-jawed detective with swept-back black hair, joined Sergeant Marx in the interview room, where the two veteran cops grilled Father Robinson for nearly eight hours, hammering at inconsistencies in his statements about his activities, his whereabouts, and the timing of events on April 5.

Father Robinson said afterward that the detectives were "forceful" in their questioning, but that they never directly accused him of murdering Sister Margaret Ann.

Toward the end of the interrogation, sometime around 10:00 p.m., Father Robinson stared directly at Sergeant Marx and blurted out a sentence that shocked the detective more than anything he had ever heard from the mouth of a suspect.

"Someone came up to me on Wednesday, and confessed he was responsible for Sister Margaret Ann's murder," Father Robinson said.

Sergeant Marx pushed himself back from the table in disbelief. A lifelong Roman Catholic, he knew that anything that someone told a priest during confession was held in the absolutely strictest confidence. A priest would never reveal what was said in confession. In fact, he would be excommunicated from the Catholic Church for doing so.

"Who was it?" Marx asked the priest.

"I can't say," Father Robinson replied.

"Was it a male or female?" Kina asked.

"I can't say," the priest responded again, shaking his head from side to side.

The detectives continued to press him for details about the confession—where was he, what time did it occur, some hint of who had confessed.

After the series of hard questions, Father Robinson dropped his head into his hands and rubbed his hands up and down his face.

He was physically and emotionally exhausted. Drained.

"Father, do you realize how serious this is?" Marx said sternly. "You're telling us that someone confessed to murdering Sister Margaret Ann Pahl. And you won't give us any details. You know this is a murder investigation, Father."

Robinson took a deep breath, then exhaled slowly.

"I made that up," he said.

"You what?" Marx shouted, slamming his hand on the table.

"It's not true. I made that up, that thing about the confession."

Marx stood up and glared at the priest.

"Father, why would you make up such a thing?" he asked.

"I was trying to protect myself," he replied. "I'm tired. I want to go home. I was just trying to give you something to get this over with."

Marx shook his head.

"Father, that was definitely not the way to get this over with."

Kina looked at his watch and then looked at Marx.

"Well, maybe you're right. That might be enough for tonight. We'll pick this up again tomorrow," Marx said. "And if it's all right with you, we would like to take a look at your apartment."

"Okay," the priest said, and signed a waiver allowing the detectives to search his apartment without a warrant.

As Marx and Kina walked out of the room with Father Robinson, Father Jerome Swiatecki was coming toward them, walking down the hallway with another officer.

The big, outspoken priest, walking briskly, came right up to Father Robinson and bent down, face to face.

The detectives thought he might strike the smaller cleric.

"Just tell them the truth!" Father Swiatecki said loudly, glaring at the priest. "For God's sake, tell them what you know!"

Father Robinson just stared at Father Swiatecki with a blank expression. He didn't say a word. Detective Kina grabbed Father Robinson by the elbow and gave him a nudge, leading him down the hall and away from the confrontation.

"What was that all about?" Kina asked Father Robinson.

"I have no idea," the priest replied.

Chapter 13

Arriving at Mercy Hospital, Father Robinson and the two detectives entered through the lobby at Madison and 23rd Street, took an elevator up one floor, and walked down a dimly lighted hallway to the priest's apartment.

Father Robinson reached into a pocket for his keys, unlocked the door, and let the detectives in.

"Help yourselves," he said, stepping back out of their way. "I'll see if there are any patients to visit."

"This won't take long," Lieutenant Kina said, looking around the small apartment.

Father Robinson walked out, leaving the two detectives alone in his apartment.

The cops were looking for whatever evidence they could find.

Doctor Fazekas, from the coroner's office, told them to look for a fairly small knife with a four-sided blade. She pointed out that the punctures in the nun's body were all about three inches deep.

Kina looked around, peeked inside the bathroom, and opened the medicine cabinet. A bottle of Valium was disbursed from Mercy Hospital's pharmacy, dated 4-5-80—the date of the murder.

There were two pairs of black oxford shoes in the closet, some clerical shirts, collars, and a cassock, and a couple of plaid shirts and jeans.

Marx, meanwhile, was looking around the priest's desk.

"Well, well, what have we got here?" Sergeant Marx said.

Lieutenant Kina walked out and saw Sergeant Marx standing in front of a wooden desk with the center drawer wide open. The detective reached down and pulled out a silver, sword-shaped instrument, maybe a letter opener or a souvenir.

He smiled as held it up for Lieutenant Kina, holding it carefully by its ends.

The silver dagger was shaped like a saber, about nine inches long, with a slightly curved, four-sided blade. It had a ribbed metal handle, a knuckle guard, and a circular medallion on the handle. The bronze medallion was embossed with a picture of the U.S. Capitol Building and the words "Wax Museum, Washington, D.C."

"Bill, get an evidence envelope," Sergeant Marx said.

Lieutenant Kina reached into a case and took out a white, six-by-eight-inch evidence envelope, then held it open for Sergeant Marx to slip the letter opener inside.

"Let's get this to the crime lab," the sergeant said, patting the lieutenant on the back.

The two detectives felt confident that, after almost two weeks of frustration, they had finally found a piece of evidence that could be a breakthrough in this case.

Driving back to the Safety Building, Lieutenant Kina turned on the radio. A smooth DJ with a rich baritone voice was introducing one of the top hits of the day, the Eagles' ballad, "I Can't Tell You Why."

He looked at Sergeant Marx.

"Can you tell me why?" the Lieutenant asked. "I'd bet the farm we have the murder weapon right here in our hands, but for the life of me, I can't figure out why—just like the song says, I can't tell you why."

"Well, we have the weapon," Sergeant Marx said. "That's a big step. Let's see where that takes us."

By the time they got back and typed up their report, it was after midnight. Sergeant Marx locked the letter opener in a safe in the detectives' bureau.

The next morning, a Saturday, Marx called Josh Franks, his friend and a top criminalist in the police lab, at home, and asked if he could come in for a few hours and run some tests.

"What kind of tests?" Franks asked warily. He had been looking forward to a day off.

"On a murder weapon," Marx replied.

"Murder weapon? Get outta here! In the nun case?" Franks exclaimed.

"I think so, but we'll know a lot more after we run some tests."

"I'll be down there quicker than a bull in a candy shop," Franks said.

"Quicker than what?" Sergeant Marx asked, but Franks had already hung up the phone.

Sergeant Marx unlocked the detectives' safe and removed the envelope with the letter opener, then headed downstairs to the crime lab to wait for Franks

Franks liked to laugh and joke around, but this day he was all business. He realized the nun's murder case had gotten stale for lack of evidence. He always said his job was "to give the evidence a voice."

Sergeant Marx opened the envelope and slid the saber-shaped letter opener onto Franks' desk. The criminalist put on a pair of surgical gloves and picked up the instrument with a pair of devices that looked like stainless steel spatulas.

He gave the sword-like object a close look, top to bottom.

"Hmmmm," he said.

"Hmmmmm what?" Marx asked impatiently.

"Nothing . . . literally, nothing," Franks said, then walked across the room to a microscope. He adjusted the lenses and slowly examined the letter opener from the tip of the blade to the acorn-shaped knob at the end of the handle.

"Well, Arthur, this is one extremely clean letter opener," Franks said. "In fact, it looks like it's just been polished."

Franks took it back to his desk and pulled a fingerprint kit from the shelf. He took out a small camel's hair brush and dipped it into a jar of dark powder, then brushed lightly on the letter opener's silver blade.

Nothing.

He dusted the handle. No prints. He dusted every square centimeter of the letter opener. No prints anywhere.

"Hmmmm. This is very strange," he said. "If he ever opened letters with this, you'd think there would be fingerprints on it somewhere."

"Well, who would write that guy a letter?" Sergeant Marx said. "Except maybe the bishop or a bill collector."

"Very funny, Arthur," Franks said. "But if this is a murder weapon, it is suspiciously devoid of fingerprints, dust, smears, or any marks of any kind. It looks like it just came off the assembly line."

"Maybe he was wearing gloves when he killed her," Sergeant Marx said. "But if this was the weapon, it probably was soaked in blood at one time. Maybe there's still a trace of blood on it somewhere?"

"Well, it doesn't look like it, but let's see what we can find," Franks said.

Sergeant Marx watched Franks take out a jar of phenothaline, a chemical used to test for the presence of blood, and dip another small brush into the jar.

"If there's any blood on this thing, even just a drop the size of a pinhead, the phenothaline will turn purple," Franks said.

He took the brush and coated the blade of the letter opener with the chemical. No purple spots.

He coated the metal handle. No reaction. Same with the knuckle guard and the Capitol medallion—no sign of blood.

On the side of the letter opener opposite the medallion, there was a concave circle engraved with two symbols—five-sided stars, or pentagrams. One was pointing up and the other was pointing down. Franks coated the concave surface with phenothaline. Negative.

The criminalist stared closely at the letter opener, then turned to the sergeant.

"Arthur, I would say that this letter opener is *sumptuously* clean," Franks said.

"Damn!" Sergeant Marx said, pounding the desk with his fist.

The detective looked down at the dagger-like instrument on the desk, then bent down to take an even closer look.

"Say, Josh, what about this medallion? Is it glued in, or is it just pressed in snugly? Maybe some blood seeped under it during the murder?"

The metal medallion, with its embossed image of the U.S. Capitol Building and the words "Wax Museum, Washington D.C.," was about an inch in diameter. Franks took a thin metal blade from his desk drawer and slipped the tip of it between the medallion and its circular frame. He pushed down, and the medallion popped out, clattering onto the desk.

He gave Marx a wink. The bottom of the medallion and the empty space where it used to be appeared to be clean. No visual signs of blood.

Franks walked over to the microscope and focused its lenses. Nothing visible, even with the microscope.

He went back to this desk, opened the jar of phenothaline and dipped the brush into it.

"Ready?" he asked Marx.

"Ready," Marx replied.

"Watch closely," Franks said. "Don't blink."

The criminalist took the brush and coated the small metal circle on the handle with the chemical. No reaction.

He took the medallion, turned it upside down, and coated the bottom with phenothaline. Suddenly, a small purple dot, just larger than a pin head, glowed brightly for a few seconds, then turned red, then pink, then faded out completely.

"Did you see that? Did you see it?" Franks asked.

"Absolutely. Unmistakably positive," Marx replied with a smile.

It was small, but it was definitely positive. Unfortunately, it was too small an amount to conduct further tests. And phenothaline could react with some other materials besides blood. It was only a preliminary indication of the presence of blood. By itself, it proved nothing.

"Write that up, Josh. A positive test result," Sergeant Marx said.

Franks sat down in front of a typewriter while the sergeant took the blade and the medallion and put them back in the evidence envelope.

The criminalist began typing on a sheet labeled "Toledo Police Regional Crime Laboratory/Laboratory Report."

"Objective: Saber-style letter opener analyzed for possible presence of known blood.

"Data: Analysis was performed by using biochemical techniques.

"Conclusion: The wax museum medallion affixed to the letter opener gave a weak positive result to a presumptive screening test for blood, indicating the possible presence of blood.

"Remarks: There was insufficient material present for the conduct of confirmatory tests."

Chapter 14

At noon that day, Sergeant Marx and Lieutenant Kina returned to Mercy Hospital to pick up Father Robinson and take him downtown for another interview.

Again, the priest barely said a word to the detectives as they drove to the Safety Building. The two detectives escorted Father Robinson to a room on the second floor, where Lieutenant James Wiegand was preparing a polygraph machine for an examination.

Lieutenant Wiegand told Father Robinson to have a seat. Sergeant Marx and Lieutenant Kina left.

The lieutenant told the priest that he was going to ask a few simple questions at first, just some straightforward background information.

Then he was going to hook him up to the polygraph machine.

He explained that he would connect several rubber tubes to the priest's chest and abdomen to measure his respiratory activity. Two small metal plates would then be attached to his fingertips to monitor sweat gland activity. The last piece would be a blood pressure cuff that he would wrap around an arm.

Father Robinson nodded. "Okay," he said.

Lieutenant Wiegand asked if he was doing all right.

"I'm tired," the priest replied. "I didn't get to bed until 2:00 a.m."

Lieutenant Wiegand showed him a piece of paper he had prepared that included a Miranda rights warning—the one that says, "You have the right to remain silent, anything you say can be used against you in a court of law, you have the right to have an attorney present. . . ."

The lieutenant read the warning aloud, then passed it over to Father Robinson and handed him a pen. The priest signed the document.

Lieutenant Wiegand then started off with biographical questions: Where were you born? How old are you? Parents' names? What schools did you attend? What was the date of your ordination?

After half an hour of such pretest questions, Lieutenant Wiegand began asking Father Robinson about his activities on the morning of the murder.

The priest paused before giving many of his answers, giving a great deal of thought to what Lieutenant Wiegand considered to be straightforward questions: What time did you wake up? When did you leave your room? When did you first learn about Sister Margaret Ann Pahl's murder?

After about an hour, Lieutenant Wiegand wrapped up with two questions.

"Do you have any idea who could have killed the nun?"

"No, none at all," Father Robinson replied.

"Do you know why anyone would have killed Sister Margaret Ann?" Lieutenant Wiegand asked.

"Well, she had a dominant personality," Father Robinson replied.

"Excuse me?" Lieutenant Wiegand asked, raising an eyebrow as he looked up from his notes.

"She was a dominant woman," the priest repeated.

"Okay, I see," Lieutenant Wiegand said, writing the phrase down in his notes: "He said she was a dominant woman."

He thanked Father Robinson for his cooperation and unhooked him from the polygraph machine.

Sergeant Marx and Lieutenant Kina returned to the polygraph room to get the priest, and asked him if he was hungry or thirsty or wanted to take a break before starting another interview.

"Yes, I am a bit hungry," Father Robinson said.

Lieutenant Kina went out and came back with a couple of hamburgers and fries from a White Tower stand around the corner.

Lieutenant Wiegand, meanwhile, was filling out a police report on the results of the polygraph exam.

He noted several curious contradictions during questioning, such as the priest saying he had just stepped out of the shower and was drying off with a towel when Sister Phyllis Ann called him about the murder, then later saying he was buttoning his cassock when the call came.

In his conclusion, Lieutenant Wiegand wrote: "It is the opinion of this polygraph examiner that truthfulness could not be verified. Deception was indicated on relevant questions concerning the murder of Sister Margaret Ann Pahl."

He added that he felt the priest "needs to relax, to be in a calmer state, because of the previous evening's lengthy examination that lasted until approximately 2:00 a.m."

Sister Phyllis Ann, when told about the polygraph results, challenged police about the conditions under which the test was administered. She felt that they needed to give the father another test, this time after he was rested and with the polygraph administered in a more neutral site than the police station.

She asked Detective Marx and Deputy Chief Vetter if they would consider a second lie-detector test, one whose results would not be so questionable.

"It couldn't hurt anything to give him another exam, and maybe it would verify the results of the first test," Sister Phyllis Ann said.

Sergeant Marx and Deputy Chief Vetter agreed, and they scheduled a second lie-detector test for the following week. This one was conducted by an examiner chosen by Father Robinson's attorney, Henry Herschel, and administered in the headquarters of the Toledo diocese, a site more amenable to the priest than the Safety Building.

According to the report from the second polygraph exam, Father Robinson passed, but the test results were deemed "inconclusive."

"Subject's polygrams contained a high background of emotionality and inconsistent specific responses indicative of emotional stress were noted on several of the relevant questions set forth above at various times during the testing sequence. For these reasons, the polygrams themselves are of marginal utility for diagnostic purposes."

On the day of the first polygraph, after eating his burgers in the police dining room, Father Robinson was taken by detectives to the same interview room where he had been questioned until late the previous night.

It was around five o'clock when Sergeant Marx and Lieutenant Kina started the interrogation, and they were all expecting another marathon session. The detectives had found the letter opener the night before in Father Robinson's apartment and they had plenty of new questions to ask the priest.

About an hour into the session, Sergeant Marx left the interview room to get some more paper for taking notes. While he was gone, there was a knock on the door. Lieutenant Kina opened the door and there stood Deputy Chief Vetter, Monsignor Jerome Schmit—one of the most powerful clerics in the diocese—and Toledo attorney Henry Herschel.

Deputy Chief Vetter asked Lieutenant Kina to please step outside. The detective glared at the deputy chief, but did as he asked, walking though the door into the wide gray hallway.

Sergeant Marx returned and heatedly asked Lieutenant Kina what the heck he was doing standing out in the hallway.

"Vetter, Monsignor Schmit, and the priest's attorney are all inside," Lieutenant Kina said. "Vetter asked me to wait out here."

"Holy crap," Sergeant Marx said. "You've got to be kidding me. That's an outrage! You know the unwritten rule—you never, never, *never* interrupt an interrogation!"

Five minutes later, the door popped open. Deputy Chief Vetter walked out first, followed by Monsignor Schmit—chomping on an unlit cigar—and the lawyer. The last one to leave was Father Robinson.

The foursome walked past the two detectives and did not say a word.

Sergeant Marx watched the four men walk down the hallway to the elevators.

"I guess the interview's over," Sergeant Marx said.

"Looks like it," Lieutenant Kina said. "When the suspect walks out of an interrogation with an attorney, you can assume it's pretty much over. He's not talking any more tonight. Or maybe ever."

Chapter 15

Monsignor Jerome Schmit was a man who had a way of taking a "no" and turning it into a "yes."

The cigar-smoking Toledo priest, born with a cleft palate, was asked to leave the seminary at Pontifical College in Worthington, Ohio, after one year because of his speech impediment.

"They told me there I could not be a priest because of my speech," Monsignor Schmit said.

He went back to Toledo and took a job in the county welfare department. But four years later, he enrolled at Sulpician Seminary in Baltimore, Maryland, then transferred to Catholic University in Washington.

He was ordained in Toledo's Rosary Cathedral in June 1941, the third of four Schmit brothers to enter the priesthood, and ultimately became one of the city's most powerful dealmakers. A Toledo street near the Mud Hens' ballpark is named in his honor, Jerome Schmit Way.

"He was just well-placed, the monsignor was," a friend said. "He chummed with the right guys. He was always very effective. He could always go out and get money [for the diocese] when he needed it."

One of the local leaders he could turn to was Deputy Chief Ray Vetter of the Toledo Police Department.

"I was a close personal friend of Monsignor Schmit," Deputy Chief Vetter said. "He told me, 'If ever I can help you in a case, just give me a call.'"

In April 1980, as the investigation into the murder of Sister Margaret Ann Pahl began to center on a priest, the deputy chief gave the monsignor a call.

"I told him, 'All I want you to do is talk with Father Robinson, make him feel sort of at home,'" Chief Vetter said. "'Whatever you can find out, and if you find out anything, let's talk.'"

Monsignor Schmit had been one of the men who interrupted a police interrogation of the priest on April 19, 1980, walking out of the interview room with Father Robinson.

There was no indication where Monsignor Schmit and Deputy Chief Vetter went with Father Robinson after springing him from the interview with Marx and Kina, but no report ever surfaced about whether the monsignor had gotten the priest to say anything about the nun's murder.

The intervention of a Toledo Catholic cleric into a police murder investigation came as no surprise to people familiar with the power and influence of the Toledo diocese in 1980.

"You took care of the Catholic Church," said Bill Gray, a retired Toledo police officer. "There was no negotiation. If you were a Jewish rabbi, a Baptist minister, or an Episcopalian priest, you're shit out of luck. But the police had to take care of the priests. It was an absolute."

In the 1960s, Police Chief Anthony Bosch, a devout Catholic, had ordered his officers to direct traffic outside Catholic churches on Sunday mornings if they had a parish in their district, Gray said.

"And there was a Catholic church in every district in the city," Gray said. "You had to sit there, you could not write a parking ticket or a speeding ticket—nothing. And then after the service, you had to personally escort the ushers to a bank."

Bosch retired in 1970, but the favoritism he had shown to the church remained in force.

"It wasn't even an 'unwritten policy,'" Gray said. "It was out in the open, public knowledge."

Gene Fodor, who was on the force from 1960 to 1987, said there was no way a Toledo policeman could ever arrest a priest.

"You would have been fired," Fodor said.

In 1960, a Catholic parishioner in a working-class East Toledo neighborhood complained to Officer Fodor about Father Alexander Pinter, saying he believed the priest was raping and molesting altar boys at a lakefront cottage.

"It was becoming a scandal, but they did not want to arrest him," Officer Fodor said. "People would come up to me and say, 'When are you going to arrest that Pinter? He's a pervert.' But I couldn't."

Instead, Officer Fodor's supervisors met with then-Bishop George Rehring and gave him an ultimatum: You take care of Father Pinter, or we're going to arrest him.

The 41-year-old priest quickly and quietly left Toledo and was admitted to a treatment center in Canada in July 1960. He later taught in several U.S. seminaries and became a parish priest in Louisiana, where he died in 1974 at age 59.

The Toledo diocese's covert handling of priests who molested children dates back to at least the 1950s, when Father Leo Welch was accused of molesting altar boys at a lakefront cottage.

Father Welch's abuse occurred between 1956 and 1961, when the priest was serving at Immaculate Conception Parish in Bellevue, Ohio, a small town in the nineteen-county diocese about an hour east of Toledo.

The young priest would invite altar boys to a small, three-bedroom cottage on two acres of land fronting a large pond.

The cottage was set up with a dirt track circling the pond for go-kart racing and a boat that the priest would use to take the boys fishing or waterskiing.

"It was a Never-Never Land for kids," said George Keller, one of the children whom Father Welch used to invite to the cottage.

At night, however, the children's wonderland turned into a place of nightmares.

Father Welch would have a few drinks and retire to his bedroom, summoning the young teenage boys, one at a time, to join him.

The priest would start out wrestling with the youngster on his bed, playfully at first, but then he would turn mean. He would force the boys into sex acts, making them perform oral sex on him or else sodomizing the young teenagers.

Dozens of Immaculate Conception altar boys were taken to Father Welch's cottage over the years, usually in groups of two or four. The children's parents encouraged them to go, feeling honored that a Catholic priest would take an interest in their boys, unaware that the weekends had such a sinister twist.

None of the boys had the nerve to tell their parents or the parish pastor until the summer of 1961, when two of the children decided they had had enough of the priest's shameful sessions and banded together to tell their parents.

Harold Lee said the turning point for him was in the fourth grade, when he saw one of the older boys refusing to step inside Father Welch's bedroom. The boy kept screaming, "No way! No way! I'm not going to do this! No more!"

The next day, the boy who had balked asked young Lee to tell his parents. He said he had told his mother but she didn't believe him. Maybe Lee's parents would believe it.

Immediately after Lee told his mother, Vivian, about the abuse, the woman drove to the church and stormed into the rectory, confronting the parish's pastor, Father Albert Bishop.

The next day, Father Welch was gone from Immaculate Conception Parish. His picture removed from the parish wall with no explanation.

In 2002, Father Welch told a *Toledo Blade* reporter that he had no explanation for his criminal behavior, other than "sexual experimentation."

Having quit the priesthood in 1965, the ex-priest now worked as a social worker in a Detroit suburb.

He admitted he had been "too affectionate" with the teens at the cottage.

"I was drinking heavily. I was lonely. I went too far. I'm not denying it," Father Welch said.

After he was shipped out of town, Father Bishop spoke harshly from the pulpit during the next Sunday morning Mass, denying the "rumors" over Father Welch's abrupt departure.

In the middle of his rant from the pulpit, Vivian Lee stood up in the front row, grabbed her children by the hands, and stormed out of the church.

Harold Lee's parents went on to report the allegations to their family lawyer, Charles Sliter, who also was the Bellevue city prosecutor.

Instead of turning Father Welch over to police, as he would have done with any other offender besides a Catholic priest, Sliter called Toledo Bishop George

Rehring and the diocese's chancellor, Father Robert Yates, and told them to take care of the problem.

Father Yates told Father Welch to get out of the Bellevue rectory immediately, so the priest left the small town behind and moved in with his parents. The chancellor also ordered the priest to undergo a psychiatric evaluation.

Four months after being removed from Immaculate Conception, Father Welch was reassigned as assistant pastor of Christ the King, a large parish in West Toledo.

In 2002, the Toledo diocese said it had no record of any allegations against Father Welch.

Father Thomas Quinn, the diocese's spokesman, said the diocese had not been in contact with Father Welch for years, since he left the priesthood, and was not sure if the former priest was alive or dead.

Bishop James Hoffman, who led the diocese from 1981 until his death in 2003—the longest reign of any Toledo bishop—told the *Blade* in a 2003 interview that from the 1960s through the 1970s, if church leaders found out that one of their priests had sexually abused a child, they would treat it "as a kind of moral failure. . . . It was sinful."

After sending the offender to a retreat house or a monastery, they would "urge him to make a good confession" and then put him back into ministry, saying, "Now let's get back going. . . . Your prayer life has to be renewed and things like that."

Bishop Hoffman compared it to the way society used to treat alcoholism as a moral failure, rather than a sickness or disease.

He said that if the church had known back then what it knows today, "the approach we would have taken would have been different," and that if he had had a better of understanding of sexual abuse in 1981, when he became bishop, "Yeah, I'm sure I would have handled things differently."

In July 2002, Minneapolis attorney Jeff Anderson, who has filed more than one thousand lawsuits against the Catholic Church nationwide over the last twenty-five years, held a press conference outside the Lucas County Courthouse in Toledo to announce that George Keller and Harold Lee were filing civil lawsuits against Leo Welch and the Toledo diocese.

The case was settled out of court two years later. The terms were not disclosed.

Chapter 16

Toledo Police Officer Bill Gray knew it was department policy not to arrest priests, but he went ahead and made an arrest anyway when he caught a 53-year-old priest having sex with a 16-year-old boy in a public restroom.

At 1:15 p.m. on December 9, 1984, Officer Gray and a security guard at a large department store in a South Toledo mall were called to a men's room on a report that there was trouble between a man and a boy. When they barged in, they caught the youth on his knees performing oral sex on Robert Thomas.

Hours earlier, Thomas had worn priest's vestments and celebrated Mass at Our Lady of Perpetual Help Catholic Church in South Toledo. Now, as Officer Gray took him downtown in handcuffs, the lanky, blonde-haired, blue-eyed priest was wearing tight white jeans and a muscle shirt.

In his police report, Officer Gray quoted the priest as saying: "He motioned me with his eyes to follow him. . . . I did want him to do it, as I did not stop him as I should have done."

As soon as word got out that Officer Gray had arrested a priest, the policeman said he began getting harassing calls from fellow officers and diocesan officials.

When he went to court to testify against Father Thomas, Officer Gray said he asked the judge if he could speak to him in private. The judge said only if all the attorneys and the defendant were present.

They went back to the judge's chambers, away from the media.

"Your honor, I've been getting phone calls from everywhere. I think the Pope even called me," Officer Gray said, getting a chuckle from Father Thomas. "I've been getting phone calls saying, 'Don't come back to the Catholic Church, I'm an embarrassment to the Catholic Church—and my phone number is unlisted. I have all the faith in the world in you, your honor, but there's a chance you'll probably get phone calls.'"

Just then, two lights on the judge's phone began blinking. The judge excused himself and answered the calls. Then he turned to the small group in his chambers.

"Gentlemen, the callers on those two flashing lines were giving me hell, asking me how I, being a Catholic, could sit on the trial of a Catholic priest."

The group went back into the courtroom and the judge found the priest guilty, but he agreed to seal the record of the arrest and the charges. The priest avoided a jail sentence. Eventually, his criminal record was expunged.

It wasn't long before Officer Gray's report disappeared from the police files, and today the department has no record of Father Thomas's ever having been arrested.

"I knew damn well the police report would get lost or sealed," Officer Gray said. "That's why I xeroxed a copy."

Father Thomas was sent to a treatment center in Minnesota, after which he was allowed to transfer to Arizona and serve as a parish priest for nearly eighteen years.

In 2002, a *Toledo Blade* reporter called the Tucson diocese for a comment on an article about Father Thomas's 1984 arrest. The spokesman said he was unaware of any arrest in the priest's past. Within weeks, Father Thomas was banned from ministry.

Officer Dave Davison, the first policeman on the scene of Sister Margaret Ann's murder, said neither the Toledo police nor the local diocese wanted to see a priest charged with any crime, let alone murder.

"There's no doubt the police department sat on this," Davison said. "The five-man task force that investigated the murder, they were all Roman Catholics as far as I know. They sat on it as a courtesy to the church. I'd ask [lead detective] Art Marx what was going on and he'd say, 'Yeah, we know he did it but we don't have enough evidence.'"

Davison said he wrote two police reports on the murder, a general crime report and a more elaborate supplemental report. The supplemental report disappeared.

"Marx told me and [partner Dan] Deeter not to put anything in writing," Davison said. "I kind of knew from day one that there was going to be a cover-up. Marx was a good cop but you could tell he was frustrated. To go up against Vetter—the deputy chief was like the Pope. Nobody approached him. He was an arrogant ass."

Deputy Chief Vetter, now in his eighties, bristles at allegations of a police cover-up.

"I can't believe anyone with any sense, who knows us as investigators and us as people, would say that we would cover this up. We just wouldn't do it," he said.

A practicing Catholic, Vetter pointed out that the victim was a Roman Catholic nun. When he retired in 1986, he told *Toledo Blade* police reporter Mike Bartell that the brutal slaying of Sister Margaret Ann Pahl was the biggest disappointment of his thirty-four-year career.

"It's especially perplexing because we know who committed the crime, but we were never able to come up with enough evidence to arrest anyone," Vetter said.

Bartell said the deputy chief asked him to include that specific statement, hoping the quote might spur the killer to confess.

Davison, 55, kept writing to authorities asking them to reopen the 1980 murder investigation and claiming the 1980 investigation covered up for Father Robinson.

Toledo Bishop James Hoffman replied to Davison in a letter by saying that in 1980, when the homicide occurred, "my predecessor, John A. Donovan, was the

Bishop of the Diocese of Toledo. I was serving as the pastor of St. Joseph Parish, Sylvania. I was not privy to the details of any contact that may have taken place between police investigators and Bishop Donovan."

Monsignor L. Sandri, Vatican assessor based in Washington, D.C., wrote to Davison to "acknowledge your most recent letter to His Holiness Pope John Paul II, and I would assure you that the contents have been carefully noted."

Representatives from the Ohio governor's office and the U.S. attorney general in Washington wrote that the investigation and an alleged cover-up were not in their jurisdictions

In March 1995, Davison requested copies of the 1980 police reports from the original investigation.

After receiving three hundred pages of police reports, paying twenty cents a page, Davison asked for a copy of the nun's autopsy and was abruptly cut short. He was told that no more records would be available because the murder investigation was being reopened.

"They panicked. They thought I was writing a book. [Prosecutor] Anthony Pizza called me and said, 'You better prove everything in that book. We're gonna sue you, we're gonna ruin your life, you'll never own anything.'"

Davison said the only motive he ever had was justice, to bring Sister Margaret Ann's killer to court.

"By '95, there were advances in DNA testing," he said. "but I knew the department was not doing anything. It galled me."

He also was upset that some people think a priest is not capable of committing a crime.

"People won't admit that priests are human, that they're not above it all. That's just stupid. . . . The collar doesn't make you holy. It's just a fashion accessory. My dog's got a collar. He doesn't do Masses, either. The only way some people would ever believe Robinson killed Sister Margaret Ann was if they saw it with their own eyes, or they saw it on videotape. And even then, some people probably wouldn't believe it."

Chapter 17

A wave of Polish immigrants flooded into Toledo in the late nineteenth century seeking factory work and the new arrivals settled into two geographic camps within the city limits.

Immigrants from the eastern regions of Poland tended to congregate in a community a little north of downtown that became known as Lagrainka.

A sprawling neighborhood with Lagrange Street as its main artery, Lagrainka had its own Polish grocery stores, butcher shops, bakeries, and even a weekly Polish-language newspaper. With most of the Polish immigrants being devout Roman Catholics, Lagrainka had two large Polish parishes, St. Adalbert's and St. Hedwig's, to meet the spiritual needs of its residents.

Immigrants from Poznan and the western region of Poland settled mostly in a neighborhood about four miles east of Lagrainka, known as Kuschwantz, or "Cow's Tail," for its rural setting at the time.

Smaller than Lagrainka, the cultural and religious center of Kuschwantz was St. Anthony's Parish, an ornately decorated Roman Catholic church with a steeple towering 211 feet in the air. Parish membership in the 1950s was as high as eight thousand.

Most of the homes in Lagrainka and Kuschwantz were modest, wood-frame buildings with large porches and neatly tended green lawns and colorful flower gardens.

Gerald John Robinson was born in Toledo on April 14, 1938, and was raised in the Kuschwantz section of the city. His family was equally dedicated to Catholicism and its Polish heritage, with his mother, Mary Sieja, being entirely of Polish descent, and his father, John, half Polish.

As a child in the 1940s, Robinson was immersed in Polish-American culture, learning both the Polish and English languages and attending Nativity Elementary, a Toledo parochial school run by one of the Polish ethnic parishes in Kuschwantz.

Some of Robinson's acquaintances felt that his mother was pushing him to become a priest, but his close friends have said that was not true, it was just a persistent rumor.

Mrs. Robinson was a "rigid" person, according to a family friend, who came across at first as cold and authoritarian. "You did not want to get on her bad side," the friend said.

All agreed that Mary Sieja Robinson, known to her friends as "Balbina," bragged to everyone in the Altar Society of St. Hyacinth Church, another local Polish ethnic parish, about her son Gerald choosing to go into the priesthood.

"She was elated by his choice of life as a priest," said Gerald Mazuchowski, an unofficial historian of the Toledo Polish Catholic community. "That was her pride and joy—my boy, the priest. It was like the highest calling you choose."

Robinson went to St. Mary's High School, a four-year minor seminary in the Detroit suburb of Orchard Lake, Michigan, about sixty miles north of Toledo. After high school, he attended Sts. Cyril and Methodius Seminary, on the same estate in Orchard Lake as St. Mary's High.

The Orchard Lake schools were founded by Polish priests in the 1800s who sought to provide a seminary education with an emphasis on Polish culture and heritage to young men seeking a vocation in the church.

"If the Orchard Lake schools did not exist, it would be necessary to establish them," Polish-born Pope John Paul II once said proudly.

In high school, Robinson was known as a quiet student who took his faith and his studies seriously.

"He was considered to be very mild and one that would rarely break any rules," said the Reverend Ralph Biernacki, a classmate of Robinson who is now a priest in the Orthodox Church in America.

"Jerry kept pretty much in the tradition of the seminary discipline at the time, which was really very monastic. I don't know if he ever dated," the priest said.

One of the jobs he held at school was overseeing the audio-visual department, and the seminarian took the role very seriously, Father Biernacki said.

"Looking back at it now, it seems almost laughable, but Jerry would choose very carefully the movies that were shown periodically to the student body. He made sure they were never controversial," the priest said. "He was not given to controversy whatsoever. He pretty much would walk the line and was not the questioning kind."

One time, when he was a young priest in Toledo, some of his contemporaries were having conflicts with the older priests and Robinson was so upset about it that he broke out in hives. "He couldn't stand it," Father Biernacki said.

Although a serious and quiet seminarian, Robinson was not without a sense of humor, Father Biernacki said.

"In our day, we used to present stage productions on our vacation—usually comedies—in Polish parishes in the Detroit area and Ohio, in Toledo and even Cleveland," Father Biernacki said.

"They were comedies in the Polish language and Jerry played some interesting roles. He played a janitor one time, and he dressed in drag to play female characters in some of the plays. He was good. He wasn't afraid of anything. He wasn't shy on the stage."

After graduating from the seminary, Robinson was ordained a priest in the Toledo Catholic Diocese on May 30, 1964, in a Mass celebrated by Bishop George Rehring, the fourth bishop of Toledo, in the diocese's towering and majestic Rosary Cathedral.

Father Robinson, one of the few American-born priests to speak fluent Polish in Toledo, was first assigned as assistant pro tem at St. Adalbert's Church, a Lagrainka neighborhood parish.

"He always had a very close circle of friends," Father Biernacki said. "You didn't become his intimate friend very easily."

Father Biernacki was assigned to St. Hyacinth's, the Kuschwantz church where Father Robinson's mother had served in the Altar Society.

"The cultural atmosphere at that time was still very guarded as far as the parishes went," he said. "When you were assigned to a Polish parish, it was a very closed circle. We still gave Polish sermons, celebrated a lot of the devotions in Polish, and had a lot of Polish pastoral duties—confessions and sick calls and the like. In 1965 and 1966, 60 percent of my confessions were still in the Polish language."

Jon Schoonmaker, a former seminarian and Catholic youth leader, served as a volunteer at St. Hedwig's Parish when he was 18 years old and said he was amazed by how much the Polish community revered its priests.

"The Polish community is very tight-knit and very church-oriented," he said. "The church was the center of the neighborhood. Really, I was kind of taken aback by this, but the thought was that the priest could do no wrong.

"Where I grew up, in St. Patrick's of Heatherdowns Parish, the priest was on a pedestal, but here the priest was god."

Father Robinson served at several parishes, his longest assignment being pastor of a cluster of three Polish ethnic churches in Kuschwantz—St. Anthony's, Nativity, and St. Stanislaus.

He was named pastor of the three Polish parishes in 1981, a year after Sister Margaret Ann Pahl's murder, and served there until 1989, although Nativity was dissolved by Bishop James Hoffman in 1982 and its assets given to the two other Polish parishes.

Everyone who knew Father Robinson, even his good friends, said that the priest often tuned out the world around him and was likely to pass by without even acknowledging your existence.

"He could be very friendly on one occasion, and on another occasion he would just ignore you," said Father David Lis, a former Toledo Catholic priest who converted to the Russian Orthodox Church.

"Father Jerry was very moody," Father Biernacki said. "There were those days when he would smile and say something; other days, nothing. He was just a little unpredictable that way."

"He's very quiet and a loner," said Jerry Hiltman, a Toledoan who plays the organ at local Catholic churches. "In the sacristy at St. Anthony's, sometimes he'd be very talkative; other times, he'd walk in and not say a word. He'd walk right past you like you're a wall."

After Father Biernacki left the Roman Catholic Church to join the Byzantine Catholic Church in 1968, eventually switching to the Orthodox Church in America in 1972, Father Robinson turned a cold shoulder to his old friend.

"Once I left and was in the Orthodox Church, he was extremely negative and noncommunicative to me," Father Biernacki said. "I had a chance to be at a number of functions with him—relatives' funerals in the Polish community—and he wouldn't even turn around and say hello."

Although Father Robinson served as a priest in the Toledo diocese for forty years, he was not very well known by his colleagues.

"He was not much of a socializer," said Father Joseph Jaros, a retired priest.

Auxiliary Bishop Robert Donnelly, who retired in 2006, was ordained alongside Father Robinson in 1964, but said he never really knew the priest.

Father Robinson lived with his mother in a modest brick house in West Toledo, near the University of Toledo and next door to a police station, for years.

His next-door neighbor for over ten years, Jackie Powell, said the priest never said a word to her or her family. "Not even a 'hello,'" she said.

Edward and Martha Wesley, an elderly couple who live around the corner from the priest, said they would sometimes see him mowing the grass or tending to flowers in his meticulously kept yard. They said Father Robinson's parents were talkative and polite, but that the priest rarely, if ever, interacted with them.

One neighbor said Father Robinson used to blast music by the British heavy-metal band Black Sabbath while he washed his car in the driveway or puttered around the yard.

He was known for being kind and considerate to senior citizens, especially in his hospital visitations and when conducting funerals, Mrs. Wesley, the neighbor, said.

"As far as I know, he was very well liked by the elderly," she said.

Several longtime members of Polish Catholic parishes said Father Robinson was extraordinarily devoted to his flock.

"He's a good, good man," said Mary Ann Plewa, a lifelong member of St. Anthony's Parish. "He's a real quiet priest. At parties, he would go stand in a corner. But he always dressed as a priest. He would never wear T-shirts or something. He's just wonderful. You would never find a priest like him, I don't care what anybody says.

"When my sister lost her husband, she called Father Jerry and he was there in a second. He's a very dedicated priest."

Bea Orlowski, Father Robinson's secretary for eleven years, said the clergyman is "very compassionate, very concerned for the people who are sick and also people in general. He's there for them in a time of need, no matter what time of night or day."

She also said Father Robinson is "a quiet man, but there are a lot of people that are quiet."

Father Paul Kwiatkowski, a Toledo priest who celebrated his fortieth anniversary of ordination in 2005, said Father Robinson lived with him for four years while they were assigned to St. Hedwig's Parish.

"He's such a quiet guy, a simple guy. He's a nice fellow," Father Kwiatkowski said.

Judge Mary Chrzanowski of Macomb County circuit court in Michigan said she has known Father Robinson since she was a child and that the priest would join her family for Thanksgiving dinner every year from the late 1970s until 1991.

"Father Jerry is a very humble person who always had very little to say. He always respected your opinion and never initiated an argument," Judge Chrzanowski said.

Hiltman, the church organist, said Father Robinson created strong feelings one way or another.

"There are those that just loved him, and those who just could not stand him," he said.

Chapter 18

Sister Mary Curtiss* is a petite, high-strung woman in her early forties. When she tells her life story, it is amazing she is able to carry on what appears to be a normal life.

For years, the sister has been teaching students at a Catholic school in Toledo and also works with children who have special-education needs.

With short-cropped gray hair and wire-rim glasses, the nun admits that despite her calm exterior, she lives in terror.

Part of the terror comes from childhood memories that flash into her mind, shattering her nerves and even causing physical pain.

The memories include being raped as a pig-tailed grade-school student, or witnessing horrific rituals in which men wearing dark robes killed her pet dog and forced her to drink blood.

In January 2002, as she read the daily newspaper reports and saw television accounts of Catholic Church's clerical sexual-abuse scandal that erupted in Boston, Sister Mary Curtiss began to steel herself to take action.

She had been undergoing years of psychological counseling, paying for the expensive therapy out of her own modest salary, with help from her religious order.

She read how many of the people who had been raped and molested by priests were now asking for dioceses to pay for counseling. It was time for some justice, she told herself.

The nun built up her courage and called Frank DiLallo, the case manager for the Catholic Diocese of Toledo, and requested a meeting.

Sister Mary Curtiss went downtown to the Catholic Center and met with DiLallo, a licensed counselor whose job is to be the liaison between the Toledo diocese and victims of clerical sexual abuse.

At the time, he was working only part-time for the diocese and had his own private practice. But by the middle of 2002, DiLallo's job as case manager became a full-time position.

---

* Her name has been changed to protect her identity.

The nun told him at the start of their meeting that she wanted the diocese to pay $50,000 to cover the costs of her counseling and prescription medicines that she and her religious order had been paying since 1993.

DiLallo asked her why the diocese should pay her therapy bills and who the perpetrator was.

"Because Father Warren raped and abused me," she replied.

"Father Chet Warren?" DiLallo asked.

"Yes. Him," Sister Mary Curtiss said curtly. The name triggered a cold chill down her spine.

"Well, Sister, he is not a Toledo diocesan priest. As you know, he's an Oblate of St. Francis de Sales," DiLallo said, sounding patronizing to the nun.

She had anticipated that response.

"Yes, I know he is an Oblate of St. Francis de Sales. But he is serving as a priest in Toledo, and he can only do so with the permission of Bishop Hoffman," the nun stated firmly.

DiLallo said he would have to investigate the situation; it was something new for him. He promised to get back to her as soon as possible. Warren had been defrocked in 1996 and had been sued by a number of women who claimed he had raped and abused them when they were children. In every case, the alleged abuse occurred so long ago that the statutes of limitations had expired and the Lucas County prosecutor's office said it could not pursue charges against the cleric.

Four months after Sister Mary Curtiss first sat down with DiLallo, she contacted the case manager again and requested a second meeting. This time she brought a statement from her pharmacist that detailed the money she had spent on medication, plus a letter from the mother superior of her order demanding that the Toledo diocese take action on the sister's request for payment.

DiLallo said representatives of the diocese wanted to sit down with officials of the Oblates of St. Francis de Sales, a religious community with its regional headquarters in Toledo, to try to develop a joint plan to handle the nun's complaints.

The nun, her attorney, and the head of her religious order exchanged letters and phone calls with the Toledo diocese and the Oblates for months.

Eventually, diocesan officials asked Sister Mary Curtiss to testify before the church's review board, a panel of six Catholic laypersons appointed by the diocese to listen to allegations of clerical sexual abuse and determine if the charges are credible.

The Toledo diocesan panel, established according to the U.S. Conference of Catholic Bishops' sex-abuse policy adopted in Dallas, Texas, in June 2002, included an attorney, a medical doctor, a psychologist, a canon lawyer, a victim of clerical sexual abuse, and a retired city manager.

"Frank DiLallo told me that if the review board thinks I'm credible, the diocese will pay for your therapy to a certain amount," Sister Mary Curtiss later told a reporter. "I thought it would be a pretty clear-cut deal. I didn't think my integrity would be in question."

The nun went to the Catholic Center on June 11, 2003, and faced the review board, revealing to them the disturbing secrets of her childhood. She told them she had been sexually, physically, and emotionally abused and tortured by a group of men and women when she was a child, and that group included several priests.

There were a number of priests who abused her, she said, including Chet Warren and Toledo diocesan priest Father Gerald Robinson.

Then she handed each member of the review board a four-page statement, typed and single-spaced, giving an overview of her allegations.

"This report is written for the Diocesan Review Board Members to chronicle the severe abuse I experienced beginning at age 2," she wrote.

"During my preschool years, my mother suffered a severe depression. Chet Warren would often visit during the day to offer her pastoral counseling. After these sessions he would encourage her to go upstairs and rest—he'd watch me. On these occasions he began sexually abusing me. . . ."

The statement included shocking descriptions of molestation by the priest that began with fondling, led to oral sex while the victim was still a preschooler, and continued to escalate into her elementary school years.

"By the time I was in third grade, he became physically violent as well," she wrote. "Sexual contact was becoming rougher and I would cry. Once he pulled my pigtails, slapped me across the face several times and told me this was just the beginning. Another time he sodomized me."

Then her allegations got darker—much darker.

"This abuse, awful as it was, represents only a portion of a much larger abusive context."

She claimed that some priests were involved in "a satanic group that performed rituals in honor of Satan on a regular basis."

Sister Mary Curtiss named three priests, a well-known pediatrician, two female teachers, and her own father and grandfather as members of the cult who abused her.

"The rituals were horrifying and sadistic, designed to break our wills and internalize whatever core programmed message they wished to use to further our powerlessness."

When she was 5 years old, she wrote, her pet Labrador Retriever Smoky died.

"A few nights later, my dad told me we were going to see Smoky. Thinking he was somehow better now, I was excited. We arrived at an old house and down in the basement was a large table on which Smoky was lying. Dad and other adults changed into black robes. My sister . . . was given a meat cleaver and she began to hack Smoky apart. The priest told me that because I was such a bad girl, [my sister] had to hurt Smoky like this. He then told me if I really loved Smoky, I would be able to put him back together again and make him come back to life. . . . I learned that anything I loved would be annihilated and that everything was my fault."

Also at age 5, she said, she was taken to Calvary Cemetery and placed inside a coffin-like pine box during a cult ceremony. "Cockroaches were released into the box. I was in the box for several minutes and thought I was going crazy. They told me the bugs were marking me for Satan," she wrote.

She said the cult members raped her in an initiation ceremony when she was 6.

"The cult members beat drums and [a priest] carried me to a table and vaginally raped me," she said.

The cult also killed, Sister Mary Curtiss stated.

"At age 11, they made me ingest an eyeball. They wanted me to know they were always watching me. . . . After the eyeball incident, they killed a little girl who was about three. I don't know who she was or where she was from. All of the adults left, leaving me alone in the room—a sea of blood and stench. I found an old cardboard piece and sat on it for hours. It was a little island. I told myself if I stayed on the cardboard, I wouldn't go crazy. I wished I had died."

Sister Mary Curtiss said that when she was in high school, Chet Warren was serving as chaplain at St. Vincent Hospital. Her father would drive her to the hospital and turn her over to Warren, who would take her to his quarters where men would pay him to have sadomasochistic sex with the girl.

"One of these S&M perpetrators was Father Gerald Robinson, a diocesan priest," she wrote. "I do not know who the others were."

As result of the abuse, Sister Mary Curtiss said she suffers from dissociative disorder and post-traumatic stress disorder.

Afterward, the nun said two members of the review board—psychologist Dr. Robert Cooley and pediatrician Dr. Pamela Oatis—seemed to understand what she was telling them and showed compassion.

"They cared, they understood the context, they knew what I was saying. I wasn't necessarily troubled by the fact that the others looked like they had been hit by a truck, because I pretty much expected that," Sister Mary Curtiss said.

Chapter 19

As soon as Sister Mary Curtiss walked out of the review board meeting, Dr. Cooley turned to the chairman, Frank Link.

"We have to report these allegations to law-enforcement authorities," Dr. Cooley said.

"Now wait a minute, Bob. Let's not act in haste. We need to discuss this," Link said.

"But there's nothing to discuss, Frank. These are not only allegations of sexual abuse of a child; she's claiming the cult murdered a child. At *least* one child. She implied there may have been more murders."

"Yes, well, Sister Mary Curtiss made a lot of allegations—a lot of very bizarre allegations," Link said. "Think about that. Our job as a review board is to decide if allegations are credible. If they're not credible, why would we report them to police? We'd just be wasting their time. It would be irresponsible of us."

"No, you've got it wrong," Dr. Cooley responded. "Our job is to determine the credibility of sexual-abuse allegations, but this is a murder allegation. As a licensed psychologist, I am obligated by law to report criminal allegations to appropriate law-enforcement authorities. And as far as I can tell, murder is a crime. Is it not, Frank?"

The rest of the board members jumped into the conversation before Link could answer. There were plenty of shouts and fists slammed onto tables. The meeting digressed into momentary chaos.

"*Now wait! Hold it!*" One voice rose above the clatter.

It was Frank DiLallo, the diocese's case manager, who had sat in on the nun's testimony—the only time he had ever done so.

"We're all professionals here. We all want to fulfill our obligations to the church and to the law," DiLallo said. "I'm a licensed professional counselor. I know there are mandatory reporting laws. We're not going to withhold anything from the police. We're not going to interfere with the legal process.

"First, let's all calm down and discuss exactly what we heard today in this room. First things first: We need to come to a consensus on the credibility of Sister

Mary Curtiss's allegations that she was sexually abused as a minor by priests. That's our first obligation. Then we can get into the other allegations. It's still early. We've got all day."

After more than hour of discussion, Dr. Cooley—the only non-Catholic on the review board—was alone in the belief that the nun's allegations should be reported to law-enforcement authorities.

He also was the only one of the six members of the panel who felt that Sister Mary Curtiss's allegations of sexual abuse were credible.

Doctor Cooley, 37, had been counseling both victims and perpetrators of sexual abuse for more than a decade, ever since earning his doctorate from the University of Toledo. He knew how victims of child sexual abuse deal with their emotions, and how many of them struggle to cope with the trauma inflicted upon them that stole their youth and their innocence and, in some cases, their lives.

He explained to the review board members that some victims of child sexual abuse sink into a life of depression, or turn to alcohol and drug abuse, or live in emotional isolation, become dysfunctional in relationships, or seek refuge in sexual promiscuity.

Some cannot cope at all and try to end their suffering through suicide.

In Sister Mary Curtiss's case, her subconscious mind blocked the horrific abuse from her own consciousness, Dr. Cooley said. It's a defensive mechanism—a way of protecting herself and holding onto her sanity.

The psychological term is called repressed memory syndrome. When these long-buried memories return to the surface, they're called recovered memories. A news report, a photograph, a smell, a touch—something comes along that triggers a memory that had been buried deep within, bringing it back to the surface, to the person's conscious mind.

Yes, the theory of recovered memories is a controversial one among psychologists and researchers today, he said. There have been numerous cases of people whose recovered memories ultimately proved to be false, the result of the way police or psychologists asked them certain questions. The "memories" were planted through subtle suggestions, either deliberately or innocently, that were made to people in anguish who were vulnerable and easily swayed.

But there have been recovered memories that have proved true, Dr. Cooley said.

The way the mind stores and recovers memories is a complex system that is far from being fully analyzed or understood by psychologists today. The human brain is capable of doing strange things when it is subjected to horrors that nobody should ever have to deal with—like people who survived concentration camps in Nazi Germany, or a 5-year-old girl being abused by a satanic cult, or a girl of 11 witnessing the murder of a 3-year-old child.

Some argued that Sister Mary Curtiss may be telling the truth—as she sees it. But she could be a victim not of an adult perpetrator in real life, but of her own overactive imagination. A satanic cult in Toledo? Priests worshiping Satan? Human sacrifices? Maybe she watched too many horror movies or read too many

Stephen King novels. She could have some kind of mental instability that makes her unable to separate fact from fantasy, they contended.

"But just suppose," another board member ventured, "that there really is a murderous satanic cult in Toledo in which priests have been—or still are—involved? I'm just playing the devil's advocate here—sorry, poor choice of words. But you know what I mean. What if there really is such a demonic cult? Kids who try to tell adults about it would be dismissed as crazy. And most of the children dragged into these rituals are probably dragged in by their own parents. These kids have nowhere to turn. And the cult continues, because the allegations are just too far out for most people to believe."

The purpose of the Dallas Charter—the landmark document adopted by the U.S. Conference of Catholic Bishops—is not just to punish perpetrators, but to prevent more abuse, Dr. Cooley pointed out.

"Sister Mary Curtiss believes the cult is still active and dangerous. I say we report her allegations to the proper authorities, and let them investigate," he said.

Link called for a vote.

All who felt that Sister Mary Curtiss's allegations were credible and needed to be reported to law-enforcement officials were asked to raise their hand.

Only one hand went up—Dr. Cooley's.

With the vote 5-1, the meeting was quickly adjourned.

Doctor Cooley grabbed his papers—including the nun's four-page testimony—and tucked them into his briefcase and headed for the door.

DiLallo stopped him with a hand on his shoulder.

"Bob, I would never interfere with the review board, but the board has voted. I know you mean well, but you've got to respect the board's decision. Right?"

"Yeah, right," Dr. Cooley said icily, brushing DiLallo's hand away and walking out the door.

Chapter 20

Before Dr. Cooley had left the four-story, brown brick Catholic Center, DiLallo was knocking on the door of Father Michael Billian's top-floor office.

A stocky priest in his forties with dark black hair, a neatly trimmed salt-and-pepper beard, and a deep baritone voice—he sometimes sings the National Anthem at Toledo Mud Hens baseball games—Father Billian held the dual titles of chancellor and episcopal vicar of the Toledo diocese.

The charismatic cleric, one of the most powerful men in the local church, was responsible for the day-to-day operations of the sprawling diocese that stretches across 19 counties in northwest Ohio and has more than 150 parishes and 320,000 members. While the bishop is the overall head of the diocese, it's clerics like Father Billian who take care of details and make sure many of the problems are dealt with.

DiLallo nervously reported the events as they unfolded during the nun's review board meeting.

Father Billian asked DiLallo if he believed Dr. Cooley might take Sister Mary Curtiss's allegations to law-enforcement authorities, despite the review board's vote against doing so.

DiLallo replied that the psychologist seemed convinced that his profession is mandated by law to report such allegations to police, especially since the nun claimed the cult murdered a child, and there is no statute of limitations for murder.

Even though the review board as a whole was convinced that her testimony failed to meet the standards for being considered credible, Dr. Cooley was adamant that law-enforcement authorities should be the ones to look into the allegations and decide their credibility.

Father Billian asked DiLallo about the reliability of recovered memories, like those of Sister Mary Curtiss.

The case manager said his research showed that recovered memories can only be considered valid if there is external corroboration. They can never be considered credible in and of themselves.

In Sister Mary Curtiss's case, she offered no evidence and produced no witnesses to back up her allegations that a satanic cult had killed children and continues to pose a threat to society.

Nevertheless, Dr. Cooley was probably poised to notify authorities. If the nun's allegations hit the news media, it would be one more black eye for the Catholic Church—perhaps the biggest, blackest eye yet.

Father Billian picked up the phone and began dialing.

Later that day, Thomas G. Pletz, the diocese's counsel with the high-powered law firm of Shumaker, Loop & Kendrick, sent a letter by fax addressed to Mr. Frank DiLallo, Diocesan Case Manager, Diocese of Toledo, and although it arrived on June 11, it was dated June 12, 2003.

Dear Frank,

You have asked on behalf of the Diocesan Review Board whether its members have a professional obligation to report to any law enforcement authorities the information reported to it by the religious sister who appeared before the Board this week. I appreciate that its members are taking their responsibilities very seriously. I also know that they are aware of the sensitivity of this information, which they must hold closely as privileged, with no disclosure except as required by law.

I can report that this person's Diocesan file was reviewed by the Lucas County Prosecutor's office last year. Its contents thus have already been reported to the proper legal authorities who decide whether to prosecute persons for criminal offenses in this county. On the level of whether any member of the Board has any present independent duty to report these facts to any one else, I enclose a copy of the Ohio Attorney General Opinion No. 2001-035, which provides a negative conclusion.

Pletz included a five-page legal opinion by the Ohio attorney general addressing whether the law requires professional counselors or licensed social workers who learn of child abuse after the victim has reached adulthood to report the abuse to authorities.

He also stated in the letter that "it appears that the Review Board members are not acting in 'an official or professional capacity' of providing professional counseling or advice so as to trigger any duty to report. Both this victim's legal counsel and her treating therapists are acting in those capacities. . . ."

The letter was copied to Rev. Michael Billian and John F. Hayward, another Shumaker, Loop & Kendrick attorney who had been representing the Toledo diocese for decades.

Claudia Vercellotti, a Toledo victim's advocate, said Pletz's letter was disturbing.

"The letter had people shook up. It was meant to intimidate Cooley—and it worked," she said.

And she questioned its accuracy, especially Pletz's claim that the nun's diocesan file had been reviewed by the Lucas County prosecutor's office in 2002. Vercellotti had been in close and frequent contact with Sister Mary Curtiss and knew that the nun had not written that four-page testimony until just before the review board hearing.

Previously, she had revealed only bits and pieces of information about her abuse to DiLallo, feeling that if she told the whole story she would immediately be dismissed as a raving lunatic.

Vercellotti said that if in fact the prosecutor's office had reviewed Sister Mary Curtiss's file in 2002, those allegations did not include any reference to a murderous satanic cult in which priests were members.

Vercellotti, a bold and doggedly determined woman in her mid-thirties, had been challenging the diocese since early 2002 over its handling of the clerical sexual-abuse scandal.

Abused as a minor by a diocesan lay leader, Vercellotti co-founded the Toledo chapter of SNAP—the Survivors Network of those Abused by Priests. That national organization, with more than 4,300 members, was founded by Barbara Blaine.

A Toledo native now living in Chicago, Blaine was sexually abused as a child by Father Chet Warren, her former pastor at St. Pius Parish who has been accused by eight women of sexually abusing them when they were children.

Vercellotti said she received copies of Pletz's threatening letter from several sources on the afternoon of Sister Mary Curtiss's hearing. The extraordinarily quick reaction seemed to indicate to her that the diocese was quite concerned over the allegations against a religious-order priest—someone who was not even one of its own.

The response from Pletz made Vercellotti think the diocese was not just worried about Chet Warren, but about the nun dredging up the name of Father Gerald Robinson.

She knew, as did most people who had been around the diocese for a while, that police considered Father Robinson the prime suspect in the 1980 murder of Sister Margaret Ann Pahl. That case was one that the diocese did not wish to revisit, and it may be why church officials were so jumpy over the nun's testimony, Vercellotti reasoned.

Odd, too, that the diocese was forgetting the cooperation agreement that Bishop James Hoffman and the Lucas County prosecutor's office had signed in August 2002.

Father Billian said at the time that Bishop Hoffman initiated the agreement, modeled after one adopted in other cities, because he wanted the Toledo diocese "to do business in a very transparent way."

The bishop pledged to "provide the prosecutor with information regarding allegations involving a priest, deacon, member of a religious community, volunteer, or other authorized representative of the diocese."

Vercellotti said that in light of the agreement and the pledge of transparency, it made no sense for the diocese to be fighting Dr. Cooley so aggressively.

"The diocese should have gone running to the prosecutor's office with the nun's allegations, especially after signing that cooperation agreement in August 2002," she said.

After Pletz's letter, Dr. Cooley and Vercellotti met with Sister Mary Curtiss and told her that they thought it was time to take her allegations to law-enforcement authorities.

The nun refused.

"She still wanted to play by the diocese's rules," Vercellotti said. "Dr. Cooley told her that he didn't think the diocese had her best interests at heart, but she, like so many victims of clerical sexual abuse, was determined to follow the diocese's procedures."

"I wanted to give the diocese the benefit of the doubt," Sister Mary Curtiss acknowledged.

On June 27, as debates raged among the review board members and the diocese, Pletz penned another letter regarding the nun's allegations. This time he wrote to Frank Link, chair of the diocese's review board.

"First, I am concerned whether the review board believes it should report something to the Lucas County Prosecutor and/or Toledo Police Department. Respectfully, I believe that any such reporting remains the responsibility of the Diocesan Case Manager or legal counsel for the Diocese. . . .

"Secondly, in our opinion, any Board member's individual investigation separate from that of the Board is not appropriate. . . ."

This Pletz letter "seemed like an act of desperation," according to Vercellotti. "We thought they protesteth too much. They were obviously practicing damage control."

The letter also stated that any review board members who conducted their own investigations into allegations risked "breaches of confidentiality" that "could compromise the integrity of the review board."

For psychologists, confidentiality is a vital part of their practice and something they guard zealously. Pletz's letter seemed not only to be insulting, but a veiled threat against Dr. Cooley's integrity, hinting that some board members couldn't be trusted to keep the confidentiality of abuse victims who testify before them.

Doctor Cooley again urged Sister Mary Curtiss to report her allegations to law-enforcement authorities, but the nun was determined not to step out of line but rather to follow the diocese's procedures to the letter.

"I know Cooley's position was, and remains, that he is a state-mandated reporter," the nun said, "and he was not going to sit on a crime that may be credible. He asked me, in his professional capacity, to share that information with police," the nun said.

Over the next few months, as Dr. Cooley jousted with the diocese, Sister Mary Curtiss slowly began to change her point of view to align with the psychologist.

"The diocese was saying that they didn't think my allegations were credible, but even if they felt it was a pile of cockadoodie, they should be mandated to report it because of the murder allegation," she said.

In September, she gave Dr. Cooley and Vercellotti permission to meet with law-enforcement authorities on her behalf, and to give them a copy of the four-page testimony she had typed up and delivered to the review board.

Chapter 21

Early on a crisp September morning in 2003, Claudia Vercellotti picked up Dr. Robert Cooley in her tidy but well-worn Toyota and headed south on I-75 to Bowling Green, Ohio.

The feisty Vercellotti had become consumed with her holy war against abuses and cover-ups by the rulers of her church. When she first participated in a news conference in 2002, she gladly stood in the background while Jeff Anderson, a nationally known Minnesota attorney who has been suing Catholic dioceses for decades, and Barbara Blaine, a Chicago attorney and Toledo native who founded the national group SNAP, blasted the Toledo diocese for its mishandling of clerical sexual-abuse cases.

It was a difficult time for Vercellotti, and she was glad to stay on the fringes of the media spotlight. Not only was she being forced to deal with the disturbing memories of her own abuse—and to discuss these dark secrets with family, friends, and even the media—but her father was suffering from terminal cancer.

Doctor Cooley, meanwhile, was not personally affected by the Catholic Church scandal, but he felt an obligation to use the knowledge and expertise he had gained as a clinical psychologist to help the church chart a new course through this unprecedented and painful crisis.

Meanwhile, his wife was pregnant with their third child and he was struggling to keep a healthy balance between family life and his psychology practice when the church asked him to serve on its newly created review board. A non-Catholic attending a contemporary "seeker-sensitive" suburban church, Dr. Cooley hesitated to cram one more time-consuming commitment into his already full schedule.

But he knew that what he had learned in ten years of counseling both victims and perpetrators of abuse could help the diocese make informed decisions in dealing with its crisis.

Today, however, Dr. Cooley regretted those good intentions. He had not expected his review board assignment to spiral downward into a quandary of ethical, moral, spiritual, and legal dimensions.

As a licensed psychologist, he knew he was required by law to report to civil authorities any possible crimes he learned about through therapy. Failure to do so could result in criminal and civil penalties, including the potential loss of his psychologist's license—an action that would devastate his career and cause hardship for his family.

When Sister Mary Curtiss told the review board that she had witnessed the murder of a 3-year-old child by a satanic cult, Dr. Cooley felt it was an allegation that he was compelled to report to law enforcement authorities.

What harm would it do, letting trained investigators decide whether or not a crime had been committed? And yet the church immediately set about pressuring him not to take the allegations to law-enforcement officials.

Their reasoning didn't ring true to him.

If the Toledo diocese was so sure the nun's allegations were not credible, why not let the police handle it? Sure, if her claims that local priests were involved in a satanic cult reached the media, the press would have a feeding frenzy. But he knew the police could keep a lid on it while they were investigating.

After months of discussing the situation with his wife, and with Sister Mary Curtiss and Vercellotti, Dr. Cooley was now en route to the attorney general's office in Bowling Green, armed with a copy of the nun's shocking four-page testimony.

The two whistleblowers had ruled out going to the Lucas County prosecutor's office with the allegations. SNAP, Dr. Cooley, and Sister Mary Curtiss all felt they could not trust the local prosecutor's office to pursue the allegations, based on the way it had handled other cases of clerical sexual abuse.

No criminal charges had been filed against priests accused of molesting children in Lucas County. True, virtually all of the allegations involved cases of rape and molestation that happened decades earlier, which meant the statutes of limitations had long ago expired.

But Jeff Anderson, the Minnesota attorney who specialized in suing Catholic dioceses, asserted that if a prosecutor was interested in pursuing charges against abusive priests and church officials who covered up the crimes, he or she could find a way.

For example, Anderson said, federal and state RICO acts—which stands for Racketeer Influenced and Corrupt Organizations—allow charges to be filed if there was a conspiracy to cover up the crimes. Prosecutors in some cities were using the RICO laws against dioceses, claiming that bishops knew their priests had abused children but conspired to bury the crimes rather than report them to authorities.

"Where there's a will to prosecute, there's a way," Anderson said. "Sadly, the Lucas County prosecutor's office has shown no will to prosecute abusive priests."

When several people contacted SNAP and a newspaper reporter claiming that a cleric, now deceased, had molested them when they were children, the reporter called assistant Lucas County prosecutor John Weglian to ask if he would investigate such allegations.

"If the priest is dead," Weglian said, "we don't give a shit."

With that kind of response, Dr. Cooley and Vercellotti decided to take Sister Mary Curtiss's allegations to authorities outside of Lucas County.

Vercellotti had called the Ohio attorney general's office in neighboring Wood County and made an appointment for 7:30 a.m. with Special Agent Phil Lucas in Bowling Green, about twenty miles south of Toledo.

She and Dr. Cooley met with Lucas for more than hour that morning and gave him a copy of the nun's typed testimony.

"He was not overly enthusiastic, but he did not dismiss the allegations outright," Vercellotti said.

Lucas wanted more information, and Vercellotti made several more trips to Bowling Green to deliver copies of documents, including Pletz's letters to the review board.

Shortly after Dr. Cooley's visit to Bowling Green, he received a phone call from Carol Collins, chairperson of the Toledo diocese's review board, telling him that his services were no longer needed. He was off the review board.

Father Billian, episcopal vicar of the diocese, told the *Blade* newspaper that the work of the review board is confidential, and "I think there were some issues about him doing that work confidentially."

On December 2, Lucas sent a copy of the nun's testimony to the Lucas County prosecutor's office by fax, with a cover letter suggesting that they look into the allegations.

"It was different this time because it came from the attorney general's office," Vercellotti said. "If we had given it directly to the prosecutor's office, I doubt they would have done a thing with it."

Prosecutor Julia Bates turned the file over to her cold-case team, a task force of law-enforcement experts she had put together in 1997 to investigate unsolved homicides. With no statute of limitations for murder, a killer can be prosecuted years or decades after the crime.

The Lucas County cold-case squad was composed of law-enforcement authorities and scientific experts from the Toledo police department, the Lucas County sheriff's department, the Federal Bureau of Investigation, the Ohio Bureau of Criminal Investigation and Identification, the Lucas County coroner's office, and the Lucas County prosecutor's office.

One of the veteran law-enforcement officials on the cold-case team was Tom Ross, who had retired from the Toledo police department and then joined the prosecutor's office as an investigator.

When Ross reviewed Sister Mary Curtiss's case file, sent to the prosecutor's office by Special Agent Lucas, one name popped out to him: Father Gerald Robinson.

Ross had been working for the Toledo police department in April 1980, when Sister Margaret Ann Pahl was murdered. He wasn't on the team of detectives that investigated the murder, but he remembered hearing all the talk around the office: Robinson was the only suspect.

Ross walked down to the Safety Building and knocked on the wall outside Sergeant Steve Forrester's cubicle, then plopped into a chair.

"Steve, Sister Mary Curtiss mentions Father Robinson in this testimony. You weren't around back then, but the priest was the main suspect in 1980 when a nun was murdered in Mercy Hospital."

"I heard his name mentioned a few times here and there," Sergeant Forrester said.

"He wasn't just one of the suspects," Investigator Ross said. "The detectives all said he was the *only* suspect. They just didn't have enough evidence to arrest him."

"And so you're saying we should go back and look at that evidence?"

"Well, I'm thinking about it," Ross said. "What do you think?"

"It doesn't have anything to do with the nun's claims about the satanic cult and the murder charge," said Sergeant Forrester, who had read her four-page testimony to the review board. "She only mentions Robinson later, about S&M sex."

"Yes, but she claims Robinson paid Chet Warren. Maybe there is a connection between the two priests," Ross said. "And the nun that was killed, it was a weird case. Some people thought it was a ritual killing."

"You know, Tom, with all those angles involved, maybe it is worth looking into," Forrester said.

Chapter 22

Steve Forrester, 50, an athletic-looking detective with twenty-seven years on the Toledo police force, and Tom Ross, 58, nicknamed "Father Confessor" for the way his friendly demeanor gets criminals talking, had been working together on cold-case investigations for more than six years.

The cold-case team had an impressive record—thirty-five of the fifty unsolved homicides it opened up had resulted in convictions. Among them was the high-profile case of Toledo serial killers Anthony and Nathaniel Cook, who confessed to murdering nine people in a bloody spree that started in 1973 and continued until 1981. One of the Cook brothers' victims was Detective Ross's young niece.

On December 4, 2003, the two investigators met in the Safety Building, where they took the elevator to the basement and signed out a key to the property room.

Sifting through row after row of dusty cases and boxes, they found the shelf they were looking for:

Item No. 4330

Sister Margaret Ann Pahl

Murdered

Mercy Hospital, Toledo, April 5, 1980

The two checked out the boxes from the property room and carried them upstairs to Sergeant Forrester's office.

Inside one box, they found a brown-paper grocery sack with a neatly folded white linen cloth inside. The detectives put on surgical gloves and pulled the cloth out of the bag, then placed it, folded, on a desk.

According to the evidence label, it was an altar cloth, slightly yellowed, about ten feet long and two and a half feet wide, with lace trim on three sides. Scattered around the cloth were seemingly random patches of bloodstains. In one section, there was a cluster of odd-shaped puncture holes.

There also was another, smaller altar cloth that had been found by one of the Sisters of Mercy on the floor outside the Mercy Hospital chapel on the morning of the nun's murder. A security guard had turned that one over to detectives, who then placed it in storage at the Safety Building two days after the slaying. The two altar cloths had not been looked at again until now.

The detectives next opened a six-inch-by-eight-inch white envelope and dumped its contents on the table. Clattering out was a silver-colored letter opener, shaped like a sword, about nine or ten inches long. Also spilling out was a small circular medallion that looked as though it had been part of the letter opener. It had an engraving of the U.S. Capitol Building and the words "Wax Museum, Washington, D.C."

Sergeant Arthur Marx had typed the evidence tag. The letter opener was taken from Father Robinson's apartment at Mercy Hospital thirteen days after the murder of the nun.

The investigators also looked at other evidence from the case: a pair of black, rubber-soled men's shoes; a Valium bottle prescribed to Gerald Robinson on April 5, 1980; the nun's clothing, eerily punctured and stained with blood, and items such as fingernail clippings, hair samples, and bodily swabs taken from the victim.

When Sister Margaret Ann Pahl was killed, DNA was not available as a tool for identifying suspects. Today, even a tiny sample of DNA can make or break a case. It looked, however, like the detectives now might possibly find some useful DNA from the items kept in storage all these years.

The first item Detectives Ross and Forrester thought they should have tested was the altar cloth. The bloodstains and the puncture marks could contain vital clues. The letter opener was another item they wanted to examine closely.

Detectives Forrester and Ross, along with Lieutenant Rick Reed and Detective Snider of the Scientific Investigations Unit, met in a conference room in the Safety Building where there was table large enough to spread out the altar cloth.

"Look at this bloodstain," Ross said, pointing to a five-inch dark-brown mark with thin, parallel lines. "And then look at the handle on the letter opener."

The letter opener's metal handle had thin ribbing, its parallel metal edges about an eighth of an inch apart. The thin dark lines on the altar cloth's stain seemed a likely match.

There were other stains that seemed to match the shape of the letter opener, all three officers agreed.

Looking at the holes in the cloth, they looked as if they could have been made by the blade of the letter opener, which had four sides in a diamond-shaped cross section. The holes in the cloth were wider than ones that would have been made by a typical flat blade.

The officers said they should look for law-enforcement officials in the area who could analyze the puncture defects and the bloodstains on the altar cloth and compare them with the size and shape of the letter opener.

On December 5, detectives Ross and Forrester drove to Bowling Green, taking the altar cloth and letter opener with them, where they met with Dan Davison of the Ohio Bureau of Criminal Investigation and Identification (BCI).

Davison's specialty was trace evidence—examining fingerprints, hairs, fibers, gunshot residue, and blood spatter for clues.

They left the items with Davison, who spent a day and a half comparing the letter opener's size, shape, and details with the holes in the altar cloth and the bloodstains on the fabric.

A few days later, Davison called the cold-case investigators with disappointing news.

He could not determine if the letter opener was the source of the punctures or the bloodstains.

"I cannot include nor exclude the letter opener as the potential weapon," he wrote in a report he handed them.

At the monthly meeting of the Lucas County cold-case team in January, one of the members, Cassandra Agosti of the Ohio BCI, asked if she could look at the evidence and try to find DNA.

Agosti had been part of the cold-case squad since 1999, and shortly after joining the team conducted tests on the priest's saber-shaped letter opener, searching for traces of blood. She had swabbed TMB—tetramethylbenzadrene—on the surfaces of the letter opener and noted a reaction in one area—the recessed circle where the Capitol Building medallion used to be. But the chemical reagent had produced only tentative results, and the amount of blood was so small that nothing conclusive could be determined.

Now, five years later, Agosti wanted to further pursue DNA testing, but warned the team that it would be a long shot for two reasons. First, DNA is a biological material that degrades over time and exposure to the elements, and twenty-four years had passed since the murder. Second, police in 1980 were unaware of DNA usage and did not take precautions to avoid contaminating the evidence.

Agosti took several pieces of evidence to the BCI crime lab in London, Ohio— the altar cloth, swabs that Ed Marok had taken from Sister Margaret Ann's body in 1980, the nun's underwear, and the medallion from the letter opener.

While she was able to find some DNA, almost all of it was below reporting standards, despite the fact that it took only microscopic amounts—as little as a billionth of a gram—to reach some conclusions.

One test Agosti performed that did produce some results involved a small stain found on the inner waistband of the nun's underwear. The scientist discovered a "mixture" of DNA, meaning there was more than one person's DNA found in the stain. That mixture contained a Y chromosome, which meant that it was from a male, and she was able to analyze enough general characteristics to limit the donor to 1 out of 83 Caucasian males.

Agosti also obtained partial results from a DNA mixture on the altar cloth.

She was unable to match the DNA results, however, to any of the individuals in the Sister Margaret Ann Pahl case, because at that point she had no "standards"— or positive DNA identifications—to compare the mixtures to.

In February, 2004, Agosti tested ten fingernail clippings that had been taken from the victim's body in 1980. The researcher tested each one for the presumptive presence of blood, and got a positive result on just one nail, from the right hand. Once again, however, the results could not be confirmed because the amount was too small for conclusive testing.

Agosti recommended to the detectives that they try to obtain DNA samples from the people who were at the scene in 1980, from the investigators who worked on the case, to medical personnel who treated her, to any of the suspects.

The blood and DNA tests at that point were no help to the prosecutors, and neither was BCI's examination of the holes and bloodstains on the altar cloth.

Yet when members of the Lucas County cold-case squad looked at Father Robinson's letter opener and compared it to the stains and the puncture defects, they were convinced the sword-shaped letter opener was a match with the holes and the bloodstains.

They asked Dr. Diane Barnett, deputy Lucas County coroner, to analyze the altar cloth and the letter opener, and she told investigators that the instrument's blade was compatible with the holes in the altar cloth.

The cold-case team decided to get the opinions of national experts.

Chapter 23

Detectives Forrester and Ross called around to local law-enforcement agencies looking for someone who had training in bloodstain-pattern analysis, and were referred by several people to Detective Terry Cousino of the Toledo police department's Scientific Investigations Unit (SIU).

Cousino, who had joined SIU in 1995, had attended a number of workshops on bloodstain-pattern transfer analysis, a relatively new field of forensics that looks to connect a weapon or other piece of evidence with impressions made by a blood-covered instrument that comes in contact with a smooth surface.

One expert compared the process to that of a rubber stamp and ink—you put ink on the rubber stamp and press it down, and it leaves an ink-stained image. It's the same principle with bloodstains: When a blood-covered gun or knife is placed on a table, it leaves behind an image in blood that can be used as evidence.

One reason Cousino had been selected for training in bloodstain-pattern transfer analysis was because he had an artist's eye. The detective had earned a degree in art education at the University of Toledo before deciding to go into law enforcement, and he had the ability to spot patterns in blood that other police officers might overlook.

Not only did Cousino have expertise in bloodstain patterns, he also was an expert with fingerprint evidence and was a forensic artist, drawing composite sketches of suspects and creating portraits to illustrate age progression or provide facial reconstruction.

On February 27, 2004, Cousino met with detectives Forrester and Ross and assistant Lucas County prosecutors J. Christopher Anderson and Dean Mandros to examine the altar cloth and the letter opener.

Almost as soon as Cousino looked at the linen cloth, he spotted definite patterns in the blood. One that seemed unmistakably clear, he said, was an acorn-shaped stain that looked to be a perfect match with the knob at the end of the letter opener's handle.

Another stain that seemed clearly defined was a curved line in blood that matched the size, shape, and curvature of the letter opener's blade when laid on its side.

"I could see the transfer pattern had a definite shape and curve to it," Cousino said. "When I compared it to the letter opener, I felt it was consistent with the shape and the curve of the blade."

To verify his observations, Cousino recommended that the cold-case squad consult with national experts in bloodstain-pattern transfer analysis.

Anderson, a member of the American Academy of Forensic Scientists, said prosecutors and police wanted to follow Cousino's lead and consult with more specialists.

"We decided to check with the experts and see if they could confirm that we had what we thought we had," Anderson said.

There were only five people in the world certified in bloodstain-pattern transfer analysis. Those credentials were carefully meted out by Professor Herbert MacDonnell of the Institute on the Physical Significance of Human Bloodstain Evidence.

Prosecutors planned to see which experts would be willing and able to examine the evidence in Sister Margaret Ann's murder.

In addition to the bloodstains, Cousino also examined the holes in the altar cloth.

On the inside of the cloth, the edges of the holes had small defects that indicated the blade had been pushed through the material, rather than slicing through it. In other words, Cousino told the detectives and prosecutors, it appeared that the very tip of the instrument was dull.

And the puncture defects were not ordinary slits, but had a Y shape to them.

Cousino then pointed out a group of puncture marks centered in one section of the cloth.

He counted eighteen holes, in two groups of nine. Looking at the way the holes lined up, he said it was obvious that there were actually nine stab wounds—the cloth had been folded over. Each stab wound left two holes, one in the top layer and one in the bottom, Cousino said.

"The two sets of nine lined up perfectly," he said.

"One side had more blood. That was the side closer to the blood source. So the left side was up, and the right side was underneath," Cousino said.

He noticed something peculiar in the way the holes lined up.

"These puncture defects had a definite form and symmetry," Cousino said.

He took a piece of tracing paper and placed it over the holes, then marked the spots where the cloth had been punctured.

Cousino then picked up a ruler and drew lines connecting the dots on the tracing paper.

"It fits the form of a cross," he said, pointing it out to the detectives and prosecutors. "It is so symmetrical and precise that it suggests to me the person had placed an actual cross down on the cloth and used it as a template, stabbing around the form of the cross."

Detectives Forrester and Ross looked at one another. Based on the wounds in Sister Margaret Ann's upper left chest, the altar cloth had to have been placed in a certain orientation.

The stab wounds formed a perfect cross, that was clear. But there was something more: It was not just a cross, but an upside-down cross.

Chapter 24

The day after Detective Cousino examined the altar cloth, finding patterns that linked Father Robinson's letter opener to the murder, Sergeant Forrester called T. Paulette Sutton in Memphis.

Sutton was one of the world's five certified bloodstain-pattern transfer analysis experts, and one of three authors of the definitive textbook, *Principles of Bloodstain Pattern Analysis: Theory and Practice.*

Sutton agreed to review the evidence and, on March 10, 2004, Sergeant Forrester and Detective Cousino flew to Memphis with a carry-on suitcase containing the actual altar cloth and a piece of linen the same size and texture for a sample, the priest's letter opener with the medallion, and some of Sister Margaret Ann's clothing.

A stocky woman with glasses and a short wave of salt-and-pepper hair, Sutton told the police officers that her specialty is studying "the static aftermath of a bloodletting event."

She took the letter opener and the sample piece of linen and began making arrangements for some preliminary tests.

The first step in examining bloodstain patterns, she said, was to see if she could eliminate the letter opener from being the object that left the images on the altar cloth. It's much easier to exclude an object than it is to include one as a possible cause of a bloodstain pattern, she said.

Sutton then wrapped the letter opener with a thin, form-fitting piece of plastic, snugly following every curve and indentation on the metal instrument. She then soaked it in stage blood and began placing the letter opener on the test cloth.

"As I tried to eliminate the dagger from being the object that made the stains on the altar cloth, instead I found that it was consistent with the patterns made," Sutton noted in a report.

The ribs of the handle, the curved hand guard, the knob at the end of the handle, the curve of the blade itself—all the different sections of the letter opener left distinct stains on the test cloth that appeared to match the ones on the actual altar cloth found at the scene.

Examining one large bloodstain near a corner of the actual altar cloth, Sutton said it looked as though something, maybe the blade of the letter opener, had been wiped off with that section of linen, creating a double image. "It had a distinctive mirror imaging and the transfer pattern was twice as large as the letter opener," she stated in her report.

She then took the letter opener, dipped it again in a container of stage blood, and wiped the blade with the clean linen. The resulting stain was almost identical to the one in the corner of the altar cloth.

Sutton found that another distinctive bloodstain on the altar cloth, consisting of thin parallel lines, matched the size and the separation of the ribs on the letter opener's metal handle.

"The distance between the 'hash mark' lines on the altar cloth did appear to be consistent with the distance between ribs on the dagger's handle," she said.

Further examining the ribbed stain pattern, Sutton took a piece of cloth from Sister Margaret Ann's blue jumper. The material in the dress had a linear pattern in its design, with its angled lines spaced similarly to the distance between the ribs of the letter opener's handle. Sutton wanted to see if a section of the nun's blood-soaked dress could have made the ribbed pattern when it came in contact with the altar cloth.

She cut off a piece of material from the victim's dress, dipped it in animal blood, and placed the cloth lightly on the white linen. It did leave a ribbed pattern, but this time there was a lot of "chatter" between the hash marks. The cloth between the ribbed lines had come into contact with the altar cloth, muddying up the stain.

In comparison, the stain on the original altar cloth was much more clearly defined, with no marks between horizontal lines. Sutton said she would exclude the dress from consideration as an object that could have made the ribbed pattern in blood.

Of the eighteen bloodstains she examined, one small, circular mark made a strong connection between the letter opener and the altar cloth.

Sutton magnified a photograph of the circular stain and could see the clear outline of a rectangle which, at its midpoint, was topped with an oval shape. The bloodstain mirrored the image of the U.S. Capitol Building that was embossed on the letter opener's medallion.

When Sutton made a rubbing of the medallion and placed it over the altar cloth's bloodstain, the shapes and sizes of the images lined up exactly.

When she scanned photographs of the medallion and the bloodstain into a computer and digitally placed them one on top of the other, she noted six specific points that lined up perfectly.

"The letter opener is consistent with the bloodstains found on the altar cloth," she concluded. "If it wasn't this letter opener, then the stains were made by an instrument of the same shape, same size, and same configuration."

Chapter 25

Sergeant Forrester called Father Michael Billian at the Catholic Center in Toledo and said he had a few questions about the occult. He offered no further explanation, but the chancellor assumed it had something to do with the Father Robinson case.

Father Billian suggested he call Father Jeffrey Grob, a Roman Catholic priest in the Archdiocese of Chicago who was researching his doctoral dissertation on the ritual of exorcism. Father Grob was the associate vicar for canonical services for the archdiocese and also served as assistant to the exorcist.

Sergeant Forrester called Father Grob and ended up talking with him for nearly two hours. Two weeks later, he drove to Chicago to meet with the priest, and after that, Father Grob made several trips to Toledo to examine the crime scene and evidence and to consult with the cold-case team.

From the start, Father Grob told detectives that there were strong indications that Sister Margaret Ann Pahl's murder had been an occult killing.

"People who prefer to worship beings other than God will seek a reversal of all things sacred," Father Grob said. "They take something that's sacred and turn it upside down, literally. They defile the very thing that is sacred,"

For Christians, he said, the cross symbolizes the death of Jesus, their Messiah, who sacrificed his life by being nailed to a cross two thousand years ago. For satanists and others who are out to mock Christianity, the inverted cross is a powerful symbol.

Sister Margaret Ann's killer had taken a cross and placed it, upside down, over her barely beating heart while the nun lay immobile on the sacristy floor, then plunged a dagger nine times into her chest, tracing the outline of the anti-Christian symbol of an upside-down cross.

It wasn't just a coincidence, Father Grob told them.

"There are two ways to interpret the inverted cross," he said. "The more ancient understanding of the inverted cross is of St. Peter who, according to tradition, was crucified on an inverted cross. When it came time for him to be executed, he felt he was not worthy to die on the cross as the Lord did, so he asked that he be crucified on an inverted cross.

"It's been part of the Catholic tradition. Unfortunately, the other way to look at it is that for centuries now the image has been usurped and is used in satanic worship."

The killer could have stabbed the nun in the shape of an inverted cross as a means of mocking St. Peter, whom Catholics revere as the first Pope, thereby mocking the Roman Catholic Church.

Or, he could have been making a symbolic reference, or paying homage, to Satan, the lord of evil, the fallen angel.

The murderer also may have intended the inverted cross as a double meaning—mocking both the Catholic Church and Jesus Christ, Father Grob said.

Were there other symbols of an occult killing, the detectives asked him.

"Where does one begin?" he replied.

"We're talking about a woman who had consecrated her life to God, who was the bride of Christ, who was, I presume, in a virginal state, forsaking all others. To be so degraded and violated, it was not only an affront to the person of Sister Margaret Ann Pahl, but it was an affront to so many things," Father Grob said.

The more pure the sacrifice, the greater the power it brings to satanists and other anti-Christian worshippers, the priest said.

Just as God told the Israelites to bring him animals without defect for sacrifice, satanists seek to bring their lord a perfect sacrifice.

"When we talk about Sister Margaret Ann Pahl, she wears a wedding band," Father Grob said. "She believes she has consecrated her life to God and God alone. Her killer took what was innocent and sought to destroy it."

Father Grob said it also was significant that the killer covered Sister Margaret Ann with an altar cloth before stabbing her.

In Catholic liturgy, when the priest consecrates the bread and wine—literally transforming them into the body and blood of Christ—he does so over the altar of sacrifice, which is covered with a cloth.

"The altar cloth is something to cover the altar, the place where the sacrifice is going to take place," Father Grob said. "When the altar cloth was placed over the dying or deceased person, the person herself then became the altar of sacrifice."

The penetration of both the altar cloth and the victim's flesh with a blade is itself a dark symbol, he said.

"In this image of penetration, you are stabbing through something that is sacred," Father Grob said.

The victim's blood also was part of the ritual, representing a mockery of the blood of Christ and the sacrament of Communion, he said.

"You are committing an affront to God, to the altar, to Communion, and to Sister Margaret Ann," he said.

Crime scene photos showed what appeared to be blood marks on the nun's forehead. Father Grob suggested that the killer had "anointed" his victim with her own blood, using the blood to make a sign of the cross on her forehead—possibly an upside-down cross.

"In the larger picture of all these symbols, I think that again it is a reversal of what normally would be done for a good Catholic person going to be with God. Instead of anointing her head with oil and performing the sacrament of the sick, he anoints her by marking her with her own blood. It's another travesty."

The time and the location of the slaying also were extraordinarily significant, he said.

The nun was murdered on Holy Saturday, during the most sacred time of the year for followers of Jesus.

And the killing took place in the sacristy, the room where preparations are made to celebrate Mass.

According to tradition, Jesus was crucified on a Friday and rose from the grave on Sunday. Holy Saturday is the day between those monumental events. At the time when Christians are mourning the death of their Savior and anticipating his resurrection, it would be a powerful time to kill one of God's most devout followers as an affront to God and to all who believe in him.

Following Roman Catholic tradition, the Holy Eucharist, which is the very embodiment of Christ, is removed from the chapel's tabernacle on Good Friday and carried in a procession into the sacristy, where it remains until his resurrection on Easter.

"The transfer of the Blessed Sacrament to the sacristy makes it a place of decorum, a place of genuflection," Father Grob said.

A final act of rebellion and degradation was still to come, the priest said, when the killer carefully folded Sister Margaret Ann's dress up to her chest and pulled her undergarments down.

As she lay there, helpless and exposed, he violated her. In her autopsy, Dr. Fazekas stated that the victim's hymen was intact but that there were abrasions on the inside of her vagina.

Police did not know what the killer used to violate the nun, but there was speculation that it could have been the same cross the killer used for a template when he stabbed her over the heart.

With all the symbols surrounding the nun's murder, investigators still had one disturbing question: Could a Roman Catholic priest actually be involved in satanic worship and commit a ritual sacrifice?

"As a Catholic, I believe the devil exists," Father Grob said. "Just as there are those who give their lives to God, there are those who have given themselves over to the devil. Priests are not immune from such temptation."

The priest said that the preponderance of symbols had convinced him that the killer was someone with extensive knowledge of Catholic and Christian ritual.

"All these different things were done to her within a specific context," he said. "These aren't random acts. If you take them in isolation, they can be lots of things.

If I see an inverted cross here and a soiled altar cloth over there, and something else over here, you can say, okay, there's a problem. Maybe there are extenuating circumstances. But all these things done in this case, clearly it was committed by someone with specialized knowledge of ritual.

"A religious sister would certainly have such knowledge. A priest would have such knowledge. Perhaps a seminarian. I would be surprised if Catholics in general would have the aggregate meaning of all these things when put together," he said.

Chapter 26

Anyone who lived in northwest Ohio in the 1980s will never forget the "Satanic Panic" frenzy that swept through the area.

It all started on June 20, 1985, when Lucas County Sheriff James Telb called a 7:00 a.m. news conference to announce that deputies were about to begin searching for the bodies of up to seventy-five people they believed had been killed in satanic rituals in a rural area northwest of Toledo.

Sheriff Telb told reporters that he had received reliable information from several confidential informants who claimed that a group of up to two hundred Satan worshippers had been sacrificing people during rituals and burying the victims in a wooded area in Spencer Township.

Furthermore, Sheriff Telb said, the informants warned police that another human sacrifice had been planned for the next day—June 21, the summer solstice.

At the center of the informants' allegations was a 59-year-old man named Leroy Freeman, who had disappeared two and a half years earlier with his 9-year-old granddaughter, Charity.

Before starting the search for the bodies, deputies raided Freeman's former home, expecting to find cult paraphernalia as well as shotguns and drugs.

Lieutenant Kirk Surprise of the sheriff's department said none of the items listed in the search warrant was found, but that deputies had confiscated a Bible, two Ozzy Osbourne records, two blank cassette tapes, a poster of *Raiders of the Lost Ark*, and an animal bone.

More than a hundred reporters from major networks and national newspapers as well as Toledo, Detroit, and Cleveland media converged on the scene to cover the satanic dig. The reporters and photographers watched the events from ground level and also from helicopters and planes circling overhead.

Sheriff's deputies used a backhoe, a bulldozer, and rakes and shovels to scrape away and sift through layers of dirt, pausing to let the evidence technicians photograph each layer as it was uncovered.

The home's current resident, Patricia Litton, said she never met Leroy Freeman and had no clue why deputies were digging up her yard with heavy earth-moving equipment.

Deputies looked suspiciously at a goat in her backyard, thinking it might be targeted for a satanic sacrifice. Litton shooed them away, saying it was a family pet and nothing more.

Sheriff Telb told reporters the cult had been operating in the area for sixteen years, sacrificing an average of five people each year. Most of the victims were infants or young children, but their ages ranged up to 13 years old, and the majority had been suffocated to death, the sheriff said.

Dale W. Griffis, a captain with the Tiffin police department and one of the area's leading experts on the occult, was flown to the site by helicopter at Sheriff Telb's request.

After the first day of digging, sheriff's deputies failed to uncover any human remains. But they did find some items that Captain Griffis said could be associated with occult rituals: an eight-inch ritual knife, called an athame, and a headless doll with its feet nailed to a piece of wood and a small pentagram tied to its wrist.

Mr. Griffis pointed out four possible burial sites in the wooded area, including one that he said was particularly suspicious because it had been covered with wire mesh, possibly to keep animals out.

Sheriff Telb said he had promised the informants he would not reveal their identities, saying, "I don't want anybody to get hurt."

To his knowledge, he said, the informants had not personally witnessed the human sacrifices. Later, however, Lieutenant Surprise gave a contradictory account.

"I have information that they [the ritual killings] have been seen. We have talked to someone who has observed someone [being sacrificed]," Surprise told the media.

The sheriff said the killings allegedly occurred in cult members' homes and that the location of the rituals was changed for each meeting.

The digging resumed early the next morning, and although deputies searched three separate areas, they did not uncover any signs of human—or even animal—sacrifices.

Besides the headless doll with the pentagram and the ritual knife, deputies uncovered two more knives, a hypodermic needle, rags, written correspondence, and seven containers of body paint.

Despite the lack of evidence, Sheriff Telb insisted his information was reliable and that his department had investigated the allegations for three months before undertaking the dig. He said surveillance by his deputies had revealed ritual activity on the property.

"We're still going to continue our investigation," he said. "There still may be bodies out there."

True to his word, Sheriff Telb ordered another search of the area two weeks later. Seven hours of digging, however, produced no human bones or signs of satanic activity. The only items found were children's clothing and shoes, two pairs of glasses, a radio with a list of phone numbers inside it, an aluminum jug, a wooden object that could have been a cross, and a birthday card with a cartoon red devil.

A month later, the media reported that the confidential informant was a Baptist minister.

Charity Freeman was found four years later, living with her grandfather in Huntington Beach, California.

Chapter 27

After Sister Mary Curtiss shocked the Toledo diocese's review board with her allegations, the diocese's attorneys and Frank DiLallo, the diocese's case manager, hired two retired police detectives to investigate her claims.

A meeting was held in the Catholic Center on July 23, 2003, in which DiLallo outlined the situation to John Connors, a veteran investigator and a former Catholic seminarian, and White Knannlien, another police veteran and a devout Catholic who was considering becoming an ordained deacon.

The two detectives had investigated dozens of cases while moonlighting for the Toledo diocese, quietly stepping in to handle problems that, for anyone other than Catholic priests, would have been turned over to law-enforcement authorities.

"I can tell you that there was always somebody the diocese could go to in the police department, and I can tell you that, at one time, I was that man," Connors said.

One Toledo priest whose abuses were covered up for years was Father Denny Gray, a tough-talking cleric who left the priesthood with a clean record and a positive recommendation from the diocese, helping him land a job as dean of students in the Toledo public school system.

In 1985, a woman from the Toledo suburb of Maumee called the diocese and said a priest had attacked her 11-year-old son, an altar boy, in the sacristy of St. Joseph's Church. She said the priest, Father Gray, had grabbed her son in a "nerve hold" and told him that he "must submit to punishment."

The priest released the boy after a deacon entered the sacristy, but the child was shaken up for weeks afterward. The mother called to warn the diocese that "Father Denny" was a menace and a threat to children.

Father Archie Thomas, superintendent of diocesan schools, summoned Connors, then a Toledo police sergeant, to Toledo's Central Catholic High School for an urgent meeting.

"We've got a problem," the high-ranking cleric told Connors.

The mother's allegations were not the only ones surfacing around Dennis Gray, who was teaching religion at Central Catholic, Father Thomas said.

He told Connors that the outgoing and outspoken young cleric was suspected of taking teenage boys to a cottage in Michigan, getting them drunk, then raping and molesting them.

Connors advised Father Thomas to keep Denny Gray away from kids.

That was the end of the case. No police report, no further investigation.

Chapter 28

One of Denny Gray's victims in the 1980s was a troubled teenage kid named Tony Comes, now a 34-year-old Toledo firefighter and the father of two children.

Comes's childhood abuse by the Toledo priest and the fallout that plagued him through adulthood were the focus of a 2004 documentary film, *Twist of Faith*.

On February 27, 2005, Comes, with his wife and his mother beside him, walked on the red carpet and into the star-studded Kodak Theatre in Hollywood.

Filmmakers Kirby Dick and Eddie Schmidt of Chain Camera Productions in Los Angeles had followed Comes around his work, his home, and his Catholic church in Toledo, documenting his struggles dealing with the anguish, pain, and embarrassment of being an abuse victim, and filming his frustrations in dealing with the diocese.

The film was nominated for an Academy Award, and so here was Tony, in a tuxedo, sitting with his wife, Wendy, his mother, Sandra, and the documentary filmmakers in the Kodak's plush red-velvet seats.

He felt both blessed and cursed to be there on a night when the whole world seemed to be tuning in to see the stars and who would get the Oscars.

Deep in his heart and mind, he knew he didn't belong there. And if it were a perfect world, he would be nowhere near the place.

The middle child in a devout Catholic family with seven children, Comes was small and clumsy and not very good at sports. He was so poor, he liked to joke, that his hand-me-down pants were just "roys" because "the cords had worn off."

The jocks at Central Catholic High School used to harass him, calling him "wuss" and "homo."

Father Gray, then in his thirties, was a priest who cussed and swore and drank beer and attracted troubled teens to him like moths to a flame.

The Central Catholic High School religion teacher took young Comes under his wing, promising to teach him how to be a man and to stand up for himself.

For six months, Comes was captivated by Father Denny, who seemed to generate excitement wherever he went.

"He was like a hero to me," Comes said.

And Tony wasn't the only boy whom Father Denny was "helping." The wise-cracking priest surrounded himself with high school students whom he proudly called "my boys." Most of them were social misfits who needed a father figure or were otherwise desperate for someone to believe in them and show them attention. But the priest's concern for young Tony took a dark turn in the rectory of St. Joseph's Church in Maumee, in suburban Toledo, when he began touching the boy's privates. Confused that a man of God and a mentor would do such a thing, Comes said he gave in to Father Denny's advances. More sexual abuse soon fol-lowed, at the rectory and then at a cottage on Crystal Lake in Michigan, where Father Denny would invite a group of his boys for summer getaways.

At the cottage, the priest would let the teenage boys drink all the alcohol they wanted, then would invite them one at a time into his bedroom. Playful wrestling would turn into sexual groping, then sodomy and oral sex, his victims said.

Father Gray was a mean drunk, insulting the boys after abusing them, call-ing them queers and faggots and telling them that they enjoyed what he had done to them.

During the summer before his senior year, Comes said he finally got up the nerve to distance himself from the priest, and Father Denny stopped inviting him to his cottage.

It wasn't until Comes turned 21 that he was able to tell his parents. They believed him immediately, but they said their son was not ready for a confronta-tion with the powerful Catholic Church and its high-priced lawyers. They could not imagine Tony having to sit on the witness stand and be interviewed by the dio-cese's slick attorneys.

Then, in 2002, as the U.S. Catholic Church's clerical sexual-abuse crisis made headlines day in and day out, Comes started feeling edgy. He was nervous and irri-table, and had trouble sleeping.

Over Memorial Day weekend, a few months after he and Wendy and the kids moved into their dream home in a middle-class neighborhood not far from where he grew up, Comes said he was driving his pickup truck down his street when he noticed a neighbor pushing a lawnmower.

He did a double take, then parked the truck and walked straight to the man. It was Father Denny, living five houses away.

"It was like my worst nightmare," Comes said. "I walked up to him and he backed away and fell on his ass, and I just said, 'Stay the hell away from my family.'"

Irate, Comes called the Toledo diocese and made an appointment to meet with Bishop James Hoffman.

Comes came to the Catholic Center with his mother and told the bishop that he was sexually abused as a child by Father Gray. Bishop Hoffman listened com-passionately, apologized profusely, and said it was the first time he had ever heard that kind of allegation against Father Gray.

Comes asked him to use whatever influence he could to get the ex-priest out of his neighborhood, and sure enough, a "for sale" sign soon went up in Gray's yard. Within a few months, Gray moved to a Toledo suburb.

Then, on September 15, 2002, about three months after meeting with the bishop, Comes picked up a copy of the *Blade* and read about another man in his thirties, Matthew Simon, who had told Bishop Hoffman in 1995 that Father Gray repeatedly abused him when he was a minor at the same cottage where Comes had been molested.

The *Blade* reported that the former vicar of priests, Father Raymond Sheperd, wrote to Simon in 1995 saying that the ex-priest "has admitted to us that he was guilty of child abuse" when he was a priest and that "he was remorseful and wished to apologize."

Comes was furious. He had believed Bishop Hoffman when the church leader said it was the first time he had heard abuse allegations against Gray.

"I still can't believe the bishop lied to me," Comes said. "He looked me and my mother right in the eye and lied to us. What Bishop Hoffman did to me hurt me as much as Denny Gray."

After that, Comes said, "the gloves came off."

Within weeks of the story's publication, Comes sued the Toledo diocese, Bishop Hoffman, and Dennis Gray, filing anonymously as John Doe.

"We did not want to sue. We wanted honesty," Comes said.

In December 2002, Comes made the rare move of amending his lawsuit to include his name. "It's time to stand up and do this with dignity," he explained.

The emotional stress from the lawsuit almost cost him his marriage, creating so much stress and upheaval that he and Wendy had contacted lawyers and had divorce papers drawn up.

Comes was losing weight because he couldn't eat, and he was having trouble sleeping. In such a condition, he felt he was a risk to his fellow firefighters and asked to be assigned temporarily to a desk job.

The macho father also was forced to talk to his 10-year-old daughter and 6-year-old son about things he never wanted to expose innocent children to—that not all priests are good people, and that one of the bad priests had hurt him when he was a boy.

He told his daughter that the priest who hurt him lived in the house five doors down, and that if she fell off her bike and scraped her knee on the sidewalk and that man tried to help, she should scream and run away.

The distrust and fear run so deep, Comes said, that he winces every time he sees his young son run up to a priest after Mass and give the cleric a hug.

One of a dozen men who sued ex-priest Denny Gray, Comes eventually received an out-of-court settlement from the diocese for $55,000.

His case caught the eye the filmmakers Dick and Schmidt, who hoped to capture the devastation of clerical sexual abuse by focusing on one victim, rather than on the broad, overwhelming picture resulting from the national scandal.

Comes agreed to be in the movie, refusing any payment and saying it would be worthwhile if it helped prevent even one child from being abused.

He said he believes his story is typical, and that "you could plug almost any other abuse victim into the movie and it would be the same."

The movie was shown to standing ovations at the Sundance Film Festival, and landed Tony a night at the Oscars.

But it was not all glamour and glitter for the world-weary firefighter.

"I don't particularly like seeing myself as a 34-year-old guy talking on a thirty-foot screen about how a priest performed oral sex on me when I was 14 years old," he said. "It's not what I wanted to be known for. It's not what I expected to be known for."

When Dennis Gray left the priesthood in 1987, voluntarily in order to get married, he did so with positive references from the Toledo diocese.

Auxiliary Bishop Robert W. Donnelly wrote a note saying that he would gladly rehire Gray if he ever decided to return to the priesthood.

Gray later became a dean at two Toledo high schools and was the dean of students at Rogers High when the *Blade* reported that the former priest had been sued over allegations of child abuse.

The ex-priest, who holds two master's degrees, was immediately suspended, then transferred to another school building, working the night shift supervising janitors. He showed up for work a few times, then filed for disability.

Gray has been sued a dozen times—more than any other Toledo priest—by men who claim they were raped and molested by the priest when they were children.

All of the lawsuits were settled out of court through mediation in August 2004. The Toledo diocese paid a total of $1.9 million to twenty-four plaintiffs who claimed they were sexually abused as children by priests.

Three months before the abuse cases were settled, the Toledo diocese moved its $117 million investment portfolio out of Toledo brokerages and gave the funds to a Detroit firm, saying it was better stewardship of the people's money.

Chapter 29

The heart-wrenching feeling that Tony Comes experienced when he learned that the Toledo bishop had deceived him mirrored the pain felt a decade earlier by Barbara Blaine, the Toledo native and founder of SNAP, Survivors Network of those Abused by Priests.

A bright and determined woman with a mane of thick red hair, Blaine was molested by Father Chet Warren beginning when she was 13, during the summer between her seventh and eighth grades at St. Pius parochial school.

She had helped clean up after Mass and was watching TV with Father Warren and several other children. Eventually, the other kids had all left and it was just the priest and the teenage girl.

"He looked at me and said he knew I had feelings for him just like he had feelings for me," Blaine said.

Father Warren moved beside her and started groping her. Blaine said she wanted to tell him to stop, but just froze.

"Stop shaking," he told the young girl. "You don't have to be afraid of anything. I'm not going to hurt you."

Afterward, Father Warren told Blaine not to tell anyone else about their encounter.

"No one else is as holy and close to Jesus as you and me," he said. "They wouldn't understand that God wants us to do this."

The sexual abuse continued for four years.

"I believed I had sinned," Blaine said. "I felt dirty and ashamed and that it was my fault. I made this good, holy man sin."

After Father Warren was abruptly transferred out of the parish and out of Toledo—with no explanation to parishioners—Blaine said she went to confession and felt that she was done with that unpleasant chapter of her life.

"I had this sense that I would be forgiven and not commit this sin again and move on with my life," she said.

She buried the disturbing memories, putting them out of her mind, and went to school in St. Louis, then Washington, D.C. She earned a law degree from DePaul

University and settled in Chicago, where she worked as a court advocate for juveniles.

One day in the fall of 1985, when Blaine was 29 years old, she picked up an old copy of the *National Catholic Reporter*, a national newspaper, and read articles about a priest in Louisiana who had molested numerous altar boys.

The stories stirred feelings that she thought had disappeared long ago.

"The article came out in June but I didn't read it until September," Blaine said. "When I read those articles, I had a physiological response. I was sitting at my desk. It was a warm autumn day. I was breathing heavy, perspiring, shaking. It was like, 'Oh my God, something's wrong with me!'

"After that I was experiencing nightmares, flashbacks, and I was truly troubled by it. I realized that these reactions were triggered by reading these articles, and it made me realize that what happened to these altar boys was what happened to me."

She contacted the Oblates of St. Francis headquarters and the Catholic Diocese of Toledo.

"Initially they both acted like they cared and they said that they were going to investigate it," Blaine said. "They led me to believe that they were going to deal with the problem. Unfortunately, they didn't. They both strung me along," she said.

Bishop Hoffman and the head of the Oblates kept promising to meet with her, then canceling the appointments at the last minute, Blaine said.

"I wanted to make sure he [Warren] was not abusing anyone else, that he'd be monitored and that he would get help," she said

"The bishop and the Oblates told me basically the same thing: 'Oh, we're so sorry. Oh, we didn't understand. We'll never let that happen again.' They led me to believe they'd correct the problem," Blaine said.

One thing she demanded was that the church warn the people at St. Vincent Hospital, where Father Warren was serving as chaplain.

"They told me—the diocese and the Oblates—that they would make sure the people at St. Vincent's knew," Blaine said.

"I later learned that the hospital was never informed of the charges against Chet Warren. It was devastating to me that these church leaders would not tell the truth, that they would break promises and actually lied to me. It was more devastating than the sexual abuse itself," she said.

"It pulled the floor out from under me. The church was the rootedness of my life. Everything I stood for was rooted in the church teachings. Everything I did, morning, noon, and night, was the church. I was a church worker twenty-four hours a day, seven days a week."

Blaine fought the Oblates and the Toledo diocese for years over Father Warren, trying to get him removed from ministry and trying to warn people that he was a child molester. She started SNAP in 1989 and began appearing on television talk shows, but not mentioning Father Warren by name.

In 1992, when she was asked to appear on *The Oprah Winfrey Show*, Blaine decided it was time to name Warren as her abuser. She called the Oblates and Bishop Hoffman of Toledo on a Friday and told them she was going to name Father Warren on Tuesday when she appeared on *Oprah*.

That weekend, Father James Cryan, the Oblates' regional leader, put Warren on a leave of absence.

Blaine threatened to sue over the lack of action taken by the church, and in 1995 received an $80,000 settlement, split between the Oblates of St. Francis and the Toledo diocese. The diocese said the Oblates paid the majority of the settlement.

In September 2002, Blaine came to Toledo to give a lecture at the University of Toledo law school. By then, her years of speaking out for victims' rights and her determination to bring about change within the church had made her one of the most prominent victims' advocates during the national clerical sexual-abuse crisis.

The *Blade* was set to publish a profile of Blaine in advance of her Toledo appearance, and the reporter called the Toledo diocese for a comment on the Toledo native's impact on the church crisis.

Father Thomas Quinn, the 68-year-old director of communications for the Toledo diocese and a cousin of Auxiliary Bishop Robert Donnelly, was known for his sardonic humor and his enthusiasm for his alma mater, the University of Notre Dame.

"Yes, I have a comment about Barbara Blaine," Father Quinn told the reporter. "Where do we place the bombs? And you can quote me on that."

The comment did not make it into print until December, when the *Blade* published an award-winning investigative series looking into the diocese's handling of priests who abused children.

As soon as the comment hit the streets, local and national representatives for the Survivors Network of those Abused by Priests called for Father Quinn to resign over his "extremely dangerous and insensitive" remarks.

Father Quinn apologized in the media for what he called "an inappropriate" comment, but never apologized personally to Blaine. The diocese kept him on as spokesman, although it revamped the communications department the following year and assigned him to a less prominent role.

He died of a heart attack two years later, in January 2005, at age 70.

Chapter 30

Just as the altar boys' stories had triggered a physical reaction in Blaine, articles about Blaine's lawsuit caused physical and emotional reactions in Sister Mary Curtiss. She began shaking and shivering, felt pain from abuse that had occurred decades ago, and began to feel a sense of uncontrollable anger rising from somewhere deep inside.

She wrote to Bishop James Hoffman, leader of the 325,000-member Catholic Diocese of Toledo, telling him she had been abused by Father Warren when she was a child.

The bishop responded with a handwritten letter, dated June 23, 1993.

"I am saddened to know that you were abused by a priest as a child," Bishop Hoffman wrote. He promised that he would "do my best to work with others to meet this reality of clergy sexual abuse with compassion, sensitivity and honesty."

The bishop closed his letter by asking Sister Mary Curtiss to "please pray for me as I will for you."

More than ten years later—and five months after Bishop Hoffman's death from esophageal cancer—the petite nun with the steel blue eyes was still trying to get a satisfactory response from church officials.

Her testimony of being abused in satanic rituals by a group that included several Catholic priests was like a ticking time bomb for the church. The diocese had to defuse it before it exploded in the media. They had to prove the woman was a pathological liar or mentally unbalanced, or else settle the case quickly and quietly.

Retired detectives John Connors and Whitey Knannlien were told to get to the bottom of it—and fast.

They first met with Dale Griffis, a former police captain for the small northwest Ohio city of Tiffin, who was an expert on "nontraditional groups"—including satanists and occult groups.

Griffis had been a consultant for the Lucas County sheriff's department in the 1985 satanic digs outside Toledo and was one of the first policemen to seriously study cults, earning a master's degree and writing a doctoral dissertation on mind-controlling cults.

He told the two detectives that the nun's shocking allegations fit the patterns of abuse he had encountered in his investigations of satanic cults, but that they would be difficult or impossible to prove without outside corroboration.

Connors and Knannlien called Sister Mary Curtiss and arranged to meet her at her religious order's headquarters on the afternoon of September 23, 2003.

The detectives gently grilled the nun for more than two hours, and scheduled a follow-up interview for the next week.

They returned six more times, interviewing the sister for twenty hours in all.

What they heard showed that the allegations Sister Mary Curtiss made before the review board were just the tip of the iceberg.

"I was holding back with the review board," she explained to them. "I didn't want them to dismiss me out of hand by giving them too much information."

Mary Curtiss was two years old when her parents and two older sisters moved to Toledo in 1965. The family settled into the local Catholic parish, St. Pius X, attending church regularly and sending their children to the parish's parochial schools.

To most observers, little Mary enjoyed a typical midwestern upbringing, growing up in a churchgoing middle-class family in a middle-class neighborhood in the blue-collar city of Toledo.

Every summer, her family took a trip to the Shenandoah National Park in Virginia.

She liked to play with her Barbie dolls and enjoyed "playing house" with her Easy-Bake Oven, making meals for her dolls in the pink-and-yellow plastic oven that baked with the heat from a light bulb.

She was a creative child who loved to read, especially books about the mischievous monkey Curious George or Dr. Seuss's colorful characters like the Cat in the Hat.

She played animal hospital with her friends across the street, using her two beloved dogs—Smoky the black lab and Chipper the dachshund-beagle mix—as reluctant patients.

As she got older, Mary fell in love with the adventures of the four March family daughters in Louisa May Alcott's Civil War novel *Little Women*, reading the book seventeen times.

Her favorite school subject was creative writing. She hated lima beans; she loved rainbow sherbet.

But her life was divided into two polar-opposite worlds. One, the dark-haired girl with the bangs and a perpetual sadness in her eyes; the other, a girl who was repeatedly raped and tortured, physically and mentally, by a murderous satanic cult to which her parents belonged.

"I led two lives—I created 'The Waltons' early on," Sister Mary Curtiss said.

The childhood memories she could recall were only the happy ones. The summer vacations in Shenandoah Park, laughing at the silly tales of *Gilligan's Island*, playing with her friends across the street.

Deep within, hidden even from herself, were horrific memories of unimaginable abuse.

Starting in 1992, at age 29, after battling ambiguous feelings of deep-seated anger, she began to see a therapist. She had a "sick sense" that she had been sexually abused as a child, but had no specific memories.

The next year, after reading news accounts of clerical sexual abuse, fragments of her worst childhood memories began to seep into her consciousness.

"When I thought about my childhood, I began to feel nauseated and panicky," she said. "The article about Barbara Blaine jarred something loose. I began having flashbacks and body memories."

In one of her first flashbacks, Sister Mary Curtiss was transported back to her grade-school days. She was overcome with a sense of horror, but could recall few details.

"I was 6 or 7. I was lying naked on a bed and my arms were pinned down. I had a look of terror on my face. That year I had a pixie haircut and wore a blue-and-green plaid uniform five days a week," she said.

The small pieces of traumatic childhood memories continued to filter back into her conscious mind.

Sister Mary Curtiss described the earliest flashback fragments that swept through her mind and tormented her body. At the center of most of them was Father Chet Warren.

"Being 4½, curled up in a little ball in the hospital bed in terror, and rocking back and forth after he left."

"Being about as tall as his belt and having his penis in my mouth."

"Being about 6, lying on the sacristy floor with him towering above me as he exposes himself and his penis hangs down in front of me."

"Standing, shaking, as a pig-tailed 9-year-old as he kneels in front of me, bends down, and kisses my vagina."

These repressed, or recovered, memories are difficult to assess and are still a mystery to medical and psychological experts.

The American Psychiatric Association, addressing the issue in 1993, stated that "it is not known how to distinguish, with complete accuracy, memories based on true events from those derived from other sources."

The American Medical Association reported in 1994 that it "considers recovered memories of childhood sexual abuse to be of uncertain authenticity, which should be subject to external verification."

And yet there have been cases of recovered memories that have proved to be true.

Kenneth Lanning, a retired FBI official who trains law-enforcement officials around the country on how to investigate allegations of ritual sexual abuse of children, describes recovered memories as a complex issue that varies with every individual.

"Some of what the victims allege may be true and accurate, some may be misperceived or distorted, some may be screened or symbolic, and some may be 'contaminated' or false," Lanning said. "The problem for law enforcement is to determine which is which."

Connors and Knannlien focused their efforts on trying to determine whether Sister Mary Curtiss's memories were real or imagined.

She showed them a letter she wrote on November 24, 1993, to the local head of the Oblates, Father James Cryan, who was Father Warren's superior.

"When I was in preschool, Mom was having some personal problems and he [Warren] used to come to our house in the afternoons at times to talk to her," Sister Mary Curtiss wrote.

"She would be in a different part of the house and he would abuse me. When I started grade school, the abuse continued in the rectory and at least once in the sacristy. I think part of the reason I was abused at such a young age was that he had access to me through my Mom."

Father Cryan replied with a handwritten letter dated December 1, 1993.

"I received your letter of Nov. 24 in today's mail," he wrote. "I know that the terror I felt in reading it cannot compare with the terror you had in experiencing its content. . . . I appreciate receiving your letter although I received it before lunch and I admit that I had appetite neither for food nor conversation after reading it."

Two months later, Sister Mary Curtiss wrote again to Bishop Hoffman and the members of a newly appointed Toledo diocesan commission convened to create policies for handling allegations of clerical sexual abuse of children.

After giving an overview of her alleged abuse by Warren, she described her current state of suffering, including panic attacks, being afraid of the dark, and experiencing "body memories" of abuse manifested in anal and vaginal pain.

"I am particularly devastated spiritually," she wrote. "I have no clue where God was when I was on the sacristy floor or lying naked on the bed, or how He could allow someone who represented Him to do those things to me. . . . I find it difficult to attend Mass. Some days it's excruciating. I walk up to Communion and think about oral sex. . . . It's not fair."

Over time, Sister Mary Curtiss's childhood memories became more detailed and complete.

And more like nightmares than memories.

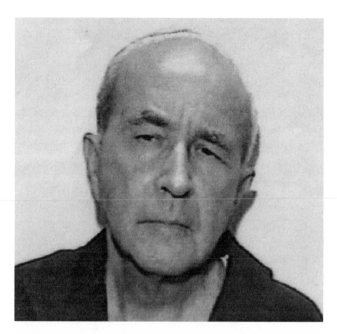

Father Gerald Robinson's booking photo taken at the Lucas County Jail after his arrest on April 23, 2004.

Sister Margaret Ann Pahl in photo taken around 1980, the year she was murdered at age 71.

Funeral service for Sister Margaret Ann Pahl in the St. Bernardine Chapel, Fremont, Ohio. Father Gerald Robinson, in center under the crucifix, is among the priests presiding. The nun's coffin, draped with a white pall, is in front of the altar.

Assistant Lucas County Prosecutor Dean Mandros questions former Toledo Police Deputy Chief Ray Vetter, who denied that he helped cover up the 1980 investigation.

Toledo Police Detective Terry Cousino displays the altar cloth found at the murder scene. A member of the Scientific Investigations Unit, Detective Cousino first noticed the blood-transfer patterns on the linen and the puncture marks in the shape of an upside cross.

Father Jeffrey Grob of the Chicago Catholic Archdiocese, an assistant to the archdiocese's exorcist, holds a cross in an inverted position, saying it is a satanic symbol used to mock God and the church.

Dr. Diane Barnett, deputy Lucas County coroner, tells jurors that the letter opener found in Father Robinson's residence was a perfect fit for the wounds found in Sister Margaret Ann's body.

Defense attorney John Thebes ponders his next move as Father Gerald Robinson looks on during the trial.

Assistant Lucas County Prosecutor Dean Mandros—his face caught in the light of a projector's beam—uses a mannequin in nun's clothing to show the court how Sister Margaret Ann Pahl's body was found in the sacristy of Mercy Hospital's chapel.

Dr. Henry Lee, renowned forensic investigator, tells the jury that the priest's letter opener matched the bloodstains and puncture marks found in the altar cloth. In the background, Father Robinson's attorneys Alan Konop and Nicole Khoury confer.

Retired Toledo Police Detective Arthur Marx, who led the 1980 murder investigation, is questioned on the witness stand by defense attorney Alan Konop.

Judge Thomas Osowik reads the verdict sheet on May 11, 2006, convicting the 68-year-old Catholic priest of murder and sentencing him to a 15-years-to-life sentence.

Father Gerald Robinson stands stone-faced as the judge reads the guilty verdict. Shocked and saddened are his defense attorneys, from left, Alan Konop, John Thebes, and Nicole Khoury.

Convicted murderer Father Gerald Robinson is led out of the Lucas County Common Pleas Court in handcuffs, escorted by court deputy Bob Detrich.

Cold-case investigators Steve Forrester and Tom Ross chat during the news conference after the priest's conviction. The two veteran officers spent more than two years investigating Sister Margaret Ann Pahl's murder.

Father Chet Warren, now barred from ministry, whom a Toledo nun accused of abusing her in satanic rituals when she was a child. The nun's allegations indirectly led cold-case detectives to reopen the 1980 murder investigation of Sister Margaret Ann Pahl.

Chapter 31

As Sister Mary Curtiss became increasingly comfortable and trusting of the two private detectives who came to her modest home week after week to conduct interviews, the nun began to relax and reveal memories that she previously was reluctant to share.

By now, her brief and troubling flashbacks had developed into more complete scenarios. Periods of her childhood that had been totally blocked out of her mind were now accessible, although many pieces were missing.

Sister Mary Curtiss told Connors and Knannlien that she remembers Father Chet Warren abusing her when she was 3 years old, and that the abuse continued until she was 18.

The nun said she recalled being abused by several priests besides Warren, including Father Gerald Robinson of the Toledo diocese.

She told them of abuse that occurred during satanic or cult-like activities in which she was the victim. A number of adults, as few as three and as many as twenty-five, took part in the rituals, wearing black robes and chanting to Satan.

Ceremonies were held to "appease the demons" and to consecrate her to Satan, she said. Her father, mother, and grandfather were all involved the cult and took part in some of the ceremonies.

When she was 5 or 6, Sister Mary Curtiss said, she was taken to a campground in Michigan where there was a cabin with a stone fireplace.

She was forced to lie on the floor, naked, in front of the burning fire. Three black-robed men stood on each side of her, twisting and twirling ceremonial knives and making "clicking" noises with their mouths. They poked her and touched her lightly with the blades, not drawing blood.

One of the cult members climbed on top of her and penetrated her vagina with his penis, she told the detectives. One robed man sat in a corner beating a drum while the others performed a strange ritual dance.

She said many of her worst memories were from events that took place in a farmhouse on Raab Road, west of Toledo, that she called "the House of Blood."

Several times, she said, she was taken out of class when she was in elementary school and driven to the farmhouse, where the cult was waiting to use her in a ritual.

One of the most horrific memories was from 1974, when Sister Mary Curtiss was 11 years old.

She said she was taken to Raab Road at one in the morning and driven down the long dirt driveway to the dark wooden farmhouse, tinted blue by the moonlight.

It was her account of that night's horrors to the Toledo diocese's review board that led Dr. Robert Cooley to report her allegations to the Ohio attorney general's office.

Sister Mary Curtiss said she was taken to the basement where ten adults— seven men and three women—were waiting, all wearing black robes.

"A bowl containing an eyeball was brought in. It looked like a human eye. One of the leaders said, 'Take it, eat it, chew it, and swallow it.' He said the eyeball would always be with me and that I would always be a part of them. The group would always be watching me," Sister Mary Curtiss said with a shiver.

She was then stripped naked. A girl about 3 years old, also naked, was brought into the room. She had long dark curly hair, Sister Mary Curtiss said, and she had never seen her before. The girl seemed to be sleepy and moved slowly, and now the nun believes the girl must have been drugged by the cult.

"They tied the girl to a wooden chair and they put a machete in my hands. They told me to kill her, but I couldn't do it," Sister Mary Curtiss told the detectives.

One of the robed men grabbed her arm tightly and forced her to swing the machete, striking the girl in the neck. Blood spurted out and the girl slumped over in the chair, but the man would not let go of Sister Mary Curtiss's arm. He kept swinging her arm and striking the girl with the machete, over and over again, hacking the young girl's body to a bloody pulp.

After what seemed like countless blows, the man let go of Sister Mary Curtiss's arm and another cult member threw her on the floor and raped her.

Then the adults all left, Sister Mary Curtiss said, locking her in the basement with the bloody corpse until sunrise.

The cement floor was covered with blood and strewn with body parts.

Sister Mary Curtiss found an old piece of cardboard and sat down, naked and vomiting. "The cardboard was a little island," she said. "I told myself if I stayed on the cardboard, I wouldn't go crazy. I wished I had died."

About six hours later, the adults returned with black plastic garbage bags and bottles of bleach and began cleaning up the room.

Another nightmare memory from the House of Blood occurred when Sister Mary Curtiss was 9 years old.

She told Connors and Knannlien that one of the cult members picked her up at school around noon and drove her in her grandfather's car to the farmhouse.

When they got to the basement, a man with a crew cut whom she had never seen before was waiting for them.

"You will get to learn what happens to little girls that talk about the Circle of Darkness," he told her.

The crew-cut man took her into a small room to the side of the basement, like a pantry, with shelves and a small window.

"There were bodies of six young girls hanging on meat hooks," Sister Mary Curtiss told the detectives. "They were all between 6 and 11 years old. Their eyes were open and there were no marks on their bodies."

The man threatened her never to tell anyone about the Circle of Darkness or they would give her medicine like they did these girls.

The nun gave detailed descriptions of each of the girls to the detectives. The crew-cut man told her she had to pick one of the girls. She resisted but eventually, forced to make a choice, she picked a girl about 6 years old with short blonde hair.

The man lifted the body off the hook and carried it into the main room of the basement. He laid it on a table, picked up a carpenter's saw, and handed it to Mary. He told her to cut the girl apart. Mary refused and the two men grabbed her arms and forced her to start sawing the body into pieces.

When she vomited, one of the men made her crawl on her knees and lick the vomit as punishment, yelling, "Damn you, Mary, can't you do anything right?".

Shaking and wiping away tears, Sister Mary Curtiss told the detectives that was about all she could handle for now, and asked if they could come back next week.

Chapter 32

Father Chet Warren, who turned 78 in 2006, was barred from ministry in 1993 but continues to wear a clerical collar, despite being banned from doing so by his religious order.

Never criminally charged with sexual abuse of children, he has been sued by at least eight women who claim the former cleric raped and molested them when they were children.

Teresa Bombrys, a 44-year-old schoolteacher who now lives in Columbus, Ohio, sued Father Chet Warren, the Oblates of St. Francis, and the Toledo Catholic Diocese in April 2002.

It was the first clerical sexual-abuse lawsuit to hit Toledo after the nationwide crisis erupted in Boston that January.

Bombrys said she had contacted the Toledo diocese and the Oblates in 1999 about Warren, before she hired an attorney.

She said she did not want to sue the church, but "when I heard they were aware of allegations against Chet and did not do anything about it, I felt then that the church was responsible."

Bombrys said Father Warren abused her for four years, beginning when she was in the fourth grade and ending when she was in seventh grade.

"It happened on a regular basis over that four-year period, from age 8 to 12. It only ended because they moved him from the church because somebody else had come forward with allegations."

She said Father Warren was manipulative and threatening.

"He used our faith, my faith, to keep me from telling anyone," Bombrys said. "He told me the acts that we were doing were acts that God wanted me to do, and to keep it secret and I will receive rewards in heaven. If I didn't do what he asked, I would spend time in hell."

She said he also mentioned satanism, as a means of controlling her.

"Chet described to me satanic rituals, and said that if I got involved with that I would have to go through an exorcism."

Bombrys also said she was taken to a farmhouse west of Toledo and forced to observe satanic rituals.

"I know it's hard for people to really understand this, but it was real," she said. "It happened, and I've lived with it for most of my life."

Investigators hired by the diocese searched the farmhouse, on the edge of a cornfield, for clues.

They knew that Bombrys' allegations were not isolated, that two other women had come forward in recent months to allege that they had been abused in strange rituals.

One woman, now in her early fifties, told police she was taken to the farmhouse in the 1960s and abused by priests in ritual sex ceremonies, while the second woman, now in her mid-twenties, told detectives that when she was a grade-school pupil she was carried into a Toledo church at night, placed on an altar, and abused by several adults.

Bombrys said members of the satanic group purposely created an atmosphere of fear among their victims and put them in situations that would seem too bizarre for most adults to believe.

When Bombrys finally told her family about the abuse, they dismissed the allegations outright and virtually disowned her, causing a rift among the staunchly Catholic clan, many of whom worked in law enforcement.

"It's very difficult for family members as well as for the victims and I think everyone has their own issues in regard to that," Bombrys said. "My family is very Catholic and they're very devout Catholics. They had never heard the church come forward and say that they believe these allegations against Chet to be true."

Bombrys told her attorney and church officials that preventing Chet Warren from abusing more children was more important to her than a monetary settlement.

When she went to Father James Cryan, head of the regional Oblates community, she said the cleric listened politely but never did a thing about it.

"Quite honestly, he listened but there was no other response. He said, 'Chet's not a priest anymore.' But yes he is a priest. He's not in a parish, but according to the Vatican he is still a priest."

According to canon law, the rules by which the Catholic Church governs itself, when a priest is ordained, he remains a priest for life. That applies to priests who are barred from ministry, although they cannot present themselves as priests in public. The only exception is when a priest is laicized, either voluntarily or by force, and either way, the decision is made by the Vatican.

"I had been in contact with the church long before the Boston scandal erupted," Bombrys said. "It just happened to be coincidental that I filed the lawsuit in April 2002. We were at a standstill. They weren't willing to discuss it, they weren't willing to negotiate, they weren't willing to do anything. When they refused to respond whatsoever, I decided to go ahead with the lawsuit."

She said it appeared to her that the Toledo diocese and the Oblates were more concerned about money than they were about helping victims heal.

"For me, I thought the church cared only about the economics. It was, 'How little money can we get away with paying this person?'"

She said Bishop James Hoffman of Toledo offered to meet with her in 1999, when she first contacted the diocese, but she declined. "I wasn't ready, quite honestly, at that point. I felt Bishop Hoffman was directly responsible for covering up Chet Warren's actions."

Bishop Hoffman's successor, Bishop Leonard Blair, installed as the seventh bishop of Toledo in December 2003, agreed to meet with Bombrys in August 2004, to discuss an out-of-court settlement of the lawsuit.

That led to one of Bombrys' biggest disappointments in her fight for justice, she said. She drove two and a half hours from her home in Columbus to the Catholic Center in downtown Toledo, only to learn that Bishop Blair was in Mexico.

"Bishop Blair was not present because he was on a month-long visit to study Hispanic culture and Spanish," she said. "To me, as a victim, it demonstrates that that's more important to him than we are. He could have planned his trip around the mediations."

Bombrys eventually settled for $80,000, plus the noneconomic conditions that were so crucial to her.

One of the noneconomic stipulations was that Bishop Blair would send a notice to all the parishes and places where Warren had served so that people would know he was a child abuser.

"The letter was to be sent to all the locations that Chet Warren had worked indicating that there was reason to believe the allegations," Bombrys said. "This was especially important to me because Chet Warren was still presenting himself as a priest, which I found absolutely amazing."

Adhering to Bombrys' demands, Bishop Blair wrote a letter that was sent to hundreds of members of St. Pius Parish in early March 2005, saying that the diocese had investigated her complaint and "determined it to be credible."

"On behalf of the Diocese of Toledo and St. Pius Parish, I apologize to Teresa Bombrys for the harm she has suffered," Bishop Leonard Blair wrote.

But there was one more obligation for the bishop, according to Bombrys' settlement.

Later that same month, on March 14, 2005, Bishop Blair stood in the pulpit of St. Pius and told more than two hundred parishioners attending a Sunday morning Mass that their former priest, Chet Warren, had committed "grievously sinful and criminal acts" while he served in their parish.

As Bombrys sat tearfully in the second row, the soft-spoken and erudite bishop read from a prepared statement for seven minutes, then paused and looked Bombrys in the eye. "I want to apologize to you, Teresa, in person and publicly as the bishop of Toledo for the harm you have suffered," he said.

Bishop Blair told the hushed crowd that Bombrys and other victims of clerical sexual abuse who had stepped forward were helping to "make it possible for the healing to begin . . . by exposing an evil that festered for decades."

Bombrys and other abuse victims "have done something truly courageous for the good of the church community," the bishop said.

That unprecedented speech, praising Bombrys and offering a heartfelt apology on behalf of the church, was a breakthrough moment for the Toledo diocese, one that filled victims' hearts with hope.

But showing how deep loyalties to a priest can run, even with the bishop's public apology, Bombrys' family never believed her allegations against Warren. She remains shut out, shunned, by most of her relatives.

Bombrys is calling for the Catholic Church to take one more action against Warren and laicize him.

Priests who are barred from ministry, like Warren, cannot celebrate Mass for anyone but themselves, cannot perform the sacraments, and cannot present themselves as priests to the public.

In the rare case of a priest who refuses to cooperate after being barred from ministry, there is little that a diocesan bishop or head of a religious order can do.

"In my opinion, the church has not done everything it could do in Chet Warren's case," Bombrys said. "If the church laicized and defrocked him, I think it would send a clear message to the public that this person is not a priest. A lot of people still believe Chet is innocent."

In December 2005, the Toledo diocese took the highly unusual step of going to court to try to keep Chet Warren out of one of its chapels.

The priest had been frequenting a secluded chapel at Blessed Sacrament Parish, set in the midst of a busy middle-class Toledo neighborhood. The chapel was on the same property as a church-run elementary school, and close to a busy city park.

A member of Blessed Sacrament called to complain about Warren frequenting the chapel, saying he posed a risk to children. When she called Frank DiLallo, the diocesan case manager, he told her: "Why don't you tell him to stay away?" Aghast, she said she did not know how to respond. DiLallo followed with another question for the woman, whom he had never met and was speaking to for the first time: "Why don't you just shoot him?"

Father Martin Donnelly, pastor of Blessed Sacrament Parish—and younger brother of Auxiliary Bishop Robert Donnelly—told Warren he could visit the chapel only if he signed an agreement restricting his visits to before 6:00 a.m., and only if he was accompanied by another male adult.

Warren refused to abide by those guidelines, and the diocese went to court.

Sally Oberski, director of communications for the Toledo diocese, issued a statement on December 28, 2005:

Because Mr. Warren failed to comply with the restrictions placed on his presence at the parish . . . the Diocese of Toledo filed a civil complaint against him to ensure that he does not enter the chapel at the parish, or any other part of the parish campus, with the exception of attending public religious worship at the church.

John Connors and Whitey Knannlien had planned to interview Warren for their report to the Toledo diocese, but the former priest refused to talk.

The private detectives conducted an investigation of Warren and found that he was living with a woman in an apartment in Sylvania, an upscale suburb northwest of Toledo. He often wore his clerical collar and did volunteer work during the day, they said.

At night, one neighbor told the detectives, Warren frequently left his apartment after midnight and returned between 3:00 and 6:00 a.m.

He also "tries to be secretive," the neighbor told the detectives, parking his dark blue Chrysler Sebring in different parking lots around the complex and sometimes leaving it a block or two away from the apartment.

On August 22, 2003, John Connors met with Father James Cryan, who had been the head of the regional Oblates community but was leaving for a sabbatical in New York.

Father Cryan said he was aware that Sister Mary Curtiss had named him as a suspect in her testimony before the diocesan review board, and denied any knowledge of occult or cult activities at St. Pius Parish while he was there.

Connors told him that in addition to the allegations Sister Mary Curtiss made to the review board, she also told him that Warren and Father Cryan picked her up in a car in 2000 and she, being in a dissociative state in which she was blocking out her bad memories, went with them and was raped by Warren while Cryan drove.

"Chet's 76 years old now," replied Cryan, who is ten years Warren's junior. "He should feel complimented that he was accused of having sex with Sister Mary Curtiss at the age of 73."

Father Cryan said he was assistant pastor of St. Pius when he first came to Toledo in 1971, then later was named pastor before being promoted to provincial of the Oblates in 1991.

"When I first arrived in Toledo, Daniel Early was the pastor and Chet Warren was the other assistant pastor," Father Cryan told Connors. "I noticed that Chet was always hanging around with the younger members of the parish, junior high and senior high ages."

After being promoted to provincial, Cryan said the first time he heard allegations against Warren, he sent him to an institute in Chicago for assessment. From there, he ordered Warren to undergo treatment at a residential facility center for sex offenders in Pennsylvania.

"After a few months of treatment, Chet refused to cooperate with the program and left the facility," Father Cryan told Connors.

The provincial ordered Warren to move to the Oblates' residence in Jackson, Michigan, where he was placed under "house arrest" and suspended from any priestly duties.

After a few weeks in Jackson, Warren complained that he could not live under those restrictions and was quitting the Oblates, Father Cryan said.

When he left Jackson, he reportedly took a car and between $30,000 and $35,000 in cash, according to Father Cryan.

The Oblates never pressed charges over the stolen car and the cash, and never formally laicized Warren. He continues to wear his clerical collar at times and he is known for sending condolence cards to people on the anniversary of the death of a loved one. He signs the cards and letters, "Father Chet," followed by the postscript, "Don't let the *Blade* be your Bible."

Father Warren was not Father Cryan's only troubled son.

On February 5, 1994, the Oblates' provincial wrote a four-page letter to John Hayward, a powerful attorney who represented the Toledo diocese for decades, detailing an hour-and-a-half meeting that he and Bishop James Hoffman had the day before with a woman who claimed she was molested by at least four Oblates when she was a child.

The abuse "included oral sex with at least two of them (one of them telling her that he was preparing her for marriage) and unwanted fondling," Father Cryan wrote.

"This activity was usually within her family home where Oblates frequently visited and where two of them were often house-guests, and where they overindulged in heavy drinking," he wrote.

One of the Oblates used to call her "luscious lips," Father Cryan said, a term that was "grossly inappropriate for a girl in her preteens."

"In recollection," Father Cryan continued, there was "an inner clique" among the thirty Toledo Oblates who "associated with the affluent-elite . . . Those of us not in the clique called them 'the Joy Boys.'"

The Joy Boys "drank heavily and partied strong, and they lived off the bounty of their benefactors," he wrote in his letter to Hayward. "Some of them seemed at times to go beyond appropriate boundaries, with either gender. . . ."

The woman said the Joy Boys destroyed her self-esteem and that she had been undergoing psychological counseling. "I was their piece of meat," she told Father Cryan.

She said Father Chet Warren had promised to marry her and then reneged on his promise.

When she went to the Toledo diocese to tell them she planned to file a lawsuit, "she claims she was snookered into delaying filing suit by [diocesan attorney] Tom Pletz's alleged promise of an extension of the statute of limitations and payment of her children's education."

Father Cryan told Hayward that the woman "recently renewed her marriage vows . . . because she claims the many Oblates who witnessed her wedding were at one time her sexual partners."

He asked Hayward for advice.

"John, I do not know where to go with this. I am no longer certain if it [is] even a legal matter. If her allegations are true, I empathize with the enormity of the issue, but I do not know what my responsibility is in the matter. Legally, I don't know. Morally, I am not the lamb of God who must take away the sins of the world or ask my brothers to take that burden."

In Connors's interview with Father Cryan in August 2003, the priest told the detective that he had learned of Sister Mary Curtiss's allegations against him from Shelly Killen, a member of the review board who had been molested by Father Warren when she was 19.

Killen, however, had told Connors that she never told Father Cryan about the allegations. After investigating further, Connors said he learned that Bill Mahoney, one of Father Warren's attorneys, had been told of the Cryan allegations by either John Hayward or Tom Pletz, two diocesan attorneys, who then told Father Cryan.

"Father Cryan's statement about Shelly was an obvious untruth," Connors wrote in his report to the diocese. "As an investigator, I had cause to wonder what other untruths he had told me."

Chapter 33

In October 2003, Connors and Knannlien met with case manager Frank DiLallo at the Catholic Center in downtown Toledo.

They reported Sister Mary Curtiss's bizarre allegations against Chet Warren, and told him about her allegations that a satanic cult had murdered a 3-year-old girl and hung the bodies of dead children in the basement of a farmhouse.

DiLallo wanted to know if there could be any truth at all to such bizarre and outrageous allegations, and if the nun had accused any Toledo diocesan priests of involvement.

The diocese was already familiar with many of Sister Mary Curtiss's allegations, which she had spelled out before the review board in June. But the stories she told the two private detectives were far more detailed and disturbing than her previous allegations.

Thankfully for diocesan officials, almost all of the priests in the center of the nun's allegations were Oblates, not members of the Toledo Catholic diocese. However, religious-order priests and nuns are allowed to serve in a diocese only with permission of the local bishop.

Furthermore, a diocesan bishop has the authority to order a religious-community priest—such as a Jesuit, Franciscan, or Oblate—to leave his diocese if he has reason to believe that the priest or monk has committed a grave sin or crime.

So although newly appointed Bishop Leonard Blair was not Chet Warren's boss, he was not completely free of responsibility for the wayward Oblate.

Connors and Knannlien told him that Sister Mary Curtiss had mentioned only one diocesan priest—Father Gerald Robinson—whose name she had already brought up before the review board.

The nun said she was not sure if Father Robinson participated in the satanic rituals at the Raab Road farmhouse.

She did tell the two detectives that Father Robinson had paid Chet Warren to use her for sex when she was a teenager.

"Chet Warren was running a little prostitution ring down at St. Vincent Hospital, where he was the chaplain," Sister Mary Curtiss told them. "I also remember Robinson being there when Warren took pornographic photos of me when I was about 15. I think that prostitution ring was a real moneymaker."

Every six to eight weeks, Sister Mary Curtiss said, she would be taken to Father Warren's chaplain's quarters at the inner-city hospital. She remembers the quarters as having a living room with red leather furniture, a bedroom, and a bathroom.

In September 1977 or 1978, when she was 14 or 15, Sister Mary Curtiss said her father drove her to the hospital about 1:00 p.m. Father Warren met them in the parking lot and the priest took her to his chaplain's quarters, leading her into the bedroom and telling her to wait.

A short time later, Father Robinson entered the room and gave Warren a white envelope containing cash.

"She's all yours. Have fun for an hour," Warren told Robinson, then walked out of the room.

She described Father Robinson as a small man, about five-feet-six inches tall, and weighing about 140 pounds. He had dark brown hair and a receding hairline, a pointy, birdlike nose, and dark, beady eyes that seemed to look right through her. That night, he was wearing a dark zippered jacket and black pants—not clerical garb.

Father Robinson told the teenager to take off all of her clothes. Then he reached into the closet and put on a black leather jacket and a pair of spiked leather cuffs, she told the detectives.

The priest took out ropes from the closet and, without saying a word, tied her wrists to the bedposts and her ankles to the other end of the bed, spreading her legs and arms.

"He licked me and he bit my thighs, arms, and breasts," Sister Mary Curtiss told the detectives. "The foreplay was painful. He was pinching me and slapping me and kept calling me 'whore' and 'pussy' and saying disgusting things like, 'You were made for this.'"

She said he reached under her buttocks and the studs on his wristbands dug into her flesh painfully. Then he took a black whip from the closet and smacked her on the thighs.

Suddenly, the priest turned angry.

"You whore!" he shouted, and smacked her hard with the whip. Then he showed her the handle, holding it in front of her face. It had a thin, black leather grip. The priest's eyes narrowed and a maniacal grin crept across his face.

"You deserve this, you whore!" he said, and shoved the whip handle into her vagina, causing a shooting pain through her body.

"He was brutal," the nun said. "He's a maniac. He wanted to humiliate me."

The nun said Father Robinson ejaculated on her body twice, then strutted around the room.

After he left the bedroom, Chet Warren came in and untied her.

"I'll bet you enjoyed that, didn't you?" he asked her with a wicked smile. She just shivered.

Warren told her to get dressed, then escorted her down to the hospital entrance where her father was waiting for them. The priest handed her father an envelope containing some bills.

"That was the only time I saw Father Robinson in the chaplain's quarters," Sister Mary Curtiss told the detectives. "There were a lot of different men. I didn't know most of them. But I know Chet Warren made a fortune running that prostitution ring."

DiLallo asked the detectives if they thought she was telling the truth.

"She came across well," Connors said. "She seemed to make a real effort to be honest and accurate. I don't have a problem with repressed memories. I know she believes what she is saying, and I have no reason not to believe her."

Knannlien said he really wasn't sure and suggested that the investigation continue.

In a written report, he said that "Sister came across as a friendly, outgoing person. She referred to disassociation and repressed memory a number of times, where these recollections of abuse have come. She told us about the memories as honestly as she could.

"From her body language during these interviews, there is little doubt that Sister believes the sexual contact actually happened with Warren, her father, Robinson, Cryan, and others.

"Her body language while she was describing the occult and satanic rituals and rapes was not as positive. She believes they actually happened, but I'm not sure if they are real or if they are fantasies. I think we need to find some evidence that would corroborate her allegations."

Chapter 34

In February 2004, Whitey Knannlien and John Connors each got a phone call from Tom Ross, an investigator with the Lucas County prosecutor's office and a member of the county's cold-case squad.

Detective Ross asked the private investigators to halt their investigation of Sister Mary Curtiss's allegations.

The cold-case squad was investigating the 1980 murder of Sister Margaret Ann Pahl at Mercy Hospital, he told them, and the prime suspect, Father Gerald Robinson, was among those Sister Mary Curtiss had accused of abusing her.

Ross said he did not want to risk having the diocese's private detectives interfere with an official investigation.

Meanwhile, the Lucas County prosecutor's office and cold-case investigators continued to gather information to build their case that Father Robinson killed the nun.

In addition to conducting scores of interviews, the cold-case investigators and the prosecutor's office had taken the priest's letter opener and the altar cloth to a number of national experts for analysis.

They also had interviewed Father Jeffrey Grob, the Chicago priest who specialized in rituals and who was convinced that Sister Margaret Ann Pahl's murder was a ritual sacrifice.

The ritual aspect of the murder was an explosive element in the case and one that prosecutor Julia Bates urged investigators to treat thoroughly and cautiously.

To follow up on Father Grob's conclusions, Sergeant Forrester and Detective Ross decided to call upon Dr. Dawn Perlmutter, director of the Institute for the Research of Organized and Ritual Violence, in eastern Pennsylvania.

The institute is a private organization providing specialized crime-scene identification and criminal-investigation assistance to law-enforcement officials around the world.

Doctor Perlmutter had been investigating ritual crimes for fifteen years and had been a consultant to law-enforcement officials in Chiavenna, Italy, in a case involving the ritual slaying of a nun on June 6, 2000.

The victim in the Italian murder, Sister Mary Laura Manetti of the Sisters of the Cross of St. Andrew, had been lured to a park late at night by a troubled teenage girl she had been counseling.

The girl and two of her friends had been waiting for the nun and ambushed her, tying her up and stabbing her to death in a crude satanic ritual. The trio of teenage girls told local police that they had formed a satanic cult and were influenced by the music of American shock rocker Marilyn Manson.

Doctor Perlmutter was invited to come to Toledo to review the evidence.

"I went back and forth to Toledo a number of times, reviewing the evidence, giving advice, and trading e-mail," Dr. Perlmutter said in an interview. "I also met with other victims [including Sister Mary Curtiss]."

She said the slaying of Sister Margaret Ann Pahl was "about as classic as it gets" for a satanic ritual murder.

Doctor Perlmutter drafted a lengthy report citing myriad reasons for such a conclusion.

To start, she said, the site of the slaying was a strong indication of satanic ritual.

"The murder was committed in a sacred place, the sacristy of a chapel," she said in a report drafted for the prosecutor's office. "In satanic crimes, perpetrators choose Christian sacred spaces because it literally and symbolically increases the desecration of Christianity and ritually enhances magical powers."

For traditional satanists, Dr. Perlmutter said, it is "ritually required" that ceremonies be held in sacred spaces. That is why satanists have been known to commit such crimes as vandalism, arson, theft, ritual sexual abuse, and, in rare cases, even murder, in churches, she said.

A second strong indication of satanic ritual was the timing of Sister Margaret Ann's murder.

"The murder occurred on April 5, 1980, Holy Saturday. Easter is the most important holiday of the Christian year and committing the murder on Easter intensifies the desecration," she said. "Ritualistic crimes frequently occur on sacred holidays and for true believers the date always has significant symbolic meaning."

The third sign, she said, was the character of the victim.

"From a traditional satanic perspective, Sister Margaret Ann Pahl was an ideal victim. In ritual killings of both animals and humans, the sacrificial offering is chosen because of its attributes. For example, historically it would be ineffective to sacrifice a sick or wounded animal; it has to be the finest specimen so that the gods are not offended.

"In satanism, the ideal victim is someone who represents a virtuous life dedicated to serving God. Sacrificing a nun would be considered a powerful accomplishment for the perpetrator."

Doctor Perlmutter also said the presence of sacred objects at the site of the murder—crosses, chalices, holy water, Communion wafers, altar cloths, etc.—was further evidence that it was a ritual murder.

In many cases of satanic rituals, she said, the devil worshippers will steal sacred Christian objects from a church and then leave them at the scene to increase the power and magic of their ceremonial rites.

"In this case, the arrangement of the holy objects (the placement of the candles, the use of the altar cloth) is clearly indicative of a ritual murder," she said.

"In satanism, it is very important to mock the Christian religion and there have been numerous cases of theft of sacred objects from churches that have later been used in satanic rituals. The significance is to desecrate the objects, which will evoke a stronger magical experience."

She told investigators that the way perpetrators use blood is the most revealing evidence of ritualistic crimes. This type of evidence involves the symbolic use of blood during the ritual, not the physical patterns left behind like the ones examined for bloodstain-pattern transfer analysis, she said.

"It is very significant that Sister Margaret Ann Pahl was alive when she was stabbed and that her body was manipulated in such a way as to emit enough blood to be used for ritual purposes," Dr. Perlmutter said. "In sacrificial rituals, it is magically more potent to keep the victim alive as long as possible so that their life force energy will be magically transformed to the perpetrator. Essentially, the perpetrator is enacting a perversion of the Catholic Mass."

Because the attacker first strangled the nun to the verge of death, the victim's heart was not pumping much blood through her body. Dr. Perlmutter surmised that the killer stabbed Sister Margaret Ann Pahl a total of thirty-one times not because of anger or in a frenzy or rage, but to draw more blood from her body to complete his dark ritual.

She said there was evidence of a circular bruise in the nun's chest area, near the multiple stab wounds, which she believes was made when the killer pressed the lip of a chalice against her body seeking to fill the cup with some blood.

"Blood is a mandatory substance for religious ritual . . . and sacrifice is the ultimate religious experience," Dr. Perlmutter stated. "Historically, people attributed sacred and magical qualities to blood. Blood is anointed, exchanged and imbibed in magical [satanic] rites of initiation, transformation, and sacrifice."

With the Catholic Church teaching that wine is transformed into the blood of Christ during a Mass, satanists seek to mock Christianity and to acquire power by using blood in a "Black Mass."

According to reviews of the 1980 crime scene photos, including close-ups of Sister Margaret Ann's face, Dr. Perlmutter said she believes the killer applied blood to the nun's forehead "as a form of being anointed, which is a very common occult ceremonial rite."

The first nine stab wounds being in the shape of an inverted cross is further evidence of ritual, with an upside-down cross being "very common in satanic crimes, the purpose of which is to mock Christianity," Dr. Perlmutter said.

Furthermore, the stab wounds were all on the left side of Sister Margaret Ann Pahl's body, and satanism is known as "the Left-Hand Path," she said.

"There have been frequent occult crimes where perpetrators deliberately stab victims on the left side of their bodies," Dr. Perlmutter told the detectives and prosecutors. "Physical mutilations are very common in ritualistic crimes and always have symbolic and magical meaning to the perpetrator."

The sexual assault of the victim also had satanic connections, she said. Sister

Margaret Ann's undergarments were pulled down over an ankle and her vagina had been penetrated by an unspecified "instrument," according to the coroner.

"In ritualistic crimes, motivations for sexual assault differ substantially from more typical sexual crimes," she said. "In traditional satanism, sexual assault is not about sexual gratification or power over the victim as much as a required ritual activity to achieve the magical goal.

"In relation to the other crime scene indicators at the scene, it is most likely that a religious object such as a cross was inserted in Sister Pahl's vagina as a part of the ritual violation."

Doctor Perlmutter said it was significant that the letter opener which police believe was the murder weapon was found in the suspect's residence.

In numerous meetings of the cold-case squad, the question had come up often: If the letter opener was, in fact, the murder weapon, why did Father Robinson hold onto it for so long rather than toss it into the depths of Lake Erie?

Doctor Perlmutter said that in her fifteen years of investigating ritual violence, she has found that perpetrators will never get rid of the knife used in a ritual.

"A ritual knife is the most sacred item of the offender and is never left at the crime scene, unless the perpetrator is caught in the act," she said. "It is often found during searches of personal areas or on the suspect. Although a suspect may dispose of incriminating evidence, they will never voluntarily relinquish their ritual knife. It is their most valuable magical tool."

She said occult sacrifices are always performed with knives, or, more specifically, with an "athame," a ceremonial knife that is usually ornately decorated with symbols corresponding to the owner's belief system.

"You are not going to find gunshot wounds at a satanic sacrifice," Dr. Perlmutter said. "It would be magically ineffective to shoot someone in a ritual."

Father Robinson's letter opener fits the description of an athame because one side of the handle is inscribed with a double pentagram—two five-pointed stars facing in opposite directions.

"The symbol of two pentagrams—one upright, one inverted—represents the duality of nature—dark and light, good and evil, always in flux," she said. "This is the ideal symbol for a priest practicing satanism."

Doctor Perlmutter said the position of Sister Margaret Ann's body in the sacristy also indicated a ritual killing.

"Sister Pahl's body was lined up with the linear pattern of the floor and placed directly in front of the window. This indicates someone who was completely familiar with the design of the room. In ritualistic crimes, everything has symbolic meaning and the positioning of her body in particular needs to be analyzed in conjunction with the deliberate placement of the other items in the room."

The way the body was positioned, in line with the pattern in the terrazzo floor, the victim's head perfectly centered over the lines, seemed an attempt to create a "magical symbol" such as a triangle or a pentagram, Dr. Perlmutter said. Occultists use pentagrams as "demon traps" that, when accompanied by spells and rituals, "summon demonic spirits into our plane of existence," she said.

Chapter 35

Within a few months, Sergeant Steve Forrester and Detective Tom Ross had managed to track down just about everybody whose name appeared in more than 350 pages of police reports from 1980. Many of them turned out to be dead ends, sometimes literally—many of the people interviewed twenty-four years ago were deceased.

One person who offered new information to cold-case investigators was Dr. Jack Baron.

A medical intern at Mercy Hospital at the time of the murder, Dr. Baron was among the throng of medical workers who had raced to the chapel after hearing the "Mr. Swift" emergency announcement that Holy Saturday morning.

Sergeant Forrester reviewed the 1980 police report by Detective Dan Foster about his interview with Dr. Baron, which took place eleven days after Sister Margaret Ann's murder.

The only item in the report that the cold-case squad had not seen before was the doctor's recollection that a patient in the hospital at the time had been convicted of killing his wife. Dr. Baron had told police about the patient soon after the murder, but when they checked on him, they found that he had been released two days earlier and was nowhere near the hospital on April 5.

Detectives Forrester and Ross wanted to ask Dr. Baron a few questions about the suspicious patient, and tracked the doctor down in Englewood, Florida, where he was a family doctor.

Sergeant Forrester called Dr. Baron and told him that the cold-case squad had reopened the investigation into Sister Margaret Ann's slaying.

"I see in the 1980 reports that you were interviewed by detectives on April 16th," Forrester said. "Do you recall that interview?"

"Yes, very clearly," Dr. Baron said.

"It says you told Detective Foster that there was a patient in Mercy Hospital who had killed his wife, and that you reported that fact to police right after Sister's slaying, is that correct?"

"Yes, sir. That is correct," Dr. Baron said. "As I recall, that patient had been checked out of the hospital several days before the murder, and was in Tiffin or Fostoria at the time that Sister Margaret Ann was killed."

"Do you remember the patient's name?"

"No. That I don't," the doctor responded.

"But you're sure police checked into it and found that he had a rock-solid alibi?"

"Yes, I'm certain of that," Dr. Baron said.

Sergeant Forrester asked the doctor if he would mind going over the day's events, as best as he could recollect.

Doctor Baron said he had worked the overnight shift, starting at 11:00 p.m. Friday, and was in a third-floor meeting room briefing the incoming day shift about the patients when the emergency call was announced over the PA system.

A "Mr. Swift" code meant that doctors, and all medical personnel, were to stop whatever they were doing and take care of the emergency, he said.

"Do you remember what time that code call came in?" Forrester asked.

"Yes, I'm pretty sure it was about 8:15," Dr. Baron said.

He said he and another doctor ran down two flights of stairs and the other doctors took a different stairwell to the first floor. But he had never been to the chapel, Dr. Baron said, and when he ran out of the stairwell, he turned the wrong way. By the time he realized it and got to the chapel, he saw that Dr. Woodard was already in the sacristy, kneeling beside Sister Margaret Ann's body. Dr. Woodard told him the victim was dead and that she possibly had been raped.

Doctor Baron recalled seeing numerous stab wounds on the nun's chest and neck and noted that her underwear was down around her ankles.

There was some blood, he said, although he was surprised there wasn't more.

He reached for her wrist to check for a pulse even though Dr. Woodard had said it was too late—probably just an instinctive action, Dr. Baron said. Her skin was cold and clammy.

The sacristy was so dark, he raised the window shade to let some light in. A nurse named Gloria was standing there and he asked her to get a blanket and cover the sister.

Then Father Swiatecki arrived in the sacristy and began giving Sister Margaret Ann her last rites.

Doctor Baron said he and Dr. Woodard suddenly realized that this was a crime scene and had just started to clear everyone out of the sacristy when two uniformed police officers arrived.

"Was there anything else you remember about that morning that might be of interest?" Sergeant Forrester asked.

There was a short pause on the other end of the line.

"As a matter of fact, yes," Dr. Baron said. "There's something that's been bothering me all these years."

The sergeant asked him to explain.

"Well, when I was being questioned by the detective, I told him something several times but he basically ignored it and went on to his next question. He kept asking me if the window shade in the sacristy was up or down when I arrived, or if I had seen the victim's watch or purse. That kind of bugged me."

"What was it that you told him that he didn't pay attention to?" Forrester asked.

"I told him that when I was running down the hallway to the chapel, after I realized I had overshot it and turned around, I encountered a priest going in the opposite direction."

"You passed a priest in the hallway?"

"Yes. I didn't know his name or recognize his face, but he certainly was wearing priest's garb—a Roman collar, dark trousers, tunic and all that."

"How close were you to him?" Forrester asked.

"Very close."

"Did you give police a physical description of the priest?"

"Yes, I told them he was about five foot seven or eight, medium build, dark hair, about 35 to 45 age range."

"And what did they say?"

"They seemed to brush it off. They weren't interested. They wrote it down but I don't think they put it in their report."

"Do you remember anything else about the priest?"

"Well, there was something pretty weird. After I passed him, running pretty much full-tilt, I turned my head and looked back at him. He had turned to look at me over his left shoulder and I'll never forget it. He gave me a stare that went right through me. He didn't say a word."

Chapter 36

There were two other people interviewed in 1980 who provided new and important information for detectives working on the cold-case investigation.

One of them was Grace Jones, who had moved from Lake Providence, Louisiana, to Toledo at age 15 to be with her older sister, Bessie, who had gotten a job at a Chinese restaurant downtown.

In 1955, Grace began working in a medical laboratory of Mercy Hospital, and a few months later Bessie joined her to work at the Catholic hospital. Her job was sterilizing needles and surgical equipment and disposing of old blood samples and other medical fluids and items that were no longer needed.

She began her shift at 4:00 a.m., taking a cab from her inner-city duplex to the hospital a mile and a half away.

Grace had a speech impediment and a hefty Southern accent, but she loved people and loved to talk. She would stop on her way to the lab to chat with the security guards and then spend a few minutes with the emergency room workers before punching in her time clock.

Sometime after 7:00 on the morning of April 5, 1980, Bessie asked Grace to get a copy of the *Blade* from the newspaper rack in front of the hospital.

Grace walked past the kitchen to the elevator and rode it from the ground floor, where the laboratory was, to the first floor one level up, and walked through the glass exit doors onto Madison Avenue. She dropped a dime into the slot of the royal blue newspaper rack and grabbed a copy of the *Blade*.

Heading back to the lab, she pressed the button for the elevator and stood against the wall and waited.

At the end of the hallway, she saw one of the wooden doors of the chapel swing open and a short, dark-haired priest walk through the opening. He was wearing a long black robe and a hat—a "beanie," Jones called it—and carried a duffel bag in one hand.

Grace had seen the priest around the hospital many times and recognized him immediately as Father Robinson.

He walked in her direction and she nodded a hello. The priest nodded back and kept walking. Just then the elevator door slid open and Grace stepped inside.

A while later, Jones was unsure exactly how long, a "Mr. Swift" emergency call came over the hospital's public-address system, directing emergency medical workers to the chapel.

The lab worker told her boss that she had seen the priest in the hallway. He looked at her sternly and told her not to say anything about it, that the priest was a man of God. If she wanted to keep her job, she'd better keep her mouth shut.

A second witness from 1980 who gave the cold-case squad something new was Leslie Ann Kerr, since married and divorced and going by Leslie Ann Kerner.

On April 5, 1980, Kerr was working in the coronary care unit of Mercy Hospital as an EKG technician, running tests on patients that monitored their heart activity.

On the day of the murder, she arrived for work a little before her scheduled 7:00 a.m. start and went straight to her office on the first floor. She then walked across the hall to punch in her time clock. It was 6:50 a.m.

Kerr had been working at the hospital for a few years and had gotten to know the Sisters of Mercy nuns, including Sister Margaret Ann Pahl. She also knew the two hospital chaplains, Father Jerome Swiatecki and Father Gerald Robinson.

Father Swiatecki was a large man who never stopped talking. He was always stopping by her office to chat, joke around, and drink a cup of coffee.

The other chaplain, Father Gerald Robinson, had quite the opposite personality. Kerr saw Father Robinson nearly every day at work, but the priest rarely said a word to her—most of the time, not even a "hello."

After punching her time, clock, Kerr prepared her EKG equipment and checked the list of patients for the day. Waiting for her coworker to arrive before getting started, she walked through the office door and looked down the long hallway toward the hospital's chapel.

That's when she saw Father Robinson standing by the chapel doors. He was wearing his priest's collar and a long black robe. She didn't think anything of it at the time.

About an hour and fifteen minutes later, Kerr heard a woman's frantic screams and ran into the hallway to see what the matter was. The screams were coming from the chapel.

She ran down the hall and through the chapel doors, where she found two nuns sobbing and wailing. Something was terribly wrong. A stream of doctors, nurses, and medical personnel came pouring into the room.

The door was open to the sacristy and she could see a doctor already inside the small room, bent down over a body. He was shaking his head.

It was clear that they did not need an EKG technician and the place was already filled with doctors and nurses. Kerr turned around and walked slowly back to her office.

Within minutes, she learned that a nun had been found murdered and possibly raped in the sacristy. She called her fiancé and then her parents to tell them the shocking news, and mentioned that she had seen a priest standing outside the chapel about an hour before all the commotion.

A week later, a detective walked into Kerr's office and asked if she would be willing to come down to the boardroom where police had set up an office.

Kerr sat down at a desk and two detectives asked her to recall the events of April 5. "Tell us about anything unusual you had seen that morning," they said.

She told them about the screams, about running down the hall, and about seeing the doctor kneeling beside the nun's body.

Kerr did not tell the detectives she had seen Father Robinson standing near the chapel doors at 7:00 a.m.

Twenty-four years later, the now-Mrs. Kerner was living in Springfield, Missouri, working in retail sales, when she turned on the television and saw Charlie Gibson report on *Good Morning America* that a Toledo priest had been arrested in the 1980 murder of a nun.

She called her mother in Toledo and asked what was going on. Her mother told her Father Robinson had been arrested and charged with murder. Her mother urged her to call police and tell them that she had seen the priest outside the chapel that morning.

Kerner agreed, promising to call, but after hanging up she began having doubts. She was living in Missouri now and had a young son. It would be an ordeal to travel to Toledo to give a deposition or testify. And the murder was so long ago. She was sure the police already had plenty of evidence against the priest or they would not have arrested him.

Her husband, Rick, from whom she had separated earlier that year, called from Texas, where he was now living and working in the food industry. He told her it was her civic duty to call authorities and tell them that she had seen Father Robinson that Holy Saturday morning.

She told him she knew he was right but that she was afraid to get involved and that her story might not mean much to police. He told her to call anyway, and let the police sort it all out.

Kerner wrestled with the decision for days, the days turned into weeks, and the weeks turned into months.

She pushed the decision aside for more than a year before finally calling the Lucas County prosecutor's office in the summer of 2005. The receptionist connected her with Sergeant Steve Forrester, one of the lead investigators.

Kerner told her story to the detective, who asked if she had told police in 1980 about seeing Father Robinson that morning.

"No," she said. "I just answered their questions as accurately as I could. They asked me if I had seen anything unusual or anyone who didn't belong, and I said, 'No.'"

Seeing a priest standing near a chapel was not unusual, she said. She saw it every day she worked at the hospital.

She didn't know at the time that Father Robinson was a suspect in the nun's murder. She also didn't know the priest had told police he never left his hospital apartment that morning until receiving a call to tell him that Sister Margaret Ann had been killed.

Chapter 37

Sergeant Steve Forrester's phone rang in the predawn stillness of April 23, 2004. The detective looked at his alarm clock—5:30 a.m.—and reached for the receiver.

"Forrester."

"Sergeant Forrester? It's Officer Middleton. I thought you should know that there are several media vehicles circling around Father Robinson's residence. It looks like they're on to something. Maybe there's been a leak."

"Okay, thanks," he said. "Just stay right there and call my cell phone if anything else develops."

He knew he'd better called Julia Bates, the Lucas County prosecutor, and his colleague on the cold-case team, Tom Ross.

They'd been staking out Father Robinson's house on Nebraska Avenue for weeks. The priest's parents had bought the house in 1966, and Father Robinson moved in with his mother after the death of his father. The small brick home with the manicured lawn and small flower garden was right next door to the Toledo police department's Scott Park substation, across the street from the University of Toledo.

Undercover police had been tailing Father Robinson since it began to appear likely that the 66-year-old cleric would be indicted in the 1980 murder of Sister Margaret Ann Pahl.

They had pulled his garbage a couple of times, looking for any conceivable clue. No luck, however. "It was just garbage," Sergeant Forrester said.

"We were focusing on Robinson for several reasons," he explained. "First, there was a limited window of opportunity in the murder, time-wise. We eliminated a lot of people who worked at the hospital right off the bat.

"[Chicago priest] Father Grob had said the person responsible for this crime had a strong knowledge of religion or anti-religion, so that narrowed our pool of suspects. We eliminated Father Jerome Swiatecki because he had been in the cafeteria with the nuns. It wasn't long until we had accounted for the whereabouts of all persons religious except one—Father Robinson."

A missing puzzle piece was the cross that they believed had been used as a template when the killer made the first nine stab wounds in Sister Margaret Ann's chest, in the shape of an inverted cross. There was still a chance the cross was in the possession of the killer.

They also knew that nothing had been stolen from the sacristy, including several jewel-encrusted gold chalices in one of the cabinets, and had ruled out robbery as a motive. There was one item missing that day: a small silver Bulova watch Sister Margaret Ann had bought for $48 from Neumann's Jewelers. If they found that watch, it would be a key piece of evidence.

The last thing police wanted now was to have the news report that the priest was being watched or was about to be indicted. Father Robinson would surely ditch any evidence that may remain. And prosecutors already were a bit worried that the physical evidence against the priest was not as strong as they would like.

Sergeant Forrester, 50, had been on the Toledo force for twenty-seven years, ever since graduating from the University of Toledo. He went on to get a law degree from UT in 1999, and joined the American Bar Association and the American Academy of Forensic Medicine.

The tall, squarely built detective with short brown hair and glasses had investigated more than two hundred homicides as lead detective, and had taught courses on constitutional law and evidence at the University of Toledo.

He was appointed to the Lucas County cold-case team when prosecutor Julia Bates put the squad together in 1999, and had worked with Investigator Tom Ross on more than fifty cases.

Investigator Ross, 58, had been a Toledo police detective for thirty years and had investigated more than two hundred murders. When the cold-case squad was being assembled, Bates coaxed the veteran investigator out of retirement.

It was Tom Ross who had recognized Father Robinson's name in Sister Mary Curtiss's testimony for the review board, remembering that the priest was the primary suspect back in 1980.

The two investigators had been reviewing evidence and consulting experts ever since the case was officially reopened five months earlier.

Sergeant Forrester quickly called Ross and Bates, and asked the prosecutor to call an emergency strategy meeting.

By 8:00 a.m., Forrester, Ross, Bates, and assistant county prosecutors Dean Mandros, J. Christopher Anderson, and Larry Kiroff had gathered in a third-floor room in the Lucas County courthouse.

After hashing out their options, Bates decided they shouldn't wait to interrogate the priest or search his home.

The group decided that Ross and Forrester would go to the suspect's home, ask him some questions about the 1980 murder, and then search his house.

Depending how the interrogation went, the investigators could arrest him on the spot, or wait. But the search would have to be done right away, because he'd know he was under investigation and could destroy the evidence.

Sergeant Forrester typed up a request for a search warrant on the priest's home and took it to Lucas County common pleas court Judge Robert Christiansen to be signed. By the time all the plans and paperwork were in place, it was already mid-afternoon.

Detectives Ross and Forrester pulled into Father Robinson's driveway, walked up the cement sidewalk, and knocked on the screen door. The priest opened it just enough to see who was there. After an awkward pause, he pushed the door open and invited the detectives inside.

The officers told the priest that they had been investigating the 1980 murder of Sister Margaret Ann Pahl at Mercy Hospital, and that they had a few questions.

Father Robinson, wearing blue jeans and a plaid shirt, took a seat in a corner chair of the living room and the detectives perched themselves on the edge of a dusty couch. The priest, his head tilted slightly, stared at the two officers, eyes narrowed to thin slits.

At first, the police officers went out of their way to be as polite and respectful to the priest as they could. They were almost apologetic in tone, as if they were being forced against their wills to ask such impertinent questions of a man of the cloth.

"Now Father, we know you were the chaplain at Mercy Hospital at the time of Sister Margaret Ann's murder. How would you describe your relationship with Sister?"

"To your knowledge, did Sister Margaret Ann have any enemies?"

"Father Robinson, is there anyone you know of who might have been capable of committing such a brutal murder in 1980?"

The priest responded slowly and cautiously to every question, answering with vague and noncommittal replies.

After about forty-five minutes, Detective Ross asked if they could move to the kitchen so that he could spread some papers out on the table. The two went into the small kitchen and sat at a wobbly dinette table while Sergeant Forrester waited in the living room, listening to every word.

Detective Ross's demeanor then took a sharp turn. The white-haired investigator opened an envelope and removed a stack of eight-by-ten black-and-white glossies of the 1980 crime scene. On top was a grisly close-up of Sister Margaret Ann Pahl's face. Her eyes were closed; there was blood on her forehead and nose. She looked strangely peaceful, despite the many stab wounds dotting her face, neck, and chest.

"Do you know recognize this woman, Father?"

"Yes, of course. Sister Margaret Ann Pahl," Father Robinson replied.

"Do you know who did this to her?" Ross asked.

The priest stared at the photo for an awkwardly long time.

"No," he said.

"How about this, Father?" Ross asked, and then showed him a photo of the nun's chest area, soaked in blood from numerous punctures. "Who could have done this to the elderly nun?"

"Don't know," Father Robinson replied, shaking his head from side to side.

"And who did this?" Ross asked, showing a photo of the slain nun's nakedness, her dress pulled up and panties down.

Father Robinson just shook his head no.

"Father, you said you were in your residence at the hospital the whole morning, but we have witnesses who will testify in court that they saw you at the chapel around the time of the murder on April 5, 1980. What do you have to say about that?"

"I don't know what you're talking about," the priest said, pursing his lips together and fidgeting in his chair.

Tough questions continued to fly for another half hour, and the priest kept giving cursory answers.

Investigator Ross put the photos back in the envelope and leaned forward in his chair to look Father Robinson in the eye.

"Gerald Robinson, I'm placing you under arrest for the murder of Sister Margaret Ann Pahl at Mercy Hospital in Lucas County, Ohio, on or about April 5, 1980."

Father Robinson sat back in his chair and gave the investigator a piercing look.

"We're going to walk next door to the police station," he said. "And while we're there, Sergeant Forrester has a search warrant signed by Judge Christiansen and he will conduct a search of your residence."

Sergeant Forrester held up the search warrant so Father Robinson could see it, but the priest barely glanced at it.

Detective Ross thought about handcuffing the priest, but instead just put a hand on his shoulder and nudged him toward the door. He walked Father Robinson to the Toledo police substation at Scott Park, about fifty yards from the priest's house.

It was, as far as most history and church experts could tell, the first time in 90 years that a U.S. priest had been arrested for murder. It definitely was the first time that a Roman Catholic priest had been charged in the murder of a Roman Catholic nun.

Chapter 38

As Detective Ross led Father Robinson to the police station, Sergeant Forrester began looking around the house. It was a small, innocuous little brick home with a detached garage along Nebraska Avenue, a street that was an uneven mix of residences and businesses. It was on the southern edge of a working-class neighborhood, near a stretch of commercial buildings, next to the police station, and across the street from the University of Toledo.

In the priest's living room, an image of Jesus looked down with compassion from a painting on a framed piece of cardboard, the Lord's glowing red heart wrapped in a crown of thorns and topped with a flaming cross.

The room's furniture looked like something Father Robinson's mother had picked out in the 1950s or '60s, Sergeant Forrester thought, from the flowered print couch to the wooden television-and-radio console.

The investigator began sifting through drawers and cabinets in the kitchen, then moved to the living room, where he scoured shelves and flipped open the small drawers in the end tables. He didn't find anything of interest.

He went into the priest's bedroom, darkened by heavy curtains. He switched on the lights and began going through the dresser drawers. Nothing unusual.

In the closet, on a shelf atop the priest's wardrobe of black jackets, cassocks, and some civilian clothes, he saw a brown cardboard box about the size of a microwave oven and pulled it down from the shelf.

Opening the flaps, Sergeant Forrester saw that the box contained photographs—hundreds of them, thrown into the box in no apparent order. Some were heavy black-and-white prints from the early 1900s, others looked as though they were printed off a computer a day ago.

All of the photographs were of dead people. They were all dressed up and lying in their coffins.

Sergeant Forrester started sifting through the pictures.

Men in dark suits, white shirts, and ties. Women in their best dresses. Grandfather and grandmother types. A few tow-headed youngsters.

All were Caucasians. All were lying in repose, eyes closed, resting in peace inside their silk-lined caskets.

Many of the pictures showed people, presumably relatives or close friends, posing around the coffins, big proud smiles on their faces.

Candles burned in the background. Most of the caskets were surrounded by bouquets of flowers.

There were at least a hundred photos in the box, maybe closer to two hundred.

"Now, *this* is strange," Sergeant Forrester said out loud. "This is *very* strange."

He put the box aside and continued searching the residence. The priest, who was paid $23,000 a year by the Toledo diocese, did not have many earthly possessions. A radio alarm clock. A nineteen-inch Zenith color television in the bedroom. Several bookshelves filled with books on church history and liturgy. A small collection of CDs, mostly classical music and Polish ethnic tunes.

Looking through the bookshelves, Forrester spotted a small volume titled *The Occult.*

Published in the 1970s by a Catholic organization, the booklet looked as if it had been read quite a bit and maybe even carried around a bit. Forrester thumbed through the pages and saw that there was handwriting in the margins and that some passages were underlined or highlighted with yellow marker.

One chapter was headlined "The Black Mass"—describing satanic rituals that mock Christianity. Underlined in that chapter was a paragraph about human sacrifices. It said satanists must select "an innocent" who is placed on an altar during a Black Mass. The innocent can be sexually abused, tortured, or even killed for the worshipper to receive power from the devil.

He took the box of photos and the occult book and carried them out to his car, putting them in the trunk. Then the sergeant locked up the priest's house and drove around the corner to the police station, where he filled out an inventory of items seized in the search.

At the station, Forrester called a Toledo priest who had emigrated from Poland to ask about the photos.

"What do you know about photos of dead people in caskets?" Forrester asked.

"You mean pictures of people who died, and are lying in their coffins?" the priest asked.

"Yes, exactly. Have you ever seen such pictures?"

"Oh, yes. They are very common where I come from," the priest said. "It's a way of remembering and honoring a loved one."

"So is this a Polish tradition, of sorts?"

"Yes, you could say that. But not just Poles. They do it in all Slavic countries. It's kind of an old custom that has been fading away. You don't see it very much anymore, especially in this country. But when I was a child in Poland it was very normal," the priest said. "Why do you ask?"

"Well," Sergeant Forrester said, "I just ran across a collection of them. I have never seen anything like it before. The suspect we arrested had hundreds of photos of dead people, all dressed up and lying in their coffins."

"Hundreds?" the priest said. "That *is* strange. Usually it's just photos of relatives and close family friends."

"Maybe he has a big family," Sergeant Forrester said with a chuckle. "Really, I don't know what to make of it, but my guess is that it's not just photos of dead family and friends. I think this guy has some kind of fetish."

"Sounds like he could use some prayer," the priest said.

"No, not *some* prayer—*lots* of prayer," Sergeant Forrester replied. "More than you know. You'll see soon enough."

He thanked the priest and leaned back in the desk chair.

Sergeant Forrester, who is both a cop and a lawyer, wondered if a judge would allow something like the coffin photos to be admitted as evidence if the priest went on trial.

And even if the judge did allow it, would it help the state's case? Father Robinson is Polish and coffin photos apparently are an old Polish tradition. His defense lawyers would surely argue that they have nothing to do with the nun's murder.

What if, he thought, there's a photo in this box of Sister Margaret Ann Pahl lying in her coffin? Now that would be a different story. Then it would be related to the nun's slaying. And Father Robinson presided at her funeral.

He figured there was a 50-50 chance that there was a photo of the dead nun in that box. The priest really did have some kind of fetish about coffins. Most people collect stamps or baseball cards. What kind of sick person collects photos of dead people?

As a lawyer, he wondered whether the book on the occult would help the state's case. Father Robinson, or whoever read that booklet, had marked certain paragraphs relating to the Black Mass. There was even a sentence underlined about selecting "an innocent" to place on the altar for a sacrifice.

But the book was published by a Catholic company. One could argue—his defense attorneys certainly would argue this—that the book was for research purposes and information only. A priest might be well advised to know how people who hate God think and act, thereby keeping up with the enemy's tactics and knowing how to recognize their behavior and spot any threats.

He asked the desk sergeant where Tom Ross was, and was told the detective had taken Father Robinson into one of the interrogation rooms at the station.

Chapter 39

Detective Ross, wearing a dark suit, white shirt, and tie, escorted Father Robinson from his home to the Toledo police department's Scott Park substation next door. He signed in with the desk sergeant, telling him that he had arrested a suspect in the 1980 murder of a nun, and was going to interrogate him further.

The investigator led the cleric into an interrogation room that was about eight feet square and sparsely furnished, with just a round table and two plastic chairs. A video camera, concealed near the top of a rear wall, recorded everything from a wide-angle view looking down into the room.

Detective Ross asked Father Robinson politely to have a seat and the priest, moving slowly, slumped into the chair.

The white-haired investigator sat in the chair opposite the priest and reached into his briefcase to take out a stack of folders and notebooks.

It was 5:50 p.m. on April 23, 2004.

"You realize, Father, that you are being investigated for the murder of Sister Margaret Ann Pahl on April 5, 1980, in the sacristy of Mercy Hospital, and that this is a very serious charge?"

"Yes, I realize that," the priest said softly.

Detective Ross read the priest his Miranda rights and the priest signed a waiver. He then began a series of questions about Father Robinson's background, his place of residence, where he went to school, when he started working at Mercy.

Sitting slumped down in the chair, folding and unfolding his hands, Father Robinson responded slowly, often mumbling his answers.

"What was Sister Margaret Ann Pahl's job?" Ross asked.

"Pastoral care," Father Robinson said. "Primarily, sacristan."

"And what was your job as chaplain?"

"The sisters made our assignments," he said. "Predominately, I visited people as they came in. They would page me or call me."

The priest leaned back in his chair.

"It was their hospital. I just worked there," he said bitterly.

"How would you schedule the chapel services, with you and Father Swiatecki both serving as chaplains?" Detective Ross asked.

"Father Swiatecki was already treated as an alcoholic," Father Robinson replied.

"But how would you schedule the chapel services?" the detective asked again.

"It was a verbal thing. There were no papers, nothing like that," Father Robinson said.

"Father, on April 5th, 1980, Sister was a homicide victim on Holy Saturday. Who do you think might have done this to Sister? Did you ever suspect anybody?"

"No. I really didn't," Father Robinson said flatly.

"The day of the murder—that was an unusual day at the hospital, was it not?" Detective Ross asked.

"Not really. It was just like any other," Father Robinson said with a shrug.

He told the detective that he had just stepped out of the shower when Sister Phyllis Ann Gerold, the hospital's administrator, called him about the murder.

"Do you remember how she broke the news to you?"

"She said Sister was killed, or something like that."

"Did she say which sister?"

He paused.

"I think she did. She told me where to come, to the sacristy."

Father Robinson said he then finished drying off, put on his clerical clothes, including a cassock, and "ran down the hallway."

When he got there, he said he saw Sister Margaret Ann's body lying on the floor and Father Swiatecki in the room with several of the nuns.

When he walked into the sacristy, Father Robinson said, Father Swiatecki confronted him immediately.

"He said, 'You did this! Why did you do it?'" Father Robinson told Detective Ross.

"And how did you respond?" Ross asked. "You must have been blown away by that."

"I just looked at him," the priest said. "I couldn't answer. I had no idea."

"You must have had thoughts about it. 'What in the heck was that all about?'" Detective Ross said.

"I did," Father Robinson replied with a wave of the hand. "I wished he would have talked to me about it and told me. . . ."

Father Robinson said he and Father Swiatecki had worked together at Mercy Hospital for three or four years, during which time the two priests ate most of their meals together, but they never talked about anything significant.

"Father and I never talked much. He had his agenda and I had my own agenda," Father Robinson said.

"You were like two ships passing in the night?" Detective Ross asked.

"That's all it was. That's how it worked over there," the priest replied.

"But you broke bread together. How often did you eat together?" the detective asked. "More so than not?"

"More so than not," Father Robinson answered. "But Father wasn't one to talk much. We only talked about unimportant things. He didn't really know me very much and I didn't really know him."

He told Ross that Father Swiatecki at one time "had a problem" with alcohol.

"Monsignor Schmit remembered he had a problem. He came there [to Mercy] as a last resort because he couldn't be in a parish anymore because of drinking," Father Robinson said.

"Was he drunk when he confronted you in the sacristy?" Detective Ross asked.

"No, no. He was not drinking at that time," Father Robinson said. "He was in AA. He gave lectures on alcoholism."

Detective Ross asked the priest about the two times in 1980 that he was interrogated by the Toledo police.

"During those eight-hour interviews, what did you glean?"

"Well, that's what I didn't understand," Father Robinson responded.

"Did they, the detectives, ever become accusatory during the eight-hour interviews?"

"Well, they were forceful," the priest said.

"They were forceful," the detective repeated. "At any time, did those detectives say, 'Father, you did it'?"

"They may have," Father Robinson said.

"How did you respond to that, Father?"

"I was dumbfounded, is what I was."

"But did you verbally respond?"

"No."

Detective Ross then explained to Father Robinson that two Mercy Hospital employees told detectives in 1980 and again in 2004 that they heard footsteps running from the chapel, down a hallway, and stopping in front of the priest's residence right about the time of the murder.

Father Robinson was the only one who had a residence on that hallway, he said. With Mercy's nursing students home for the Easter weekend, the hospital was unusually quiet that Holy Saturday morning.

"How do you account for those footsteps, Father?"

"I was in the shower stall. It was away from the door. I couldn't hear it," the priest replied.

"So after you got dressed, you ran down to the chapel?" Ross asked.

"No, I didn't run. I couldn't run because I had on a cassock."

"I'm sorry, I didn't mean to put words in your mouth," Detective Ross said. "You couldn't run because you had on a cassock, a long robe down to your ankles."

"That's right."

"So you walked quickly down to the chapel?"

"That's right."

Detective Ross then showed Father Robinson photos of the altar cloth found at the scene of the crime, and said several experts had told investigators that the puncture marks in the altar cloth and in Sister Margaret Ann's clothing and skin appeared to fit the size and shape of the blade of the priest's saber-shaped letter opener.

He showed the priest photos of the letter opener and his tone turned confrontational.

"How on earth, Father, can you possibly explain the puncture wounds through an altar cloth that match your letter opener perfectly? How do you explain that?"

The priest just stared blankly.

"Father, why do you smirk at me? This is serious," Detective Ross said.

"I'm not smirking," Father Robinson said.

The detective then slid a photograph across the table, an eight-by-ten glossy of bloodstains on the altar cloth. He told the priest that experts will testify that the stains match the size, shape, and details of his letter opener.

He asked Father Robinson how long he had owned the letter opener and where he got it from.

The priest said he was a Boy Scout chaplain when he was associate pastor of St. Adalbert's Parish, from 1964 to 1969, and that a scout troop had given him the letter opener as a present after the kids went to Washington, D.C.

He said he never used it because it was too big to open letters, but he kept it in his desk as a souvenir.

"This is your knife, this ceremonial souvenir. It is exclusively yours," Detective Ross said. "How does it end up leaving its shadow in blood on the altar cloth? How does it end up leaving its blade in the altar cloth without you being involved?"

"I wasn't involved," Father Robinson said sharply.

"Did you ever loan the knife to anyone?"

"Not that I know of," he said.

Detective Ross asked the priest if he remembered whether detectives in 1980 had seized anything else from his hospital residence besides the letter opener. Father Robinson said they took one of his cassocks, the priest's robe that he usually wore.

"And why did they take your cassock?"

"Because of a small stain on the sleeve," Father Robinson said.

"And that stain proved to be what?" Detective Ross asked.

"Gravy," the priest said.

"Okay," Detective Ross said. "Now, how would you describe your relationship with the sisters at the hospital?"

"The sisters were good to me. We got along great."

"How would you describe Sister Margaret Ann Pahl?"

"Sister was quiet. She did her job. Nothing out of the ordinary," Father Robinson said. "We had a good relationship."

He asked the priest if he had a key to the sacristy. He hesitated, then said, "Not to my knowledge."

The nuns had keys to the sacristy and were usually there before him, he said. What if he needed to get into the sacristy at an odd hour, Detective Ross asked, to get any items he might need for a sacrament, like last rites for a dying hospital patient?

Father Robinson said he would probably have borrowed a key from one of the sisters, but that scenario would have been "very unlikely."

Detective Ross also asked Father Robinson if he kept his residence locked. The priest sat silently as eleven seconds ticked by.

"I did not keep the door locked," he finally said.

"Prior to this conversation, you said you kept the door locked," Detective Ross reminded him. "Is that the truth?"

"The cleaning lady had a key," Father Robinson said.

Detective Ross said he had to leave the room for a moment and asked the priest if he wanted any refreshments—water, soda pop, food?

Father Robinson said he didn't need anything, he was fine. The detective walked out, but the video camera was still taping.

Left alone, the priest put his elbows on the table and dropped his face into his hands.

"Oh, my Jesus!" he said, with an anguished sigh. Then he whispered quietly to himself.

When the detective came back, Robinson said he realized he should have confronted Father Swiatecki when the priest accused him of killing Sister Margaret Ann.

"I didn't respond normally like a person accused of murder would respond," he told Ross. "I don't have that in me, to yell and scream and carry on."

Chapter 40

After ninety minutes of interrogation, Detective Tom Ross looked directly at Father Gerald Robinson and said there were too many inconsistencies and contradictions in his story.

The first inconsistency, he explained to the priest, was about what he was doing when he got the phone call from Sister Phyllis Ann. In the first part of the interview, Father Robinson said he was drying off after a shower when the phone rang. Later, he said he was in the shower when he got the call.

Second, the detective said, Father Robinson had said that he ran down to the sacristy after the phone call. Then, after being informed that two hospital employees had heard running footsteps in the hallway, he said he could not have run because he was wearing an ankle-length cassock, but instead "walked in a rapid fashion" toward the chapel.

During the interview in his house, Detective Ross continued, Father Robinson said he had kept his hospital residence locked and needed a key to enter. Then, at the police station, he said—after a long and awkward pause—that he did not lock his apartment.

Detective Ross told Father Robinson that he was taking him down to the Lucas County jail to be booked on a charge of murder in the April 5, 1980, slaying of Sister Margaret Ann Pahl in the sacristy of Mercy Hospital.

He asked the elderly priest to put his hands behind his back, then slipped a pair of handcuffs over his wrists. Detectives Ross and Forrester led the priest to their unmarked car and drove him downtown to the jail.

Father Robinson was booked at 10:15 on a Friday night.

Sergeant Steve Forrester signed the arrest warrant, citing Ohio Revised Code No. 2903.02 (A), stating that "the defendant, Gerald J. Robinson, caused the death of the victim, Sister Margaret Ann Pahl, with the cause of death being strangulation. Sister Margaret Ann Pahl was found to have numerous post-mortem cuts on her body and an instrument, with unique characteristics associated with Sister Margaret Ann Pahl's post-mortem cuts, was found to be in Gerald Robinson's possession. It has been established from Sister Phyllis Ann Gerold that Gerald Robinson was at or near the scene at the time of the murder."

The booking sheet listed the priest as a white male, five-feet-six inches tall, weighing 150 pounds, with gray hair and brown eyes. Date of birth: 4-14-38. His employer: the Toledo diocese.

He turned over his personal possessions: a black wallet, keys, and a set of rosary beads. The cleric had four one-dollar bills in the wallet and eighty cents in change in his pocket. He listed his brother, Thomas, as an emergency contact.

Father Robinson exchanged his black coat, plaid shirt, and blue pants for a light brown jumpsuit and was escorted to a private cell in the six-story downtown jail.

A hearing was set for 9:00 a.m. Monday before Judge Mary Trimboli in Toledo municipal court, and the case was expected to go to a grand jury sometime during the next week. Gary Cook, an assistant Lucas County prosecutor who had been involved in the investigation, said the murder charge did not carry a death-penalty specification because there was no death penalty in Ohio at the time of the 1980 murder.

Chief Mike Navarre of the Toledo police department released a brief, four-paragraph statement announcing that, "based on new information," detectives Forrester and Ross had reopened the 1980 murder investigation in December 2003, and that "their subsequent investigation resulted in today's arrest of Father Gerald Robinson and the execution of a search warrant on his Nebraska Avenue residence. Robinson, 66, has been charged with Murder."

Father Michael Billian, speaking for the Toledo diocese, said on the night of the arrest: "We're very saddened by the whole experience. It certainly saddens the diocese that any one of its ministers would be in this situation."

He added that the human condition is sinful and that priests are human.

John Thebes, a Toledo defense attorney and a Roman Catholic, received a call at his home late Friday night from Father Robinson's family, asking if he would consider taking the case.

He remembered Father Robinson from second grade when the priest was an associate pastor of Christ the King Parish, one of the largest parishes in Toledo. He hadn't seen Father Robinson in more than thirty years, but agreed to meet with Father Robinson the next day.

On Saturday, April 24, as Thebes headed for the jail, he spotted a long row of multicolored TV vans and trucks, bearing the logos of local stations and national networks, parked bumper to bumper on Michigan Avenue in a line stretching from the jail to the courthouse.

Father Robinson looked pale and fragile in the jail cell, and he said barely slept his first night behind bars.

Thebes agreed to take his case and represent his former pastor. Seeing Father Robinson at age 66, dressed in a drab brown jumpsuit, was the low point of his professional career, Thebes said.

Chapter 41

The Catholic Diocese of Toledo had barely found its footing after being slammed with a dozen lawsuits—the biggest crisis in its ninety-year history—alleging that priests had sexually abused minors. Just as the diocese was preparing to settle the lawsuits out of court, it found itself facing a different kind of crisis—one that no other U.S. diocese had ever had to deal with: one of its own priests was charged with murder.

Fifty-four-year-old Bishop Leonard Blair, installed as bishop of Toledo only four months before the priest's arrest, had previously served as auxiliary bishop in the Detroit archdiocese.

Blair succeeded the late Bishop James Hoffman, a native of the 325,000-member Toledo diocese, who had presided from 1981 until his death from cancer in February 2003, the longest reign of any Toledo bishop.

The diocese's director of communications, Sally Oberski, was relatively new to church work. A Toledo native, Oberski had worked for years in the secular business world in the field of public relations and marketing, accepting the communications position with the diocese in September 2003. She said she wanted to do something of significance in her life and felt that she could use her training and skills to help her church through the current crisis and then move forward into a more positive era.

The day after Father Robinson's arrest, Oberski received a half-dozen phone calls from national news outlets seeking comment or information.

But the real media frenzy would not begin for another day.

Bishop Blair did not meet with the media Saturday, the day after the priest's arrest, because he was out of town presiding at Confirmation ceremonies, Oberski said.

Meanwhile, Father Robinson's arrest spurred a new wave of allegations that the diocese, police, and the prosecutor's office had covered up for the priest in 1980.

Dave Davison, the first policeman on the scene of the murder, wanted to know why it took twenty-four years to arrest and charge Father Robinson in Sister Margaret Ann's slaying.

He revived allegations he had been making for years, only now the case was national news: investigators did not pursue Father Robinson because they did not want to hurt the image of the Catholic Church, Davison said.

After a letter-writing campaign in the mid-1990s to try to get the murder case reopened, he had given up, he said, because "I figured they were going to treat me like a kook. It sounded so unbelievable."

Ray Vetter, the deputy police chief at the time of the murder, again found himself having to denounce allegations of a cover-up. He asserted that the priest was a suspect in 1980, but police kept it quiet because they didn't want to "tip their hand."

Ultimately, the prosecutor's office decided there wasn't enough evidence to convict Father Robinson in 1980, which meant there was no point arresting the priest, the retired deputy chief said.

He called it "the biggest disappointment of my career."

"I can't believe anyone with any sense, who knows us as investigators and us as people, would say that we would cover this up. We just wouldn't do it," Vetter said.

He added that "no one from the diocese ever contacted me and told me to 'quote' lay off. We didn't have enough evidence to convict him. And there's no point in arresting someone unless you have evidence to convict him. We don't make the decision by ourselves. We consult with the prosecutor."

Father Billian also denied there was a cover-up in 1980.

"It's hard for me to define where any cover-up took place," he said. "There was cooperation between the diocese and police in 1980, and again last year."

The day after the arrest, Sergeant Forrester and Detective Tom Ross held an impromptu news conference in the detectives' bureau of the Safety Building.

Sitting in a cubicle with a handful of reporters, the detectives said they first decided to look at the physical evidence after a Toledo woman, whom they would not identify (but eventually revealed to be Sister Mary Curtiss), told the diocesan review board that Father Robinson had abused her in sado-masochistic acts when she was a minor.

The woman had also alleged that she was abused by a satanic cult that included several priests.

Detectives Ross and Forrester said they could neither prove nor disprove the woman's bizarre allegations, and stressed that her testimony was only indirectly linked to the reopening of the murder investigation.

Detective Ross had been on the force at the time of the nun's murder and, when the woman mentioned Father Robinson in her testimony before the review board, the veteran investigator recalled that the priest had been a suspect in 1980.

That led the detectives to go the police property room and examine the altar cloth, the nun's clothing, and other items that had been collecting dust for more than twenty-three years.

When they looked at the evidence, "we noticed something that was startling and apparent to us," Sergeant Forrester told reporters.

The investigators also said they believed they had found the murder weapon and that they could prove it was "in the control of the suspect" at the time of the nun's slaying.

The detectives said they believed Father Robinson acted alone, then added that Sister Margaret Ann was killed as part of a "ceremony" in the Mercy Hospital sacristy. They refused to elaborate on the nature of the ceremony.

When the Sunday, April 25 edition of the *Blade* hit the streets, it featured a front-page article quoting the detectives as saying that Sister Margaret Ann Pahl had been killed in a "ceremony" and that they had reopened the murder case partly because of allegations of a woman who claimed Father Robinson had abused her as a child and that she had been the victim of satanic rituals by a local cult that included priests.

The woman alleged she had been forced to eat a human eyeball, placed inside a coffin filled with cockroaches, and penetrated by a snake "to consecrate these orifices to Satan."

The *Blade* also quoted the woman's allegations that the cult had killed a 3-year-old child and that she had been subjected to a "ritual abortion."

That same day, Bishop Blair made his first public comments after the priest was jailed, saying he had been completely unaware of the case until Father Robinson's arrest.

"Having only recently been appointed to Toledo, I was very sorry to hear of this unsolved murder of Sister Margaret from twenty-four years ago. Now that Father Robinson has been arrested, I'm as shocked and troubled as anyone. I'm shocked that anyone would commit such a crime. If it's one of your own, that's troubling," Bishop Blair said.

He reminded everyone that the priest was "innocent until proven guilty" and he urged people to pray for Father Robinson and everyone involved in the case.

"I hope that truth and justice will prevail in this," Bishop Blair said.

He pointed out that police had praised the Toledo diocese for cooperating fully with their investigation.

Father Billian said the cold-case investigators had contacted him in November or December 2003 to request biographical information about Father Robinson—where he lived, where he had served.

In subsequent meetings, investigators asked him about standard religious articles, specifically crosses and cross designs, Father Billian said. He said police did not tell him why they were interested in such information or whether it was connected to the Robinson case.

By the tine Father Robinson was arraigned on Monday morning in municipal court, the case had created a full-blown media circus.

Reporters from the local media, *The Today Show, Dateline,* the *New York Times,* the *Los Angeles Times,* MSNBC, *People* magazine, and even supermarket tabloids were swarming over the story of a priest charged with murder in the ritual slaying of a nun more than two decades earlier.

Chapter 42

Father Robinson, looking weary and small in a brown jail jumpsuit, stood before Toledo municipal court Judge Mary Trimboli and stared straight ahead, his only emotion an occasional twist of the lips, apparently in disgust.

His attorney, John Thebes, told the judge that his client maintained his innocence and had been a respected member of the community since he was ordained in 1964. He said there was no risk that the priest would flee.

Judge Trimboli set bond at $200,000 and scheduled a preliminary hearing for the following Monday. Court deputies led Father Robinson out of the courtroom and through an underground tunnel to the Lucas County jail.

The priest did not say a word during the brief arraignment, and declined all requests for media interviews.

The case was assigned to Lucas County common pleas Judge Ruth Ann Franks, who later excused herself, citing a potential conflict of interest. She did not explain further, but her husband was retired Toledo police criminalist John Franks, who had investigated Sister Margaret Ann's murder in 1980, and she was an assistant county prosecutor when the murder occurred.

The priest's case was then assigned to Judge Patrick Foley.

Outside the courthouse, Claudia Vercellotti and Jon Schoonmaker of the Toledo chapter of SNAP (Survivors Network of those Abused by Priests) staged a press conference and were immediately surrounded by a throng of reporters and cameramen.

"Why didn't the Toledo diocese put Father Robinson on a leave of absence or bar him from ministry in June 2003, when a woman testified before the church review board that she was sexually molested as a child by Robinson?" Vercellotti asked.

She said that if those allegations weren't enough to suspend Father Robinson, then surely the diocese should have acted as soon as they learned that the Lucas County prosecutor's office was investigating the priest in the 1980 murder of a nun.

"Father Gerald Robinson has been on the radar for over a year," Vercellotti said.

She said the diocese had not followed its own policies for dealing with priests who were accused of sexual abuse. Vercellotti claimed that failing to bar Father Robinson from ministry the previous year had put more children at risk.

Sally Oberski, the diocese spokeswoman, was questioned later about SNAP's comments, and said the church only bars priests who face credible allegations. The bizarre allegations the woman had made to the review board were not considered credible enough to suspend Father Robinson.

She added that the priest's status had not changed after being arraigned on a murder charge.

After SNAP's press conference, Thebes walked out of the courthouse and was immediately encircled by the media.

"Father thought this whole thing was behind him in 1980 when he cooperated fully and they dropped the investigation," said the tall, dark-haired attorney.

He mentioned again that he knew Father Robinson when he was in the second grade at Christ the King Parish, but had not seen him for decades.

There were many pieces of the state's allegations against Father Robinson that would be reviewed by the defense attorneys, Thebes said.

"Twenty-four years is a heck of a long time. Things happen to evidence and memories fade," he said. "There's a reason these cases are cold cases. There was not enough evidence the first time around; there's still not enough evidence."

He declined to provide details, saying he had just accepted the case.

Thebes said he was getting calls from many of the priest's supporters who said they wanted to help get him out of jail and were willing to put up their homes as bond. The process required a lot of paperwork, however, including having the homeowners present the court with copies of their mortgage notes and property deeds.

To free Father Robinson on a $200,000 bond, supporters would have to post $400,000 in property. The priest's home on Nebraska Avenue, which he co-owned with his younger brother, Thomas, was among the properties to be held for bond.

Also putting their homes up were Thomas Robinson and his wife, Barbara, and the priest's closest friends, Gary and Kathleen Glowski of suburban Sylvania, and Dorothy Sieja of Glenview Road in south Toledo.

Judge Franks told the priest's supporters that there were no conditions placed on the property bond, but if Father Robinson failed to show up for scheduled court dates, prosecutors could start foreclosure proceedings in common pleas court and the homeowners risked the possible loss of their property.

Oberski, meanwhile, said the Toledo diocese would not pay for Father Robinson's legal expenses.

Later that day, the diocese issued a statement saying that it "will continue to cooperate with the authorities in the investigation" and also that "because of the large amount of publicity that this case has attracted both locally and nationally, the diocese will not conduct any further interviews" about the Robinson case.

The next day—four days after Father Robinson's arrest—Bishop Leonard Blair made a pastoral visit to the Lucas County jail to see the 66-year-old priest.

Afterward, he issued a statement saying that he and Father Robinson "had discussed Father's canonical status given the allegations against him."

The bishop said he had "placed Father Robinson on Leave of Absence with the following restrictions; namely, that he is excluded from public ministry, may only celebrate Mass alone with no one present; may not celebrate other sacraments." Bishop Blair said the priest "has accepted these restrictions effective today."

Barbara Blaine, founder and president of SNAP, who flew in from Chicago for the arraignment, said of the bishop's action: "Well, it's about time. It should have been done when the victim, Jane Doe, came forward back in June 2003."

Bishop Blair and Auxiliary Bishop Robert Donnelly left Toledo that Wednesday morning for Rome, where they had been scheduled for their semi-annual meeting with Pope John Paul II at the Vatican.

Lucas County prosecutors presented evidence to a grand jury on Friday, April 30, and the panel's decision to indict Father Robinson on a charge of aggravated murder was filed by the court clerk on Monday, May 3.

John Weglian, chief of the special units division of the county prosecutor's office, said the grand jury was asked to consider either murder or aggravated murder charges, both of which carried mandatory sentences of life in prison, but with slightly different specifications for parole. In aggravated murder, the killer can ask for parole after twenty years in prison. In a murder conviction, the inmate can seek parole after fifteen years. Because there was no death penalty in Ohio when the murder occurred in 1980, capital punishment did not pertain to this case, Weglian said.

Father Robinson was released from jail on Monday, May 3, ten days after his arrest. Friends and family waited outside the county jail until the frail cleric emerged from a back door, wearing his familiar clerical collar and priest's garb instead of the jail jumpsuit he had been wearing.

Supporters greeted him warmly and the priest clung tightly to the arms of his attorneys, John Thebes and the recently hired legal veteran Alan Konop. Father Robinson refused to respond to the flurry of media questions as he and his lawyers hurried to a nearby sport utility vehicle.

The crowd then regrouped for a celebratory party at the Scott Park Banquet Hall, near the priest's home. About seventy people ate hors d'oeuvres and sipped drinks while patting the priest on the back and telling him that they knew he was innocent.

Among his ardent supporters was Bea Orlowski, 74, his secretary for eleven years, and Mary Ann Plewa, 68, a lifelong member of St. Anthony's Parish, where Father Robinson sometimes celebrated Mass in Polish.

"When I heard Father Jerry had been arrested, I thought I was going to pass out," Plewa said. "He's just wonderful."

Also in attendance was Jack Sparagowski, a local entrepreneur who had recently joined St. Anthony's Parish. A former sheriff's deputy turned consultant, Sparagowski helped raise more than $13,000 for Father Robinson's defense fund.

One elderly parishioner said she was very concerned because their pastor was about to go on vacation and Father Robinson had been scheduled to fill in for him. "We've got to get him out!" she said.

Shortly after the celebration began, a woman carrying a nun doll interrupted the party by screaming and waving the black-and-white figurine.

"I am here for Sister Margaret! She is the one who suffered!" Paulinha Garcia Cleveland shouted. "Justice for Sister Margaret!"

When one of the priest's supporters, Jack Napierala, tried to talk to the woman, she swung the doll at him. He grabbed it and yanked it out of her hands, and Cleveland began yelling to give the doll back. When Napierala refused, she pulled his jacket, knocked his glasses off his face, and ripped his shirt pocket.

The 49-year-old woman then grabbed a pitcher of water and threw it at Napierala, then walked defiantly out of the banquet hall, pausing to shout at a reporter: "To honor Sister Margaret, I will go to jail!"

Chapter 43

When the cold-case team decided to arrest Father Gerald Robinson earlier than planned to prevent the media from tipping him off, they were still in the process of gathering evidence against the priest.

Their first attempts to use DNA to build their case had fallen flat. Not only were there minimal amounts of DNA on the altar cloths and the nun's clothing, but the DNA they did manage to obtain—from the nun's fingernails and a stain in her underwear—ended up excluding Father Robinson as a contributor.

Investigators also were dealing with the fact that DNA consists of biological matter and degrades over time, and that police and laboratory technicians had not taken precautions to keep DNA from being contaminated because DNA was not a forensic tool in 1980.

Despite the obstacles, they felt that it was worth looking for DNA evidence that linked the priest to the murder because it could turn out to be a powerful tool for the prosecution.

Scientists at the Ohio Bureau of Criminal Investigation and Identification in the Columbus suburb of London, Ohio, told investigators that obtaining a DNA sample from Sister Margaret Ann Pahl would be essential if they were to analyze any stains or trace evidence found on Father Robinson's clothing, on the letter opener, or on any other items they might find.

"The only way to get a DNA record is to exhume the body," said Dr. Diane Barnett, deputy Lucas County coroner.

On May 19, 2004, prosecutor Julia Bates issued an order of disinterment for the body of Sister Margaret Ann Pahl.

The nun had been buried on April 8, 1980, in a circular grassy section of St. Bernadine Cemetery, on the grounds of Our Lady of the Pines Retreat Center in Fremont, Ohio.

Her grave was marked with a simple, rectangular marble stone, just like all the Sisters of Mercy who had been buried there. The tombstone simply read:

SR. MARGARET ANN PAHL, R.S.M.
1908–1980
MAY SHE REST IN PEACE

On a hot, sticky morning of May 10, 2004, a small gathering of people assembled at the Sisters of Mercy cemetery on the grounds of Our Lady of the Pines retreat center in Fremont, Ohio.

The body of Sister Margaret Ann Pahl, buried more than twenty-four years ago, was set to be exhumed. Present were Detectives Tom Ross and Terry Cousino, Assistant Lucas County Prosecutor Tim Braun, Sisters of Mercy President Marjorie Rudemiller, Mercy's attorney Barry Hudgin, and workers from a local funeral home and the sisters' cemetery.

Sister Marjorie did not want any other nuns to have to witness the disinterment and asked them to instead gather for prayers in nearby St. Beradine's Chapel—where Sister Margaret Ann's funeral had been held in 1980.

The grave was carefully dug open and the concrete vault, with the casket inside, was hoisted by a crane and placed on the grass. The vault was then opened and the simple pine coffin was loaded into a transport van and taken to the Lucas County Coroner's Office in Toledo, forty miles north.

Doctor Barnett had extensively reviewed thirty-seven photographs of the murder and the crime scene, and had examined the bloodstains and puncture marks in the altar cloth and in the nun's clothing. She also had examined the priest's sword-shaped letter opener.

Now she had the nun's body physically in front of her, and she was anxious to put her observations and theories to the test.

The first step, however, was to obtain a DNA record, which was typically done by extracting teeth. In cases where there is no blood or bodily fluids to sample, teeth generally prove to be an excellent source of DNA. Doctor Barnett also clipped some scalp hairs to obtain DNA data.

Even after twenty-four years of interment, Sister Margaret Ann Pahl's skin was remarkably well preserved. It had turned a dark brown over the years but it was mostly intact. The deputy coroner was able to see most of the stab wounds in the skin, including a cluster of punctures in the upper left side of her chest and in the left side of her neck.

After photographing the exhumed corpse, Dr. Barnett performed a second autopsy on Sister Margaret Ann.

She noted that the killer had first choked the nun with a soft ligature—such as a cloth—pulling so tightly that he left an indentation of a cross and chain in her skin and breaking the two small hyoid bones in her neck.

Doctor Barnett also was able to find some "bone involvement," where the killer's knife or letter opener had struck a bone and left a defect.

One of the most clearly discernible wound marks was in Sister Margaret Ann's left mandible, or jawbone. It is one of the hardest bones in the human body, very rigid and not malleable at all, Dr. Barnett said.

She discovered a small but distinct impression, triangular in shape and about a quarter of an inch deep.

Although Dr. Barnett had performed thousands of autopsies in her twenty years as deputy coroner, she consulted forensic anthropologists Frank and Julie Saul, a Toledo husband-and-wife team, when the evidence involved bones. That was their area of expertise, and they had advised police and coroners' offices across the country on such cases.

Julie Saul was overseas temporarily, however, and Dr. Barnett needed to return the nun's body to her grave as soon as possible. The nun's body was reburied in a private ceremony on June 1.

To preserve the evidence for testing when the Sauls were back in Toledo, Dr. Barnett used a power saw to remove sections of bone that contained defects from the murder weapon, including a two-inch section of Sister Margaret Ann's lower jaw where the triangular defect was located.

On June 7, the Sauls and several members of the cold-case unit met at the coroner's office to conduct a "fit test."

Julie Saul used a solution to clean the nun's bones of any soft tissue.

Doctor Barnett, using what Detective Cousino described as "extreme caution," slowly pressed the tip of the priest's letter opener into the small indentation in the sister's jawbone.

On the first try, the diamond-shaped blade slid into the indentation and fit reasonably well.

But then Dr. Barnett turned the asymmetrical blade 180 degrees and tried again. This time, she said, it slipped into place and made "a perfect fit."

Dean Mandros, the assistant prosecutor, said the blade fit into the uniquely shaped hole in the jawbone "like a key in a lock."

"It is my conclusion," Dr. Barnett told the investigators, "that based on my twenty-one years of experience as a deputy coroner, and based on my knowledge and my training, that this weapon caused these injuries. Either this weapon, or a weapon exactly like it."

Less than a week after Dr. Diane Barnett conducted a fit test with the letter opener and jawbone, the cold-case squad found another expert who would review the evidence.

Doctor Steven Symes, a tall, gray-haired professor of applied forensic sciences, had recently left the University of Tennessee to teach at Mercyhurst College in Erie, Pennsylvania.

When he moved, he was able to put together a laboratory equipped with every forensic tool he could dream of, including specialized microscopes, cameras, and a wet lab for examining fresh tissue.

A forensic anthropologist with a doctorate in physical anthropology, Dr. Symes' specialty was sharp-force trauma—analyzing wounds and marks to bones caused by saws, knives, and other sharp tools. He had served as a consultant in numerous serial homicide cases where victims were mutilated or dismembered.

Doctor Symes said he typically starts with a broad category of instrument, and then narrows it down from the general class to more specific subcategories. For example, he said, he can start by finding that the wound was made by a saw, and then determine if it was a power saw or a handsaw, and then how many teeth per inch were on the saw, and continue to narrow the scope of the weapon's characteristics as he examines it further.

Detective Terry Cousino and Julie Saul drove to Mercyhurst with the letter opener, the section of the nun's jawbone, and reports and photographs from the 1980 crime scene. Doctor Symes photographed and measured each piece of physical evidence using a $2,000 Nikon digital camera that he connected to a microscope.

Doctor Symes told the Toledo investigators that he believed the defect in the mandible, at less than a tenth of an inch across, was unusually small. He initially was skeptical that he could reach any conclusions over whether the letter opener could have been the instrument that caused the defect.

But after looking at magnified photos, he saw that the letter opener was "a bit unusual" in shape, with the blade having four sides and a blunted tip, most likely because it was designed to open letters, not for use as a knife. But while the tip was blunt, the leading edge of the blade was sharp, he noted.

Doctor Symes measured the jawbone wound from different angles, seeking to quantify the instrument's angle of entry in relation to the body.

He said he always avoids, as much as possible, having to insert an instrument into a wound, but prefers instead to work with models of the evidence.

He created casts of the letter opener's blade and the nun's jawbone, then made replicas of the instrument and the wound.

Even though the wound was only two millimeters in diameter, the tip of the letter opener clearly was a good fit, he said. And the more tests he conducted, the more convinced he was that the letter opener could not be ruled out as the instrument that caused the wound to the mandible.

Chapter 44

When Father Robinson's attorneys learned that the cold-case team had had Sister Margaret Ann Pahl's body exhumed without notifying them, they were furious.

John Thebes was the first attorney on the case for the defense, but he was quickly joined by Alan Konop, John "Jack" Callahan, and Nicole Khoury.

A more diverse legal team would be hard to imagine.

Thebes, a tall and youthful 44, took the job out of personal concern for the cleric, having had Father Robinson as an associate pastor when he was a child.

Konop, 69, and Callahan, 84, were highly respected defense attorneys with long and successful track records, while Khoury was a relative newcomer at 28.

Konop, a folksy courtroom veteran with a pair of reading glasses perpetually perched on the tip of his nose, had handled a number of high-profile cases on the local and regional scene. Among them was Jeffrey Hodge, a University of Toledo campus policeman who confessed to killing female student Melissa Herstrum in 1992, and Kim Anderson, acquitted in the shooting death of her husband on grounds of self defense.

Callahan, a natty dresser known for his dark, pin-striped suits and wide smile, had defended his first murder case more than fifty years ago in the same court-house where Father Robinson's trial was scheduled.

Khoury, a tall and attractive woman with long, wavy brown hair, was just begin-ning her career in criminal law, although she had already won acquittals for two defen-dants accused of murder. Several nights a week, she left the courthouse, changed clothes, and headed to a downtown pub to sing and play guitar until 2:00 a.m.

The Toledo diocese announced shortly after Father Robinson's arrest that it would not pay any of his legal bills, and the four attorneys had volunteered to take his case pro bono, spending nearly two years preparing for the trial without pay.

While the priest's lawyers were willing to work for free, there were other expenses involved for the court battle, including the costs of DNA testing, filing fees, and travel and fees for forensic experts.

Jack Sparagowski, a local entrepreneur who went to St. Anthony's Parish, where Father Robinson had occasionally celebrated Mass, stepped in to organize a legal defense fund for the priest.

Hundreds of supporters sent checks to the priest's defense fund, raising a total of more than $13,000.

One of the biggest expenses for the defense attorneys was to hire expert witnesses, whose fees are generally several thousand dollars plus travel expenses to get them to testify in court.

Thebes, Konop, Callahan, and Khoury agreed to use the money to hire Dr. Kathleen Reichs, a noted forensic anthropologist from Charlotte, North Carolina, and a best-selling author whose crime novels inspired the Fox TV show *Bones.*

The thin, blonde-haired forensics expert said she keeps her science and her fiction careers separate by using Kathleen when working in forensics and Kathy when writing novels.

Having missed the opportunity to inspect Sister Margaret Ann's body in person, Dr. Reichs was forced to rely on the coroner's reports, photographs, and analyses by prosecution experts.

Doctor Barnett's autopsy had been performed the day after the exhumation.

It appeared from the photographs that someone from the coroner's office or the cold-case team had inserted the priest's letter opener into wounds in the jawbone and vertebrae both before and after the bones had been cleansed of soft tissue, Dr. Reichs said.

The photos contradicted parts of the reports by Dr. Barnett and Julie Saul, who stated that the "fit test" was conducted only on June 7, and only after the bones had been cleaned. Several photographs of the procedure showed, however, the tip of the letter opener inside the bone with soft tissue visible.

Doctor Reichs told Thebes and Konop that even though the mandible is a rigid bone, inserting a metal object into it while the bone still had pieces of tissue in it could potentially damage the bone and contaminate the evidence.

"Especially if the bone has osteoporosis—when it loses some mass and is not as strong as a young, healthy bone," Dr. Reichs said.

Sister Margaret Ann had been murdered the day before her seventy-second birthday and at that age a woman's bones could be exceedingly brittle, she said.

"This could have caused a modification of the edges of the defect," Dr. Reichs concluded. "The defect in the mandible is only two millimeters by two millimeters, so removing even a little bit of one edge can be significant."

"What kind of conclusion can you reach based on your review of the photographs?" Konop asked her.

"That they should not have done that," Dr. Reichs said sternly. "They should not have placed the metal letter opener in the defect of the mandible."

Thebes asked her if she wanted to examine the mandible itself, since the coroner had removed it from the nun's body.

"No, there would be no point now, because the evidence could potentially have been damaged or contaminated and I would have no way of knowing," Dr. Reichs said.

Chapter 45

In August 2004, Gary Cook, an assistant Lucas County prosecutor, and Detective Terry Cousino drove to the Dayton suburb of Kettering, Ohio, to meet with one of the most famous and respected forensic investigators on earth, Dr. Henry C. Lee.

Born in 1938 in Taipei, Taiwan, Dr. Lee studied at Central Police College and worked as police captain in his native country before coming to the United States to study at John Jay College of Criminal Justice in New York City in 1972.

Doctor Lee went on to earn a master's degree in science and a doctorate in molecular biochemistry from New York University and had consulted in hundreds of high-profile cases, including his famous "bloody footprints" testimony in the O. J. Simpson murder trial.

He had authored or coauthored two hundred books and had led more than five hundred workshops and seminars in all fifty states and thirty-nine countries regarding crime scene investigations, forensic medicine, latent fingerprints, and dozens of other forensics-related topics.

Now serving as chief emeritus for the Connecticut Division of Scientific Services, Dr. Lee is one of only five people in the world certified in the field of bloodstain-pattern transfer analysis.

When Cook and Cousino approached Dr. Lee after an afternoon seminar, they explained their case thus far against Father Robinson and asked if Lee would be willing to examine the evidence, especially the bloodstains on the altar cloth.

Doctor Lee agreed, and had his personal assistant schedule a two-day visit in December.

"I think it's a very interesting case," he said in an interview. "Of course, it's a classic cold case. I tried to inform them that basically today when you look at a cold case, you have to work out of the box. You cannot use conventional methods. You have to reach in and hopefully regenerate some energy."

The first step, he told the cold-case team, was to undertake a crime-scene reconstruction.

Because Sister Margaret Ann had been murdered so long ago and the evidence was not extensive, Dr. Lee could only create a "limited" crime-scene reconstruction.

"The photographs from 1980 were in black and white. They don't have videotapes. There was not a complete documentation of the scene," he said. "The only thing to their advantage is the preparation room, the sacristy, was still there, and the chapel was still there," he said.

In addition, it was to the police's advantage that there never was any question that the nun had been murdered. In many cold-case investigations, there is some possibility that the victim died accidentally. Not so with Sister Margaret Ann.

"Nobody questioned she's not murdered," Dr. Lee said. "Homicide was not the question as it is in many cases. We don't have any argument here, except who done it."

Doctor Lee, using his ever-present magnifying glass, carefully studied the 1980 crime-scene photos and then looked for bloodstains on the sacristy's terrazzo floor. Because the photographs were in black and white, he said it was difficult to tell whether the spots on the floor in the photos were blood or part of the brown and black spots in the terrazzo design.

But the floor in the room had not been altered since the murder, giving Dr. Lee the opportunity to compare each individual spot on the floor that was visible in the photographs with the design elements in the terrazzo today.

"If the blood spatters, most likely the stabbing was first," he said. "We painstakingly put back each spot in the photographs and, in fact, only few, very few, were blood drops."

The lack of blood at the scene—just one small pool under the victim's head—led Dr. Lee to surmise that Sister Margaret Ann must have been strangled quickly to the verge of death by her attacker, and then stabbed as she laid on the floor, immobile, her heart barely beating.

"There was no sign of blood dripping, which would have indicated the person was upright when stabbed," Dr. Lee said. "But there was no obvious pattern consistent with dripping. It indicated she had to be knocked down first, attacked and rendered unconscious pretty quickly. Most or all of the stabbing was inflicted afterward."

It was clear to him that the sacristy was the primary scene—in other words, that Sister Margaret Ann was murdered where the body was found, and not strangled or stabbed elsewhere and then carried into the room.

There was no sign of a struggle, Dr. Lee said. None of the furniture was knocked over, a tall candle was standing upright next to her body, and there were "knickknacks all over the place," he said.

This analysis of the evidence was part of his limited crime-scene reconstruction, Dr. Lee explained.

The next step was to analyze the bloodstains and the holes in the altar cloth.

"The altar cloth was very long, almost ten feet, and was actually folded," he said. "We saw the original photographs and, using a mannequin, were able to put together what's her position, and the position of the altar cloth. Also, because the cloth was folded, we were able to see how single stab wounds created multiple holes."

He said he believed that the way the nun's panties and pantyhose had been pulled down indicated that the killer attempted to "stage" the crime, hoping to mislead investigators into thinking it had been a sexual assault.

Doctor Lee also said the multiple stab wounds were signs of a "frenzy" killing, in which the murderer knew the victim and went into a rage, stabbing out of vengeance or hatred.

He said he did not seek to determine if the nun had been the victim of a ritual sacrifice, but preferred to focus on the physical evidence and leave the interpretations of religious imagery and symbols to others.

Doctor Lee said he believes the killer knew Sister Margaret Ann and knew that she would be in the sacristy, and that the room was off to the side of the hospital chapel and somewhat secluded.

"Somebody has to know where it's located and also have to know her schedule. An intruder would not know these things. Somebody has to be on the inside and know her activities," Dr. Lee said.

The forensic investigator then turned his attention to the bloodstains on the altar cloth and on the nun's dress.

The bloodstains had oxidized, turning brown and fading over the years, he said, so he sprayed the linen with a chemical enhancer that further defined the blood patterns.

"With the chemical reaction, you can see the patterns pretty well."

Doctor Lee said the bloodstains on the altar cloth clearly matched the shape and design of Father Robinson's letter opener, but he said there was no way of knowing how many saber-shaped letter openers with U.S. Capitol emblems on the handle were in existence. Because of that, Dr. Lee said, he could conclude only that the bloodstains and the puncture marks in the altar cloth were made by Father Robinson's letter opener or by an instrument exactly like it.

"You can see the pattern pretty well, but the only conclusion I can reach is that it is similar. You really don't know how many of these letter openers were made. Could be hundreds, could be thousands, could be millions—I don't know," Dr. Lee said.

Asked why detectives in 1980 put the altar cloth in storage only two days after the murder, never linking the bloodstains and punctures with the letter opener, Dr. Lee said it was not uncommon for police to overlook such patterns and connections.

"They probably just missed it," he said. "You have a lot of blood, you only see blood. If you don't see it, your mind don't know it. I joke that Caucasians have big eyes, they don't see it. We Chinese have little eyes, we have to look at it and focus on the pattern. A lot of people only see the forest, they forget to see the individual tree."

Chapter 46

In August 2002, when the Toledo diocese announced it had signed a cooperation agreement with the Lucas County prosecutor's office, Father Michael Billian said the document merely formalized the diocese's already existing policy.

He said church officials had been voluntarily opening files for the prosecutor's office ever since the national clerical sexual-abuse crisis began five months earlier, but nothing prosecutable had been discovered.

"The prosecutor's office has determined that criminal charges were not warranted," said Father Billian, the diocese's chancellor.

"We believe that civil authorities have an important role in the development of comprehensive and effective procedures for protecting children and we pledge to continue to cooperate with them. In ongoing discussions with the prosecutor's office we have agreed to provide any additional information requested so that the prosecutor's office may review pertinent information and make such determinations as are warranted."

But John Weglian, chief of the special units division of the county prosecutor's office and one of the officials in the prosecutor's office who had helped draft the agreement, said he had been reviewing church files for five months and had found no cases that were prosecutable.

The main reason, he said, was that the statute of limitations had expired in every case. Ohio law at the time required victims of child sexual abuse to report their allegations within two years after reaching the age of majority, which in most cases was 18.

"No complaints have come to this office to present, or to the police department that I am aware of, and I am in close contact with the police department in regard to these matters. There has been nobody who has brought a claim that is prosecutable," Weglian said in July 2002. "And when that happens, the claim will be pursued."

The fact that the diocese's agreement cautiously acknowledged that there had been sexual abusers in the ranks of Toledo priests—even though the offenses were not prosecutable—marked a sharp contrast from the church's stance just a few months earlier.

In March 2002, then-Bishop James Hoffman sent a letter to the 325,000 Catholics in his diocese apologizing for clerical sexual abuse in general, but asserting that the Toledo diocese had put safeguards in place to protect children, referring in particular to guidelines adopted in 1995.

At the same time, Frank DiLallo, the case manager and liaison for the diocese with all victims of clerical sexual abuse, told the *Blade* in an interview that in the six years he had been on the job, "there have been absolutely no allegations of priests abusing children."

He said only two priests in the history of the ninety-year-old diocese had been diagnosed as pedophiles. They had been sent away for treatment and by March 2002, were deceased.

But a month later, in April 2002, Teresa Bombrys burst the diocese's bubble, filing a lawsuit alleging she had been molested by Father Chet Warren, an Oblate priest, starting when she was in the fourth grade. Furthermore, she said she had notified the Toledo diocese in 1999.

Then, in June 2002, the *Blade* interviewed Leo Welch, a former Toledo priest who admitted to molesting altar boys at a cottage back in the 1950s and early 1960s. Welch said the diocese sent him for counseling, then reassigned him to a different parish before he voluntarily left the priesthood.

With the diocese pledging "transparency" in its handling of abuse cases and promising full cooperation with the county prosecutor's office, investigators Steve Forrester and Tom Ross—working on the county prosecutor's cold-case squad—went to the diocese on December 15, 2003, and asked for its files on Father Gerald Robinson.

Detective Forrester had been on the Toledo police force for twenty-six years, was a practicing Catholic, and considered Father Michael Billian, the diocese's chancellor, one of his friends.

Detectives Forrester and Ross met Father Billian in his fourth-floor office, across from the office of newly installed Bishop Leonard Blair.

The investigators explained that they had reopened the investigation into Sister Margaret Ann Pahl's 1980 murder at Mercy Hospital. They knew that Father Robinson had been a suspect at the time of the slaying and asked if they could get copies of his personnel file to see if there was information that would help their investigation.

The chancellor left the room briefly and came back with a slim manila file. Sergeant Forrester flipped it open and found a photograph of Father Robinson, a sheet containing the priest's basic biographical information, and another paper outlining his diocesan assignments.

The detectives had been expecting more in-depth information, such as performance reviews, comments from parishioners and church officials, and any internal documents related to the 1980 police investigation in which the priest had been a suspect.

Father Billian assured them that the folder he had given them contained the priest's entire file, and the detectives left, taking his word for it.

About eight and a half months later, however, with the cold-case investigation still under way, Sergeant Forrester learned from a knowledgeable source that the Toledo diocese did, indeed, have more information in its files regarding Father Robinson.

Those files were kept in a section that was separate from the standard personnel forms and diocesan documents, the detective was told.

Sergeant Forrester, who is a lawyer in addition to being a detective, dug out a copy of *The Code of Canon Law*, the book of laws that governs the Roman Catholic Church, and began researching references to secret files.

He found that church law orders dioceses to maintain secret archives—also called *sub secreto*, Latin for "under secret," files—that are to be guarded so carefully that church leaders are forbidden from volunteering information about them or consenting to them being searched.

The existence of the secret files is mandated by Canon 489, which states: "There is also to be a secret archive in the diocesan curia or at least a safe place or file in the ordinary [bishop's] archive, completely closed and locked, which cannot be removed from the place, and in which documents to be kept secret are to be protected most securely."

The code book specifies that among the types of files to be concealed are those involving moral or criminal investigations of priests and diocesan employees. Canon 1719 states: "The acts of the investigation, the decrees of the ordinary [bishop] which initiated and concluded the investigation, and everything which preceded the investigations are to be kept in the secret archive. . . ."

If the Toledo diocese had conducted its own investigation of Father Robinson in 1980, something that detectives Forrester and Ross presumed had been done, there would have been numerous documents and internal reports detailing the church's findings. Canon law specifies that even if outdated documents are removed from the secret archives and destroyed, the church must keep a summary of the documents.

After consulting with several canon lawyers, Forrester concluded that bishops and chancellors are barred by church law from even acknowledging that secret archives exist.

He said his research showed that diocesan officials were prohibited by Canon Law from volunteering such information or consenting to a search of the diocesan secret archives. Even if they were fully aware that the government was conducting a criminal investigation and that Father Robinson had been indicted by the Lucas County grand jury for aggravated murder, the diocesan leaders could not surrender their secret archives or even acknowledge them, according to Sergeant Forrester's research.

"Notably, canon law provides that canon law supersedes civil legal authority," Sergeant Forrester said.

Furious that the diocese he had trusted implicitly may have deceived him and Investigator Ross when they asked for Father Robinson's files, Sergeant Forrester called Father Billian and told him that he had been researching the church's canon law and learned that dioceses are required to keep a separate secret archive of criminal investigations.

Father Billian brushed aside the allegation, saying that yes, canon law does require such archives, but, no, the Toledo diocese did not keep such files.

It was a reflection of the U.S. Catholic Church's commitment to openness and transparency, Father Billian told him.

Although technically the diocese was in violation of canon law, he asserted that it was not likely to draw any penalties or punishment from the Vatican.

Father Thomas P. Doyle, a Dominican priest from Virginia and a canon lawyer who had been critical of most U.S. bishops for their handling of the sexual abuse crisis, said he had doubts about Father Billian's explanation.

"First off, I don't think that was a true statement," Father Doyle said. "They do have secret archives. Every diocese has them. What this process has shown over the years, in court procedures and everything else, is that diocese after diocese does not tell the truth when it gets involved in this process. So that was a lie. They do have secret archives."

He said society and the church have created a double standard in dealing with wayward priests.

"If anybody else in life is accused of a crime, it is not kept secret. In state after state, you have men who were accused of abuse but it's been kept secret. The church has moved these people around. Because of this, it will have to accept that there will be no trust."

He said that while every diocese has secret archives, their physical location and descriptions can vary and that bishops or diocesan leaders use semantics to dodge questions and to mislead investigators and the media.

"The [canon] law says you have to have secret archives, but that pertains more to the documents themselves," Father Doyle said. "We don't have a place that we call the secret archive. But they have files that are kept in deep secrecy."

Father Stephen Stanbery, a diocesan priest who has challenged both Bishop Hoffman and Bishop Blair over the way they have treated abuse victims, said he confronted Bishop Blair about why the cold-case investigators were given only three pages when they requested Father Robinson's file.

"We gave them what they asked for," Bishop Blair told him.

"He said it with a smile, in kind of a smug way," Father Stanbery said.

Chapter 47

After Sergeant Forrester's revelation that Roman Catholic law requires all dioceses to keep secret archives, he began poring over canon law for all references to *sub-secreto* files.

Working with Thomas Aquinas Matuszak, an assistant Lucas County prosecutor specializing in combating organized crime, Sergeant Forrester drafted a twenty-page affidavit outlining his reasons for his belief that the Toledo diocese had concealed documents relevant to the state's murder investigation of Father Gerald Robinson.

On September 15, 2004, Sergeant Forrester and Investigator Tom Ross brought their affidavit to Judge Robert Christiansen of the Lucas County common pleas court, seeking his approval to search the Catholic Center for secret archives.

The affidavit said the diocese was concealing "certain property including the diocesan secret archives, key(s) and/or combinations to the secret archives, and internal policies and/or procedures concerning the creation of, maintenance of, and access to the diocesan secret archives for the period 1980 through the present."

The detectives sought the authorization to search for books, documents, photographs, negatives, videotapes, computer hard drives and storage devices, e-mail, and any other records "relating, directly or indirectly, to Father Gerald Robinson, Father Jerome Swiatecki, Sister Margaret Ann Pahl, the death of Sister Margaret Ann Pahl, and/or any canonical process relative to the aforementioned persons and/or events."

They said in the affidavit that Father Gerald Robinson and Father Jerome Swiatecki were working as chaplains at Mercy Hospital at the time Sister Margaret Ann Pahl was found dead in the hospital sacristy on April 5, 1980.

They also stated that Father Robinson, on or about April 18, 1980, "failed a polygraph examination conducted by the Toledo Police Department, scoring 'deception indicated' on relevant questions concerning the murder of Sister Margaret Ann Pahl."

Father Gerald Robinson had been identified as a suspect in Sister Margaret Ann's murder "early in the criminal investigation," they pointed out in the affidavit, and the police department's investigation may have been compromised when "Toledo Police Deputy Chief Ray Vetter told Monsignor Schmit, an official serving with the Catholic Diocese of Toledo at the time, that Father Robinson was the focus of the criminal investigation."

But the detectives said the reason that no criminal charges were filed in 1980 was because "certain forensic techniques" were not available to law-enforcement authorities at the time. Since the case was reopened in 2003, however, additional forensic testing "further implicated Father Robinson as the person who murdered Sister Margaret Ann Pahl," they said.

Sergeant Forrester then detailed the series of events of December 15, 2003, when he and Investigator Tom Ross went to the diocese seeking Father Robinson's personnel files in order to obtain information relevant to the murder investigation.

The affidavit said Father Michael Billian, chancellor of the diocese, left the room for a few minutes and returned with a file that "was substantially devoid of any information concerning Father Robinson's service in ministry, his performance evaluations (or their equivalent) and/or any internal (canonical) investigation(s) conducted by the Catholic Diocese of Toledo into the death of Sister Margaret Ann Pahl or Father Robinson's fitness to serve in ministry."

He suggested that the Toledo diocese had misled investigators because officials repeatedly stated during the murder investigation that they had been "fully cooperative" with law-enforcement authorities, yet no one mentioned the secret archives.

The detective then detailed his reasons for believing that the diocese was concealing documents related to the murder investigation.

On April 26, 2004, three days after the priest was arrested, Bishop Leonard Blair issued a statement saying that the diocese "will not conduct any further interviews at this time regarding the investigation," which implied "that it had already conducted interviews into the allegations that Father Robinson had engaged in criminal misconduct."

The next day, the bishop released another statement saying that he had placed Father Robinson on a leave of absence and excluded him from public ministry.

Sergeant Forrester said he had reason to believe that the bishop's actions "stemmed from a canonical penal process conducted internally at the bishop's personal direction" and that this process "generated records and other materials that must be stored in the diocesan secret archives according to Canon Law and the statements of credentialed lawyers."

He cited Canon 380 of church law, which says bishops must make a profession of faith and an oath of fidelity to the Pope upon taking office. That oath says, in part, "I shall follow and foster the common discipline of the whole church and

I shall observe all ecclesiastical laws, especially those which are contained in the Code of Canon Law, so help me God, and God's holy Gospels, on which I place my hand."

Canons 1717 and 1719 decree that bishops must conduct investigations of any priests suspected of wrongdoing, "unless such an inquiry seems entirely superfluous," and that records of the investigation "and everything that preceded the investigation are to be kept in the secret archives."

Chapter 48

Armed with what legal experts say may have been the first search warrant filed in a murder investigation that sought access to a U.S. diocese's secret archives, the two detectives walked through the glass doors of the Catholic Center on the afternoon of September 15, ignored the receptionist's plea to sign in, and boarded an elevator for the fourth-floor chancery.

The spacious office suite, with its rows of glass-lined offices, library shelves filled with Catholic books and magazines, and a reading area with couches and coffee tables, is where Bishop Leonard Blair, Auxiliary Bishop Robert Donnelly, and Chancellor Michael Billian kept their offices.

Terrie Albert, the bishop's executive assistant, went over Bishop Blair's office and informed him that two detectives were there to see him.

Sergeant Forrester told the bishop that he and Investigator Ross had a search warrant commanding them to search for and seize certain documents they believed to be located in the diocesan secret archives.

Bishop Blair shook his head in disbelief.

He told the investigators that, contrary to what they may have been told or believed, the Toledo diocese did not follow that section of canon law and it did not maintain a secret archive.

"It simply does not exist," Bishop Blair asserted.

They asked for Father Billian and were told that the chancellor was out of town. Bishop Blair then called Father Billian and put him on speaker phone.

With detectives Forrester and Ross listening, Father Billian said there were two places where files on priests are kept: one was a set of metal filing cabinets in a document room across from the bishop's fourth-floor office, and the other was a filing cabinet in the chancellor's office.

"Father Billian did not mention during that conversation that there was a file concerning Father Robinson in his office at the time," Sergeant Forrester said afterward. He also noted that nine months previously, on December 15, 2003, he and Investigator Ross had asked Father Billian to provide "any and all documents pertaining to Father Robinson."

Sergeant Forrester then asked Bishop Blair to contact the diocese's attorney. The bishop dialed Thomas Pletz and put him on speaker phone, in front of the detectives.

"There are two detectives here in the chancery with a warrant to search the secret archives," Bishop Blair told the attorney.

Pletz quickly called Dean Mandros, assistant Lucas County prosecutor, then hurried over to the Catholic Center.

While they were waiting for Pletz, Investigator Ross asked the diocese's archivist, Susan Wietnik, how the archives were maintained.

She told him that Father Billian was responsible for the creation and the maintenance of the files, including those pertaining to Father Robinson.

She said Father Billian would ask for a file on a particular priest and that she would then retrieve the file without looking at it and give it to the chancellor.

Father Billian would then add or delete records from the file, return it to Ms. Wietnik without comment, and she would place the file in a locked cabinet.

Pletz arrived shortly after, waving a set of keys in the air.

"I have a key to Father Billian's office," the attorney said.

He then led the detectives to the documents room in the chancery, where Sergeant Forrester confiscated files on Father Swiatecki, the hospital chaplain who assisted detectives in 1980 by driving Father Robinson to the Safety Building for an interrogation, and Monsignor Schmit, the church leader who had informed Father Robinson that he was a suspect in the nun's murder.

Both the Schmit and Swiatecki files contained the same kind of bare-bones information as the file on Father Robinson that the diocese gave the detectives in December—basic biographical information, parish assignments, and photographs.

While Sergeant Forrester and Investigator Ross were in the documents room with Bishop Blair, Pletz left and returned about two minutes later carrying a thick blue file folder and plopped it down on a table.

The file was about an inch and a half to two inches thick. Sergeant Forrester believed Pletz had gotten it from the locked cabinet in Father Billian's office.

The file contained 148 separate documents pertaining to Father Robinson. Many of those documents were dated prior to the cold-case detectives' request nine months earlier for all of the Robinson files.

Clearly, the diocese had not turned over all of its Father Robinson files in December.

Chapter 49

The cold-case investigators left the Catholic Center with 145 more documents about their murder suspect than the Toledo diocese had willingly provided in December.

Dean Mandros, assistant prosecutor and head of the criminal division, said the new documents contained nothing "directly related" to the investigation, although there were some documents that, depending on how the trial went, might come into play.

That in itself was suspicious, Mandros asserted, because Father Robinson had been the subject of police and diocesan investigations in 1980 and again in 2004, but there were no references to any murder investigation in the priest's files seized in the search warrant.

The fact that the diocese had kept hidden a folder containing 145 documents about Father Robinson made Sergeant Forrester wonder if more files may be tucked away inside the Catholic Center.

He and Thomas Matuszak, the assistant prosecutor with expertise in fighting organized crime, together drafted another search warrant plus a motion to seal the affidavits.

In the motion to seal, the prosecutor's office said it wanted to search for the secret files without causing further embarrassment to the Catholic Church.

"The Lucas County Prosecutor's Office wishes to forego any possible public or professional stigmatism and/or humiliation of the Catholic Diocese of Toledo, Bishop Blair, Father Billian, and/or other administrative officials affiliated with the diocese that might otherwise result from the aforementioned being filed as public records."

In the affidavit seeking a warrant to search the church headquarters for the second time in two days, Sergeant Forrester went over the events of September 15 and noted that the diocese kept files in both a document room and in Father Billian's office on the fourth floor.

However, he wrote, "during the execution of the search warrant, no police entered Father Billian's office."

He said he believed that the file with 148 documents on Father Robinson had been retrieved from Father Billian's office.

The files that he seized from the document room about Monsignor Schmit and Father Swiatecki contained the same kind of bare-bones information like the Father Robinson files that the diocese had handed over in December.

It was reasonable to assume, therefore, that the more extensive and sensitive files were the ones kept in Father Billian's office.

"It appears that Father Billian, in contravention of Canon Law, maintains records separate and apart from the general archives and/or the secret archives," Sergeant Forrester wrote. "Furthermore, it appears Father Billian exercises control of said records to the exclusion of Bishop Blair, again, in contravention of Canon Law."

Judge Christiansen signed the documents allowing the search and sealing the affidavit.

Jeff Anderson, the Minneapolis attorney who has sued Catholic dioceses around the country, told the *Blade* that a court order was the only way the Lucas County prosecutor's office would ever get into the Toledo church's secret archives.

"A search warrant is the only effective way to get their secrets and their secret information," Anderson said. "I know the Diocese of Toledo and they have been absolutely obstructionistic."

On September 17, detectives Forrester and Ross again marched into the Catholic Center and went straight to the fourth-floor chancery, this time demanding access to the files in Father Billian's office.

They reviewed a number of files that were marked "Privileged," but found nothing related to the investigation of Father Robinson.

The detectives left the chancery empty-handed.

Officially, Sergeant Forrester said the privileged files involved cases of sexual abuse of children by priests. Off the record, a number of insiders, including a diocesan priest, said the file contained reports of abortions paid for by the diocese.

Not long after the second search, Sergeant Forrester moved his family from Toledo to Monroe, Michigan. By relocating to the small community about fifteen miles north of Toledo, the sergeant officially transferred membership from the Toledo diocese to the Detroit archdiocese. Bishop Blair was no longer his bishop, and his former friend, Father Billian, was no longer his chancellor.

The search warrant affidavits and the motion to seal the affidavits were obtained by the *Blade* in February 2005, their contents published in a front-page article about the wrestling match between the diocese and the prosecutor's office over church documents and secret archives.

Representatives of SNAP, the Survivors Network of those Abused by Priests, wrote a letter to Lucas County prosecutor Julia Bates on February 23, urging her office to subpoena all diocesan files "related to allegations of sexual abuse as well as any other files that could possibly demonstrate a pattern of diocesan cover-up."

"To stop the violence that we have experienced in the Diocese of Toledo, we are asking you to use your authority as prosecutor to uncover the hidden truths and deception that the diocese may still be carrying out," said the letter, signed by Barbara Blaine; David Clohessy, executive director of SNAP; Claudia Vercellotti, the local coordinator; and Marcia Holtz, a Toledo SNAP member.

The letter alleged that "Father Billian and other diocesan officials have repeatedly, publicly denied the existence of such files, but now it has come to light that those files do exist as evidenced by this past weekend's article in the *Toledo Blade*. The presence of these files indicates that the diocese is in violation of the 2002 agreement made between Bishop Hoffman for the diocese and your office."

Two days later, Bishop Blair released a lengthy statement defending the diocese's policies and again denying the existence of secret archives.

"Reports have been circulated in the media implying that the Diocese of Toledo has not been forthright or has withheld information concerning the Father Robinson case.

"This is based on the claim that the church's Code of Canon Law says that dioceses should maintain a 'secret' archive for certain confidential matters, and therefore the Diocese of Toledo must have such a 'secret' archive which it has hidden from the public authorities," the bishop said in the February 28, 2005, statement.

"The fact is that the Diocese of Toledo has no separate 'secret archive' to which 'only the bishop may have the key.' There is no indication that one might have existed in the past, and there is certainly none in the present. The fact that the Diocese of Toledo has no 'secret archive' was explained to the police on September 15, 2004, and nothing has been found to the contrary for the simple reason that there is nothing to find.

"All the diocese's information concerning Father Robinson, including what would be called confidential information, is filed in the records that are now in the custody of the prosecutor's office and the police," Bishop Blair said.

Chapter 50

On April 20, 2005, almost exactly one year after the arrest of Father Gerald Robinson, a woman and her husband filed a civil lawsuit in the Lucas County common pleas court alleging that she was the victim of sexual and ritual abuse by Father Robinson when she was a child.

The suit named Father Robinson, the Diocese of Toledo, St. Adalbert's Catholic Parish and school, and Toledo Catholic layman Gerald "Jerry" Mazuchowski as defendants.

The plaintiffs filed anonymously as Survivor Doe and Spouse Doe, saying in the court filing that they feared reprisal and because of the "extremely graphic, personally devastating, and deeply embarrassing aspects of the abuse."

The Toledo woman, now in her early forties, called Claudia Vercellotti of SNAP in the summer of 2004, saying that news reports about Father Robinson's arrest had triggered memories of childhood abuse.

She said she never knew the names of her abusers, but that "I recognized him the minute I seen him on TV. I recognized him through those eyes—those droopy eyes."

Vercellotti and Jon Schoonmaker of Toledo SNAP drove to Survivor Doe's home to meet with her and to offer whatever help they could.

The woman, who held a job in which she was responsible for overseeing a large number of children each day, had kept journals since 1993, detailing the memories of childhood abuse that were starting to surface.

Pages upon pages of her journals were filled with childlike drawings of men with robes and hats, frightened little girls, and priests with women's hair. Her handwritten rhymes contained simple but harrowing verses about abuse and fear.

Survivor Doe said keeping the journals was therapeutic for her.

The rhymes included such phrases as, "They say it's my turn to die, I better shut up that is why," and, "In their mouths were the color red, it was from the blood they said."

Survivor Doe said she recognized Gerald Mazuchowski from an article that had been published in the *Blade* about his involvement in an informal group called Sisters of Assumed Mary.

According to the lawsuit, the woman attended St. Adalbert's Church and school, in the heart of Toledo's Lagrainka Polish neighborhood, from 1968 to 1972. Toledo diocesan personnel files list Father Robinson as having been associate pastor of St. Adalbert's from June 16, 1972, until June 15, 1973, when he was transferred to a parish in Findlay, Ohio.

The lawsuit, filed by Toledo attorney Mark A. Davis, stated that Survivor Doe was "kidnapped and held either against her will or through beguilement in the basement of St. Adalbert's" and that "while held in the basement, Father Robinson and other clergy colleagues, including Jerry Mazuchowski, engaged in elaborate, ritualistic ceremonies dressed as nuns. While dressed as nuns, Robinson, Mazuchowski, and their clergy cohorts referred to each other with the first name of a woman and then their own name."

The suit claimed that Father Robinson was known by his group as "Mary Jerry" and that Mazuchowski was known as "Carrie Jerry."

"The clergymen, including defendants Robinson and Mazuchowski, dressed in nun drag, circled around plaintiff Survivor Doe while she was on a table and chanted satanical verses and 'Son of Sam' and their female names. They intoned that Jesus was Satan's son. They cut Survivor Doe with a knife and drew an upside down cross on her stomach. They forced Survivor Doe to drink blood of a sacrificed animal.

"At each instance, the clergymen forced Survivor Doe to masturbate the clergymen in the circle. Furthermore, the clergymen would rape and/or sodomize her. . . ."

The suit said the ritual abuse sessions also took place in a wooded location, and then when they ended, the defendants "would intimidate her, tell her she was Satan's child, force her to clean the blood off the floor, and threaten to kill her if she told."

The allegations were nearly as shocking and bizarre as the ones made by Sister Mary Curtiss.

The lawsuit claimed that Father Robinson and Mazuchowski engaged in "rituals and sexual abuse which escalated dramatically."

It said they killed rabbits and made the girl drink the blood; that they vaginally raped her with a dead snake with its head cut off, and that they burned her feet and lit matches, blew them out, then burned them into the corner of her eyes.

The lawsuit claims that the diocese knew about the abuse yet continued to conceal Father Robinson's behavior and move him from parish to parish.

Father Robinson's attorney, Alan Konop, said when the suit was filed that he would not dignify it with a response.

The civil suit by Survivor Doe and Spouse Doe was assigned to Judge Ruth Ann Franks and is scheduled for trial in May 2007.

She said she filed the lawsuit to encourage other victims of clerical sexual abuse, and especially those who were abused in satanic rituals.

"It's not about the money," Survivor Doe said. "The satanic stuff, it's very dangerous. If I don't get a dime out of this, I don't care. I just want to help people come forward and heal; to show people how hard it is but you can do it."

Mazuchowski, 53, a lifelong Catholic with encyclopedic knowledge of Toledo's Polish community, is a member of the Third Order of St. Francis, a citywide secular fraternity founded in the 1940s whose biggest event each year was a blessing of the animals service.

A heavyset man with a permanent limp and mischievous twinkle in his eye, Mazuchowski had served as a Eucharistic minister and was parish council president at St. Hedwig Parish in the Lagrainka neighborhood.

Mazuchowski said Survivor Doe's lawsuit was absurd in claiming not only that he was a Catholic priest and an Oblate, but that he had sexually abused her.

"It's impossible. I have never been intimate with a woman," Mazuchowski asserted.

He acknowledged that he and a group of friends had created an informal group they called the Sisters of Assumed Mary, or SAM.

"There was no structure, there never was an establishment."

They used nun-like names, but not the ones Survivor Doe mentioned in her lawsuit, he said. Mazuchowski was called Sister Fortunata. His friend, John, was known as Sister Mary Xaviera, and Larry was referred to as Sister Mary Lavern, minister of novices.

They all were graduates of the imaginary "Convent of Regina Mundi."

SAM members never dressed in nun drag except on Halloween, Mazuchowski said.

"Did the Sisters of Assumed Mary exist? In people's imaginations," he said with a shrug. "It was all nonsense. Inside humor. Just foolishness."

Rumors flew about the Sisters of Assumed Mary, including allegations that they held orgies dressed as nuns in the basement of St. Hedwig's Church.

Those flames were fanned when the parish's pastor, Father Paul Kwiatkowski, heard about SAM and the alleged activities in his church basement and ousted Mazuchowski from the parish council, then held a Catholic cleansing ritual at St. Hedwig's.

The Lucas County cold-case detectives interviewed Mazuchowski early in their investigation of Father Robinson, when they were looking into Sister Mary Curtiss' bizarre and wide-ranging allegations.

Mazuchowski told them he was a freshman at Central Catholic High School when he first met Father Robinson and the priest was on the faculty. He assured them that Father Robinson had nothing to do with the Sisters of Assumed Mary.

Furthermore, he told the detectives, he could not believe that Father Jerry was capable of killing anyone. He said he knew both Father Robinson and the other Mercy Hospital chaplain, Father Swiatecki, who died in 1996, and, in his opinion, Father Swiatecki was more capable of violence.

"If a priest did it, then Father Swiatecki was more likely the one," Mazuchowski said. "He was a reformed alcoholic. He had a volatile personality. He was a woodcarver with access to knives."

Mazuchowski theorized that Father Swiatecki had confessed to Father Robinson that he murdered Sister Margaret Ann.

Perhaps that was why, after being grilled by detectives for hours on end in 1980, he slipped momentarily and said that someone had confessed to him about the murder, then quickly recanted.

"He would go to prison rather than break the seal of the confessional," Mazuchowski said.

He described Father Robinson as moody and shy, but not reclusive.

"That's just the way he is. Some days he's gregarious, some days he keeps to himself. But is he violent? No. Is he satanic? No. He was *pubuznu*—holy."

Chapter 51

After Father Robinson pleaded not guilty at his arraignment, he was released on $400,000 property bond and moved back into his Nebraska Avenue home by the police substation.

Barred from ministry and suffering from early stages of Parkinson's disease, the frail and aging priest surrounded himself with a small circle of friends, many of whom visited him at his home or met him for dinner at his favorite local restaurant, the Mango Tree.

Those who spent the most time with the priest were his brother, Tom, who worked in the construction trade, and sister-in-law, Barbara; his nephew, Brian Robinson; his friends, Gary and Kathy Glowski; an aunt, Dorothy Sieja; and a Toledo priest, Father Bernard Boff.

Father Boff, a retired cleric who at one time headed up the Toledo diocese's mission in Zimbabwe, Africa, joked that he wanted to be Father Robinson's agent and earn a fee every time his picture appeared in print or on television.

Father Robinson also spent a great deal of time during the months leading up to his trial meeting with his attorneys, John Thebes, Alan Konop, John Callahan, and Nicole Khoury.

Much of the courtside maneuvering involved setting pretrial hearing dates and debating the admissibility of evidence. Under Ohio law, prosecutors are required to disclose all evidence that investigators have collected, including witness statements, photographs, coroner's findings, police reports, and scientific and physical evidence.

On May 24, 2004, about a month after the priest's arrest, assistant Lucas County prosecutor Gary Cook told Judge Patrick Foley of the Lucas County common pleas court that it was unlikely the state could be ready for trial by the end of the year.

At the next court hearing, held July 13, Cook said the county prosecutor's office had turned over 90 percent of its evidence to the priest's defense team, and that it would give the lawyers the rest of the materials within a week.

The next time both sides showed up in court was August 5, when Judge Foley set February 22, 2005 as the date the trial would begin.

But that trial date was derailed by the November elections, when assistant prosecutor Gary Cook ran for the Lucas County common pleas court seat held by Judge Foley, and ousted the incumbent.

Normally, a judge's successor would inherit his or her docket, but because Judge Cook had been deeply involved in preparing the prosecution's case against Father Robinson, it was assigned to Judge Thomas Osowik.

A Roman Catholic, Osowik was elected in November to common pleas court after serving fifteen years as a municipal court judge.

On January 28, 2005, Judge Osowik pushed the priest's murder trial back to October 17, 2005, but with little more than a month to go, Father Robinson's attorneys requested more time.

Judge Osowik agreed to postpone the trial a second time, setting the date for April 17, 2006, but he warned the attorneys that it would be the final delay.

"I am going to emphasize this is going to be the final trial date. The case will proceed to trial on that date," the judge said.

On December 29, on a Friday afternoon just before the start of the long holiday break, assistant prosecutor Dean Mandros filed a motion to amend the charge against Father Robinson, dropping the phrase "with prior calculation and design" from the indictment.

That amendment reduced the charge against the priest from aggravated murder to plain murder.

There was no immediate explanation from the prosecutor's office, but Mandros said after the trial was over that the move was simply a pragmatic one.

"With aggravated murder, you have to prove the added element that it was premeditated. In Ohio we call that 'prior calculation and design.' That's just one more thing we have to prove and the only thing we would get out of that in return is a sentence of 20 to life instead of 15 to life. And with a 68-year-old man, what's the point?

"Strategy-wise, I wanted to have my job to be to prove as few things as possible. So I didn't want to prove premeditation, although clearly it was."

One of the final pretrial hearings involved a heated dispute over a 1980 police interrogation of Father Robinson. The defense claimed the prosecution was holding out, that it had a tape of the interrogation but refused to give them a copy. The prosecutor's office, meanwhile, asserted that no such tape existed.

Detective Arthur Marx, who had conducted the interrogation on April 19, 1980, testified at the pretrial hearing that he took notes that night but did not tape record the session.

When asked by defense attorney Alan Konop whether he took notes during the interrogation, Marx said it was his policy to always take notes.

When pressed by Konop on what he recalled about whether he remembered taking notes that particular night, Marx replied: "I cannot specifically recall. But I am sure that I did."

Two months before the trial was scheduled to start, Judge Osowik held a Daubert hearing to determine which scientific evidence would be admissible in court.

The defense and prosecution had their expert witnesses take the stand for questioning about their credentials and qualifications to testify as experts.

Doctor Kathleen Reichs, the forensic anthropologist from Charlotte and best-selling *Bones* novelist, and T. Paulette Sutton, the Memphis forensic examiner who is certified in bloodstain-pattern transfer analysis, both were accepted as expert witnesses.

Unlike the other witnesses at the Daubert hearing, Father Jeffrey Grob did not take the stand or answer questions in public, but was accepted as an expert witness nonetheless.

The defense attorneys and a team of assistant prosecutors huddled in Judge Osowik's chambers for more than an hour to debate Father Grob's qualifications as an expert.

The Roman Catholic priest's area of specialty was rituals, both Christian and occult. He served as assistant to the exorcist for the Archdiocese of Chicago and had written a doctoral dissertation on exorcism.

If reporters had heard testimony from an exorcist discussing his qualifications to serve as an expert witness in Father Robinson's trial, the media circus surely would have intensified. In line with the gag order imposed on the case, Judge Osowik made sure that Father Grob's credentials and expertise were kept as far away from the media glare as possible so as not to impact the trial before it began.

Chapter 52

Judge Osowik had summonses sent to 250 prospective jurors, the largest jurors' pool ever called for a trial in Lucas County common pleas court, but 104 were promptly excused for reasons ranging from medical conditions to inabilities to find childcare.

At 9:00 a.m. on Monday, April 17, a group ranging from college students in jeans to grandmothers with coiffed hair in their Sunday best rode the elevators to the fourth floor of the 105-year-old Lucas County courthouse.

There they walked across the lobby's marble floor, beneath an arched forty-foot ceiling, and entered through the wood-and-glass-paneled doors into Courtroom 5. The prospective jurors filled every seat in the jury box, the gallery, and several rows of folding chairs set up on the main floor of the courtroom.

In a rear corner of the room, in the gallery near the entrance, an area was blocked off for Court TV's camera and sound equipment. Court TV had been designated the pool video, supplying feeds to all stations. On the other side of the railing was a small table where the *Blade*'s photographer would sit, supplying still photos to media outlets. Both Court TV and the *Blade* also had remote-controlled cameras discreetly set up behind the witness stand.

Judge Osowik reminded the media in a memo that at no time could they photograph or videotape jurors or prospective jurors.

Court deputies, with walkie-talkies in hand and pistol bulges under their jackets, announced sternly to the crowd that they were to take off all hats and sunglasses and turn off their pagers and cell phones.

About 9:15, the slightly built defendant, wearing his clerical clothes, slipped into the room, flanked by his attorneys—Konop, Thebes, Khoury, and Callahan—and took a seat at the defense table. The defense attorneys had set two tables together in an "L" shape, with Father Robinson seated facing to the side of the room, toward the jurors.

Three assistant Lucas County prosecutors, all around 50 years of age and with a couple of decades of trial experience apiece, represented the state: Dean Mandros, the articulate and precise chief of the criminal division, J. Christopher

Anderson, specializing in forensic sciences, and Larry Kiroff, who recently returned to the prosecutor's office after spending ten years handling civil litigation for the city and the federal government.

Judge Osowik, in a black robe sitting high up on the bench, told the prospective jurors that the defendant, Gerald Robinson, had been charged with murder, entered a plea of not guilty, and was presumed innocent.

The trial was expected to last three to four weeks and court would be in session Monday through Friday from approximately 9:00 a.m. to 4:30 p.m., with morning and afternoon breaks and a recess for lunch.

The judge said he and the attorneys would interview prospective jurors individually in a process known as *voir dire*—French for "speak the truth"—and that their questions would focus on three main issues: their availability to serve on a lengthy trial, the extent of their knowledge of the case based on pretrial publicity, and their opinions of the Roman Catholic Church and its clergy.

He said they would have to control their "natural inclination" to discuss the case, being barred from talking about it to anyone. Jurors were expected to form an opinion based only on the facts presented in court, the judge said, and they were not to read, review, or listen to television, Internet, or newspaper reports during the trial.

He also told them they would not be allowed to take notes during the trial and would have to concentrate on the testimony and the evidence for three or four straight weeks.

The prospective jurors were then randomly divided into four groups and each group was given a time to report to the courthouse.

Many of the candidates were eliminated right away because serving on a lengthy trial would cause them financial hardship.

One woman, for example, owned and operated a restaurant with just one other employee, and she would have had to close it for the length of the trial. The woman was excused, but before she left she gave the judge and the attorneys a copy of her menu.

Others had jobs that would pay them only for a few days of jury duty, but not for three weeks.

Religion was an issue with a handful of prospective jurors. Many said that the clerical sexual-abuse crisis of the last few years had changed their opinion of priests—they no longer "put them on a pedestal."

Even when religious beliefs were not cause for dismissal from the jury pool, it was clear that faith had a strong grip on many people's lives.

"Do you have concerns about the Roman Catholic Church?" Kiroff asked one potential juror, a man in his thirties with a buzz haircut.

"Sure. It's in a lot of hot water. A lot of it is unjust—just not built on fact. It builds up and it snowballs. The Catholic Church is the new thing to attack," he said.

Father Robinson sat quietly, face resting in his hands, rubbing his mouth thoughtfully.

"Is the Catholic Church being picked on?" Kiroff asked the juror.

"Yeah, kind of. It's not fashionable to be Catholic right now. It's an easy thing to pick on."

The juror left the courtroom.

"No objections," Kiroff said.

"No objections," Konop echoed.

Most of the jurors said they had heard of the case, either when Sister Margaret Ann Pahl was murdered in 1980 or when Father Robinson was arrested in 2004.

One 26-year-old prospective juror, with spiked hair and glasses, told Kiroff that he first heard of the murder case that morning, when he picked up a copy of the *Blade* on his way into the courthouse.

"I usually turn to the sports section, TV, and cartoons, but today I had time to read the whole thing. I read about the trial opening today."

Asked about his religious background, he said he had been to a Baptist church a few times.

"Were you baptized in the Baptist church?" Kiroff asked.

The prospective juror, Matthan K. Martin, shrugged his shoulders.

"I don't know," he said.

Martin ended up being on the jury.

One man with a red, round face and thick glasses said he would find it "difficult to believe that a priest would do something like this."

"Could you be a fair and impartial juror?" Judge Osowik asked him.

"I doubt it," he replied.

When Chris Anderson questioned him, the man said he was "an old-fashioned Catholic and I would find it difficult to believe that a person of that stature would do something like this."

"Do you want to be on the jury?" Anderson asked.

"No, I don't want to be on this jury," he stated.

The man was excused.

One middle-aged man in a Toledo Mud Hens baseball jacket sat fidgeting in the jury box.

He was raised a Catholic, he said, and now attended a Lutheran church. Visibly shaking, he said, "I would be unable to overcome the reverence for priests that was ingrained in me during childhood."

The man was dismissed.

Kiroff asked each of the prospective jurors if they felt there might be "divine consequences" if they convicted a priest of murder.

One thin man in his twenties with bushy black hair pulled back in a ponytail looked on the verge of despair when that question was posed to him.

"I don't think I could do it. I just feel wrong. I can't make that decision, I just can't," the man said, his voice barely above a whisper. "I just feel that the decision I made will affect me forever. It will always be with me."

Throughout the jury selection, a county psychologist, Lucia Hinojosa, sat behind prosecutors and passed them notes on some prospective jurors. When one man, a practicing Catholic who went to the same Catholic high school as defense attorney John Thebes, was being questioned, Hinojosa passed a note on yellow legal paper to prosecutors that read: "Strong locus of control. He will convict!!"

The man was not selected for the jury.

Mandros told the group that the state did not have to prove a motive in the murder, just that Father Robinson had committed the crime. He told them that, according to state law, they had to look at the priest as they would any defendant, and not place a higher burden of proof on the state because the defendant is a priest.

"The white collar is not some sort of halo that will prevent him from human temptation," Mandros said.

He compared the state's case to solving a jigsaw puzzle. You don't need all of the pieces to be able to tell that it is a picture of a lighthouse, Mandros said. With the trial being held twenty-four years after Sister Margaret Ann's murder, some of the nonessential pieces may be missing. But by the end of the trial, he said, the puzzle picture will be clear.

He also said that the state's case is based on circumstantial evidence and that in the courtroom, circumstantial evidence is equal in weight to direct evidence.

He used a metaphor, telling prospective jurors to imagine they saw a child on a bicycle, with a baseball glove in one hand, sitting on one side of a freshly poured concrete driveway. You turn away and then look back and the child is on the other side of the driveway. His mitt is in the middle of the wet cement and there are bicycle tracks across the driveway. The tires on the bike have traces of cement on them.

What you have in this case is circumstantial evidence, Mandros told them. Nobody saw the boy ride his bike across the driveway. But the circumstantial evidence is enough to convince you that the boy rode his bicycle across the wet concrete and dropped his glove as he did so.

The state was going to show jurors that there was enough circumstantial evidence to prove that Father Robinson killed Sister Margaret Ann Pahl, Mandros asserted.

Konop followed with a half-hour statement, telling prospective jurors that it's not the quantity but the quality of evidence that determines a defendant's guilt or innocence.

"The question will be the quality of the state's evidence," Konop said. "The burden is on the prosecutor's expert witnesses."

On Thursday, April 20, after four days of interviewing prospective jurors individually and as a group, the attorneys for both sides and Judge Osowik settled on twelve people and four alternates for the panel. They took care not to distinguish which jurors were regulars and which were alternates.

Of the sixteen chosen, ten were women and six were men. Eight were married, six single, and two widowed. Fourteen were Caucasian and two were black. Their jobs spanned a cross section of industry, from construction and engineering to medicine and education. Two were unemployed.

Four jurors were Roman Catholics, two were Lutherans, two were nondenomi-

SIN, SHAME, AND SECRETS   189

national Christians, one was Baptist, one was an agnostic, and six were unaffiliated with any religious group or denomination.

Mandros said that according to his pretrial research, he would not have minded an entire jury of Roman Catholics as long as they were "not 70-year-old, old-school Polish Catholics," whose strong sense of loyalty to their priests could cloud their judgment.

He said Roman Catholics were quick to understand the significance of religious symbol and ritual, more so than non-Catholics. When they were told that the murder occurred in front of the Blessed Sacrament, they knew immediately that according to Catholic doctrine the Eucharist is the body of Christ. Tell them that the killer made stab wounds in the shape of an inverted cross and they know that the upside-down cross is a symbol of Satan.

Judge Osowik told the jurors to be ready for the start of trial at 9:00 the next morning.

Chapter 53

Away from the courtroom, being careful not to violate Judge Osowik's gag order, the prosecution team spoke in general terms about its strategy for the murder trial.

The first part of their presentation would focus on the physical evidence from the 1980 crime scene, in particular the priest's letter opener and the bloodstained altar cloth. That would likely take most or all of the first week of the trial.

In the second part of their presentation, they would question the detectives who investigated the murder, starting with the initial police team in 1980 and then the cold-case squad's investigation in 2003 and 2004.

Prosecutors had put more than ninety names on its list of potential witnesses that it could subpoena, but as the trial approached they said they would likely call between thirty and forty.

The defense, meanwhile, said it planned to hammer at the prosecution's case every step of the way, pointing out any missing elements or inconsistencies or contradictions. The goal would be to raise reasonable doubt in the minds of the jurors, who would have to be unanimous to convict the priest. Thebes said the defense team planned to call between eight and ten witnesses to the stand.

The defense would not confirm or deny whether they were planning to put Father Robinson on the witness stand in his own defense, but court insiders virtually ruled that option out.

The main reason, they said, was that Father Robinson had admitted on the record that he lied to police when he was interrogated in 1980 by saying that another person had confessed to him about the murder, then saying he had made that up. There was no way the priest would be able to explain that on the witness stand, under questioning by the prosecutors, without destroying his credibility, the experts said. One veteran defense attorney called it "a fatal and irreversible blunder."

Technically, a defendant in a criminal case does not have to testify in his or her own defense, and jurors are instructed that a defendant's decision not to testify cannot be held against him or her. In reality, however, legal experts said that these jurors were likely to wonder why a Catholic priest would not take the stand to deny that he murdered a nun.

A few days before the trial began, Claudia Vercellotti and Jon Schoonmaker, co-coordinators of the local chapter of SNAP, tried to hand deliver a letter to Bishop Leonard Blair at the Catholic Center, asking him to bar Father Robinson from wearing his priest's collar during the trial. They said the priest's clothing might unduly influence the jury.

But the diocese sent its building supervisor to the edge of its property before the SNAP officials finished a press conference, and she blocked Vercellotti and Schoonmaker from walking to the building. In a tense and unpleasant showdown, the church employee refused to let Vercellotti and Schoonmaker step onto the private property, saying she would accept the letter to the bishop right there, and promised that the letter would be delivered to the bishop.

Diocesan officials said later that after researching the subject, they believed that a bishop can bar child molesters from wearing a priest's collar, but not murder suspects. The reason was that the Dallas Charter specifically addresses the issue in regard to child abusers, but there is no reference to the crime of murder.

On the morning of April 21, 2006, the national media turned its eye on Toledo, with television vans and portable broadcast studios parked nose to tail along Michigan Avenue, the one-way street on the east side the Lucas County Courthouse.

Along with all of the local television channels were CNN, the world's most-watched news network, and Court TV, which was planning gavel-to-gavel coverage. Reporters from the Associated Press, *Los Angeles Times*, *People* magazine, *Dateline*, and the *Cleveland Plain Dealer* were in town, and reporters from the British Broadcasting Company, National Public Radio, Canadian press, Reuters, and other major media outlets had interviewed Toledo reporters by phone about the trial.

The Toledo diocese was, reluctantly, in the spotlight again. The last time was in 2004 when ex-priest Denny Gray was accused of molesting a 14-year-old boy in the Oscar-nominated documentary *Twist of Faith*.

Today, Father Gerald Robinson, a Toledo priest for more than forty years, was going on trial in what was believed to be the first time in U.S. history—perhaps in world history—that a Roman Catholic priest was charged in the murder of a Roman Catholic nun.

Court TV's boxy blue trailer, equipped with a large studio and separate production room, featured a wall of tinted glass windows that made it appear as if correspondent and attorney Beth Karas, assigned to the trial, was standing outside under the sun-dappled maple trees on the courthouse's lush green lawn.

On the fourth floor of the century-old building, crowds were lining up to get into Courtroom 5. There were ten gallery seats assigned to the defense team, ten to the prosecution, and twenty-five to the media. Whatever seats were left would become available to the general public.

Compared to the laid-back atmosphere during four days of jury selection, the air in the courtroom the morning of the trial was electrified. A bench along the back rail, in front of the gallery, was lined shoulder to shoulder with local law-enforcement and court officials squeezing into the room, including prosecutor Julia Bates and the cold case's lead investigators, Tom Ross and Steve Forrester.

The defense team was now relegated to a single table, and Father Robinson, in his clerical collar, was told he must face the bench, not the jury. His 84-year-old lawyer, John "Jack" Callahan, was allowed to sit on the far end of the table, facing jurors.

When Father Robinson first entered the room, wearing his priest's collar and escorted by his team of attorneys, he walked briskly over to his supporters in a corner of the gallery, smiling slightly as he chatted with his brother Tom and sister-in-law Barbara, and friends Father Bernard Boff and Gary and Kathy Glowski.

Once the jury entered the room, marching silently past the defense table and staring straight ahead, never looking sideways at the priest, Father Robinson's demeanor changed dramatically. He sat stone-faced, his face propped in one hand, gazing straight ahead. He showed little emotion, if any, most of the time, especially when the prosecution's witnesses were on the stand. Occasionally he looked as if he were dozing, or perhaps meditating. The most visible reaction was an occasional roll of the eyes in disgust at a statement by a prosecutor or a witness.

The state had said beforehand that today's juries have high expectations of prosecutors—legal experts call it "The *CSI* Factor"—and so the state planned to augment its case using some high-tech tools, including DVD slide shows and charts and graphics projected on a white SMART Board™ hooked to a laptop computer.

During his opening statement, Mandros used the SMART Board™ to display a black-and-white photo of a smiling Sister Margaret Ann Pahl, followed by a color photo of Father Robinson taken in 1980, with a shock of brown hair and a much more vital appearance than the haggard old cleric sitting in the courtroom that day.

Mandros opened by methodically outlining the steps that the prosecution would take to convince jurors that Father Robinson brutally killed the nun on Holy Saturday morning, 1980.

"We will prove to you the whereabouts of Sister Margaret Ann Pahl on the day of April 5th, 1980, and we will prove to you the whereabouts of the defendant on the morning of April 5th, 1980. You will learn how the defendant and the victim were together in the sacristy of that chapel, and how one of them died an unholy death."

He explained that the sacristy, the small room adjacent to a Catholic chapel, is a place where the priests put on their vestments and where religious items are stored for use in Mass and other services.

But on Holy Saturday, the sacristy is "transformed," Mandros said, "because the Eucharist, also called the Blessed Sacrament, consecrated as the very body of Jesus Christ, is removed from the chapel on Good Friday and placed in storage in the sacristy. . . . Thus the sacristy is transformed into the holiest place in the chapel."

He then proceeded to go through the series of events that led up to the Holy Saturday slaying.

Sister Margaret Ann Pahl was an early riser, with two alarm clocks in her convent bedroom, one set for 5:00 a.m. and the other for 5:30 a.m.

While she was preparing for Holy Saturday services, the hospital's night-shift nursing supervisor, Rose Byers, stopped by the chapel to say a prayer before heading home, a routine she had followed every day for eighteen years.

"But she did not do this on April 5th. It wasn't because she forgot, and it wasn't because she didn't want to. She certainly did want to this Saturday before Easter," Mandros said. "But she couldn't. And the reason she couldn't do this is because shortly after 7 o'clock on the morning of April 5th, 1980, these chapel doors were locked. The first and only time, she'll tell you. So she went home and said her morning prayers."

That led Mandros into a dramatic description of the gruesome murder of Sister Margaret Ann.

"The chapel doors were locked because something inconceivable was about to take place. . . . It was in the sacristy of that chapel that someone took her by the neck and choked her. The killer choked her so hard that two bones inside her neck broke. He choked her so hard that the blood vessels in her eyes burst."

Sister Margaret Ann was strangled "to the very verge of death, but not quite," he said. "The killer laid her upon the floor. After laying her on the floor, he covered her with a white altar cloth. After doing that, he stabbed her over the heart nine times. Nine piercings of her flesh in the shape of an upside down cross.

"And after he did all that, he does some more. He takes off the altar cloth, he stabs her 22 more times. This time he's still not through. After doing these things, he carefully pulls up her dress, her smock, up over her chest. He pulls her girdle, her underpants, her hose, down to her ankles. He leaves her exposed, naked, stretched out like in a coffin, on the sacristy floor. Only then is the killer done."

Mandros continued, describing the discovery of the nun's body by a colleague, Sister Madeline Marie Gordon.

"She let out a scream that was heard throughout the building," he said. "All the nuns came when they heard the scream and offered their assistance . . . the nurses came running to the chapel . . . but it was too late. Sister Pahl was dead. There was nothing the doctors could do. The 71-year-old nun was murdered the day before Easter, the day before her 72nd birthday."

Mandros told jurors that a saber-shaped letter opener belonging to Father Robinson had been tested by deputy Lucas County coroner Dr. Diane Barnett on a wound found in Sister Margaret Ann's jawbone, and that the unusual shape of the blade fit the indentation in the bone "like a key fits a lock."

He also said the priest lied about his whereabouts the morning of April 5, 1980, and that the state would produce witnesses who would place him at the chapel about the time of the slaying.

Defense attorney Alan Konop, speaking to jurors as if he were their favorite uncle, followed Mandros's thirty-minute presentation by thanking the jurors for giving their time and serving such an important role in the community.

"We will share a long journey," said Konop, who had been defending criminal cases for more than forty years.

He reminded the jury that the state's case was based on circumstantial evidence.

"This is a case that will be tested by the standard of proof, which is proof beyond a reasonable doubt. That's the standard. Not hunches, not guesswork," Konop said.

He referred to Mandros's analogy that the state would build its case by putting the puzzle pieces together.

"This is like a jigsaw puzzle. The circumstantial evidence, the testimony, are pieces of a puzzle. These pieces must fit in order for the state to show beyond a reasonable doubt that Father Robinson committed this crime."

Konop said the defense will show that there are "important inconsistencies and discrepancies in their presentation. *Important* inconsistencies and discrepancies. There will be serious questions regarding the investigation."

He again asserted that the state will not be able to prove "beyond a reasonable doubt" that the defendant killed Sister Margaret Ann Pahl.

"The puzzle will not fit. The pieces do not fit," Konop said. "As much as you want to jam them in—we've all had that experience with a puzzle—you can't quite put it together and you jam and jam and jam, and it doesn't fit. That's exactly the situation we find here. Exactly."

Konop assailed the prosecutors for arresting Father Robinson on April 23, 2004, before they had collected sufficient evidence to prove his guilt.

"He's arrested. He's condemned. He's humiliated, cuffed and booked, based upon what you will find, based upon the evidence, doesn't fit the standard of proof beyond a reasonable doubt."

The defense lawyer argued that the state still was missing vital pieces of its case against the priest and continued to examine evidence and interview experts "after the humiliation and degradation of an arrest of Father Robinson."

Konop pointed out that tests conducted by the prosecution on stains found on the slain nun's underwear and on material found on her fingernails showed that the DNA could not have come from Father Robinson.

"There will be reasonable doubt, reasonable doubt, reasonable doubt—to the point that the puzzle pieces don't fit," Konop said emphatically.

Chapter 54

After the opening statements, jurors took a short break and then gathered outside the courthouse to board a small, private bus. They were driven a mile and a half to the former Mercy Hospital—now Mercy College of Northwest Ohio.

The jury was to get a firsthand look at the hospital's sacristy, where the murder took place, and Father Robinson's residence in the hospital, as well as other parts of the medical complex that would be mentioned during the trial.

As the jurors filed out of the bus, court bailiff Tanya Butler led them into the building and along a circuitous route that had been chosen through careful negotiations between the defense and the prosecution.

It was not your typical tourist trip.

Butler read from a precisely worded script, giving minimal information to the jurors as they walked in silence through the former hospital's freshly cleaned hallways and rooms.

Each word of the court's script had been agreed upon by lawyers for each side, striving to find the right balance of giving jurors sufficient information for them to notice important sights, but not too much information that the script might influence their thinking.

After entering the complex from the entrance at 23rd Street and Jefferson Avenue, Butler gathered the jurors together in the ground-floor lobby.

"Please look around the lobby, and note the overhang of the balcony above. Note the relationship of the elevators to the front door," she said, reading from the script.

The jurors were then led up to the second floor, down a dark hallway, and stopped in front of an exit door with a push bar.

"Please note this exit door which leads to a stairwell. Please note this stairwell has steps both up and down," Butler said.

The jury was then led through a door leading into Room 127 and into an adjoining room, with windows overlooking a small courtyard.

The script did not mention that the tiny two-room suite was Father Robinson's living quarters at the time of the murder.

"Please note the size of these two rooms. Note also the bathroom in the first room and the closets in the second room," Butler said.

They were then led back down the same hallway, then west along the path above the lobby. The sixteen jurors, walking slowly and paying close attention to the details, followed the bailiff down another hallway that led to a glass-walled walkway. The bridge connecting the nursing school and the old hospital provided fast, easy access between the two buildings in 1980, but now one side was sealed off with bare cement block.

After several assorted twists and turns, walking up and around the hospital complex, the jurors eventually came to St. Joseph's Chapel—the room that Sister Margaret Ann Pahl had been preparing for Mass.

"Because of the modifications to the hallway, the chapel doors are no longer in their original position," Butler informed them. "The rear of the chapel has been expanded to absorb what was originally a hallway in 1980. However, the front half of the chapel—and, specifically, the sacristy—has remained essentially unchanged."

The jurors took their time walking through the door and into the narrow sacristy, single file, no one saying a word.

There was a sense of sadness mixed with curiosity, as the jurors gazed around the room. No script was read inside the sacristy. None was needed. Everyone knew that just over twenty-six years ago, Sister Margaret Ann's lifeless body lay stabbed and strangled on this very floor.

The sacristy was about eleven feet wide and seventeen feet long, its terrazzo floor made of light-colored marble with rectangular lines and numerous dark flecks. Most of the walls were lined with dark wooden cabinets, where the priests and nuns kept vestments, chalices, altar cloths, candles, and other items used to celebrate Mass. On one wall was a small porcelain sink beneath a wooden crucifix.

The jury's tour of Mercy Hospital lasted about forty-five minutes, after which the panelists were taken back to the courthouse by bus.

Judge Osowik dismissed the jury until Monday, reminding them not to watch TV or read newspapers and not to discuss the case with anyone.

Chapter 55

The state's first witness was 76-year-old Sister Phyllis Ann Gerold, the administrator of Mercy Hospital in 1980. The nun was now in a wheelchair and living in St. Bernadine's Retirement Home in Fremont, but Mandros made it clear to jurors from the start that her mind was as sharp as ever.

Sister Phyllis Ann, in her blue nun's habit with a small gold cross pinned to her lapel, responded in detail to Mandros's questions about the history of the Sisters of Mercy of the Union, explaining that the order was founded in Ireland in 1831 by Sister Catherine McAuley and that it began its U.S. hospital ministry in 1847.

She joined the order in 1945 and said there were six thousand Sisters of Mercy worldwide today.

Sister Phyllis Ann said she had worked as a nursing supervisor for ten years before earning a degree in hospital administration.

In 1980, the year of the murder, she was president and CEO of Mercy Hospital, which had about three thousand employees and three hundred patients and an annual budget of $100 million.

In more than three hours on the witness stand, Sister Phyllis Ann said that Sister Margaret Ann Pahl was the administrator of Mercy Hospital in Tiffin when they first met in 1954, and at the time, Sister Margaret Ann was known as Sister Annunciata. She changed back to her birth name in 1968.

"She was very good to me," Sister Phyllis Ann said. She paused a moment, tilting her head thoughtfully. "She was a very good administrator."

She described Sister Margaret Ann as "a direct person. . . . She had been in positions of power, so she stated her opinions."

By 1980, Sister Margaret Ann was semi-retired, but still very active and clearheaded, Sister Phyllis Ann said. The only problem she had was her hearing, which was getting worse every year.

Sister Margaret Ann had written to Sister Phyllis Ann in the 1970s to ask if there was a position open at Mercy Toledo, "and we were very happy to have her," the administrator said.

"She was in charge of the chapel, she visited patients—she was essentially a hostess," Sister Phyllis Ann said. "She took care of the convent cleaning—she was very good at cleaning. She had a quiet sense of what she went about doing. She was very generous and would go beyond what she was asked to do. She was a very, very lovely sister. She was a devout person. She prayed."

Over the coming days in Courtroom 5, the prosecutors would present to the jury all the testimony and evidence they had meticulously compiled during the two-year investigation of the murder.

When Mandros asked Sister Phyllis Ann if she had specific recollections of the events of April 5, 1980, the elderly nun gazed down at the floor and replied, in a somber tone, "Yes, I do."

She said she had been eating breakfast in the dining room that morning when she heard "terrible screaming." The blood-curdling shrieks sent chills down her spine, and she ran into the hallway to see where they were coming from.

The nun raced toward the chapel and the screams grew louder. Inside, she found Sister Madeline Marie Gordon in hysterics, completely out of control. Sister Phyllis Ann tried desperately to find out what was wrong, and after repeating the question over and over, Sister Madeline Marie finally managed to say, gasping between every word, that Sister . . . Margaret . . . Ann . . . was . . . on . . . the . . . floor . . . of . . . the . . . sacristy.

"When I found Sister Margaret Ann, it was terribly strange and sad and horrifying," Sister Phyllis Ann testified. "I felt she needed to be saved. . . . Her face was swollen and, as a nurse, I knew she needed care now because there was air in her chest."

It was an eerie sight, she said. Sister Phyllis Ann had seen countless people die during her years as a nurse and as a hospital administrator, but this case was different, she told the hushed courtroom.

The image was still vivid in her mind.

"I did not see any blood. She was laid very neatly, in the center of the floor. Her dress was pulled up and her other clothes were rolled down to the feet."

"Did you see her nakedness?" Mandros asked.

"I saw her nakedness," she replied softly.

A gray-haired mannequin, dressed in a blue nun's habit, was then carried into the center of the courtroom. Mandros, following the nun's description of the scene, adjusted the clothing on the dummy. The mannequin provided the jurors with a chilling visual image of what Sister Phyllis Ann had seen inside the sacristy that morning.

"What was your first impression upon discovering Sister Margaret Ann's body?" Mandros asked.

"I felt horror. The weirdness of it," she said. "She was so straight. People usually don't die that straight."

Her first thought was that the death seemed "ritualistic," Sister Phyllis Ann said, at which point Alan Konop, the defense attorney, leaped up and asked Judge Osowik if he could approach the bench.

After a brief discussion among Konop, Mandros, and Osowik, Mandros resumed the questioning of Sister Phyllis Ann.

She said that by the time the doctors and nurses arrived, it was too late to save Sister Margaret Ann's life.

She left the sacristy and went to her office across the hall and "called the people that needed to be called."

Later, under cross-examination by Konop, Sister Phyllis Ann said she had no previous experience with ritual killings. She said she used that term when interviewed by detectives in 1980 and still felt it was accurate because Sister Margaret Ann's death had seemed "unnatural."

Sister Madeline Marie then took the stand and testified that she went to the chapel that morning to help Sister Margaret Ann prepare for the Holy Saturday services. When she entered the sacristy and saw the nun's body lying on the floor, her first impression was that someone had left a CPR mannequin in the room.

The room was dark and when she bent down to take a closer look, she realized that it was not a CPR dummy lying in front of her—but the body of her beloved friend and colleague.

"I was in there a matter of seconds. Then I ran out of the sacristy and screamed," she said.

The next two witnesses for the prosecution were detectives from the 1980 investigation, now retired.

Lieutenant William Kina, with a square jaw and swept-back gray hair, said he and Detective Arthur Marx searched Father Robinson's Mercy Hospital residence on April 18 and found the sword-shaped letter opener in the priest's desk drawer.

He said he and Marx interrogated Father Robinson at length on two successive nights, about two weeks after the murder, and that during the first night of intense questioning the priest claimed another person had confessed to him that he killed the nun. When asked to provide more details, the priest "admitted it was a lie," Lieutenant Kina testified.

The detective also said two Mercy employees in 1980 told him they had heard "frantic footsteps" around the time of the murder, running from the chapel down to the hallway where Father Robinson was the lone resident.

He said he personally interviewed between 150 and 200 people in the month-long investigation.

Because of the brutality of the murder, Lieutenant Kina said he believed the killer must have known Sister Margaret Ann.

"It would take someone with a vendetta to kill someone in such a ferocious manner," the lieutenant said.

On April 19, 1980, he said he and Detective Marx interrogated Father Robinson at the Safety Building. A few hours into what was expected to be an all-night affair, Marx left momentarily and Deputy Chief Ray Vetter knocked on the interrogation room door. The deputy chief entered the room, followed by Monsignor Jerome Schmit of the Toledo diocese and an attorney.

Deputy Chief Vetter asked Lieutenant Kina to leave the room, so he stepped outside, Kina testified. About five minutes later, Vetter walked out with the priest, the monsignor, and the attorney. The interrogation was over.

Konop challenged the accuracy of Lieutenant Kina's memory. Shouting angrily at the retired detective, pointing an accusatory finger, Konop asked if it was true that his testimony was based not on his own notes, but on "recall and reports supplied to you by the prosecutor's office?"

"That's true," Lieutenant Kina replied matter-of-factly, unfazed by the attorney's histrionics.

Josh Franks, a retired Toledo police criminalist with a quick and mischievous smile, testified that the letter opener was "sumptuously clean" when he first examined it. He used phenothaline to test for the possible presence of blood on the instrument, but the only place where he found a positive indication was on the back of a medallion that he had pried off. The test was only presumptive, he pointed out. There was not enough material there for a conclusive result.

Asked by assistant prosecutor Chris Anderson if he had conducted any DNA tests in 1980, Franks chuckled and said, "No DNA then. No e-mails, either."

Prosecutors then presented three witnesses who were involved in the 2003 and 2004 cold-case investigation—Detective Terry Cousino of the Toledo police Scientific Investigations Unit, Dr. Diane Barnett of the Lucas County coroner's office, and Julie Saul, a forensic anthropologist.

Detective Cousino, who had been an art major in college before entering police work, had investigated more than a thousand cases in a decade with SIU.

He testified that he noticed right away the similarities between the bloodstains on the altar cloth and the shape of the priest's letter opener. After conducting a series of tests, he recommended that investigators follow up by consulting with the top experts in bloodstain-pattern transfer analysis.

Detective Cousino then discussed the holes in the altar cloth, putting on a pair of surgical gloves and spreading the altar cloth out on the courtroom floor. Judge Osowik gave jurors permission to step down from the jury box to take a closer look at the altar cloth, and all sixteen got out of their seats and walked around the stained linen, bending down for a close-up view.

Detective Cousino said there were eighteen puncture marks in the altar cloth, and it was clear to him that the cloth had been folded over before any punctures were made. When he folded the cloth, he found that nine of the holes on one side lined up perfectly with nine holes on the other side.

"These puncture defects had definite form and symmetry," Cousino testified, using a laser pointer to outline the alignment of the holes shown in detail on the SMART Board™.

"A cross fit inside that form, as if a cross had been used as a template."

Displayed on the SMART Board™ was an image of a black cross fitting inside the puncture holes on the altar cloth.

The detective also noted that the holes in the cloth had a Y shape to them, indicating they were made by an instrument that did not have a flat blade. The punctures also showed that the instrument had pushed through the cloth, which meant the tip of the blade was not sharp enough to cut the cloth cleanly, Detective Cousino said.

"To me, this is a fairly unique blade," he said.

The shape of the holes and evidence that the instrument had a dull tip were consistent with Father Robinson's letter opener, he said.

Not knowing how many such letter openers had been manufactured, he said he looked everywhere to try to find one just like it. He searched online and found that there were Web sites devoted to letter-opener collectors. He searched through thousands of letter openers being auctioned online at eBay. He went to the library and examined dozens of books on letter openers.

"I could find nothing like this," he said, holding the priest's saber-shaped letter opener for the jury to see.

Detective Cousino said he attended the exhumation of Sister Margaret Ann Pahl's body on May 20, 2004, taking photographs of the procedure and riding back to the county coroner's office along with the nun's body in a transport van.

Dr. Diane Barnett, deputy Lucas County coroner, found several defects in the nun's bones, and used a power saw to remove a section of jawbone from the left side of the murder victim's face.

The deputy coroner also took the letter opener and inserted the tip into a container of modeling clay. The defect in the sister's mandible and the defect that the letter opener made in the clay appeared to be identical, Detective Cousino said. He showed the jury comparison photos of the defects in bone and clay.

On June 7, Cousino said he observed and photographed Dr. Barnett as she conducted a "fit test," inserting the tip of the letter opener into the hole in Sister Margaret Ann's jawbone.

Detective Cousino said Dr. Barnett used "extreme caution" during the procedure, and that the blade "did appear to fit very well" in the jawbone defect.

Chapter 56

When Dr. Diane Barnett took the stand, she brought a medical model of a life-size human throat with her to explain to jurors how Sister Margaret Ann Pahl's killer had strangled her with such force that he broke the two hyoid bones in her neck.

She said the nun, who was only five-feet-two inches tall, was choked from behind with a cloth, or "soft ligature," which the killer wrapped around her throat and pulled tight, leaving an indentation in her skin of the cross and necklace she wore as a reminder of Jesus' death and resurrection.

If the killer had strangled her with his hands, as Dr. Renate Fazekas had suggested in 1980 before doing the autopsy, it would not have left the impression of the complete necklace in the victim's skin, Dr. Barnett said. "That tells me something broader was used."

The deputy coroner said there was an abrasion on the nun's chin, as if she had lowered her jaw instinctively to try to protect her neck from the attacker.

She also noted that the thirty-one stab wounds were all three inches or less in depth. One of the wounds sliced Sister Margaret Ann's carotid artery, and three others breached her larynx and trachea, causing an air leak.

One stab wound went through the sternum and into the heart, puncturing the left ventricle.

Doctor Barnett said that about twenty-four ounces of blood collected inside the nun's chest cavity, which indicated that there was some blood pressure when she received the stab wounds. If her heart had not been beating, there would have been no blood in the chest.

Doctor Barnett displayed photos of the exhumed body, causing some jurors to gasp and cover their mouths in horror, shocked by the gruesome pictures.

Based on her review of the 1980 autopsy by Dr. Fazekas and the second autopsy she personally conducted after the exhumation, Dr. Barnett said Sister Margaret Ann Pahl died from a combination of strangulation and stab wounds.

Asked how long the nun could have survived such wounds, the deputy coroner said "not more than five or ten minutes."

She also noted that neither she nor Dr. Fazekas in 1980 found any defensive wounds whatsoever on Sister Margaret Ann's body.

Three witnesses who testified for the prosecution said they conducted DNA tests to try to find evidence linking Father Robinson with the crime, but they ended up finding nothing that proved helpful to the state.

After the expensive and time-consuming DNA testing process forced several continuations of the trial, the lab work ultimately ended up favoring the defense.

"No, we were not excited by the DNA results," assistant prosecutor Dean Mandros said after the trial. "Not only did we not get the suspect's DNA, but the evidence fit someone else's DNA."

Although the state was not relying on DNA evidence in its case against Father Robinson, prosecutors had no choice but to conduct genetics tests.

If prosecutors had not looked for DNA evidence, the priest's defense attorneys would have turned that around and used it against them, Mandros said.

"You know they would have said that 'the state could have proved a positive ID if it would have looked for DNA, but it did not,'" Mandros said.

The implication by the defense would be incompetency or conspiracy on the part of the prosecutors. "Our conducting DNA tests was more of a defensive posture, if you will," Mandros said.

Although the DNA samples found on the nun's underwear and on her fingernails excluded Father Robinson, Mandros said it was not a major concern to prosecutors. So many people had been in the sacristy after the murder that DNA contamination easily could have come from a number of sources, including anyone who entered the sacristy to try to save the nun's life and the police officers who searched for evidence.

Mandros said renowned forensics expert Dr. Henry Lee told him that he once conducted a test to see how easy it is for DNA to be transferred to an object. Doctor Lee said he bought a package of men's underwear from a department store, opened it in his laboratory, and tested for DNA evidence immediately—and he found some.

The state asked for a continuance, or delay, while it obtained DNA samples from every male who had been in the sacristy the day of the murder—more than twenty people—hoping to find a match with the DNA that had been found on the nun's nails and underwear. Even with the trial's delay, no DNA match was found. The only conclusive result was that the DNA did not come from Father Robinson.

On Wednesday, April 26, the state called T. Paulette Sutton, one of five people certified in the field of bloodstain-pattern transfer analysis.

Sutton testified for an hour and forty minutes, showing photographs on the SMART Board™ and using diagrams and charts to illustrate consistencies between the bloodstains and puncture marks on the altar cloth, and the size, shape, and details of Father Robinson's sword-shaped letter opener.

"Bloodstain-pattern transfers are sort of like a rubber stamp. You put ink on the stamp and press it, and it leaves an impression. It's the same thing," Sutton told jurors.

She explained to the jury that she conducted laboratory tests on the "dagger"—the term she used for the letter opener until defense attorney Thebes objected.

Sutton said she covered the letter opener in "stretchy" plastic, soaked it in stage blood, then used it to create stains by placing the instrument on a piece of linen that had the same texture and color as the altar cloth.

The stains made in the laboratory on the piece of test cloth were consistent with the stains found on the altar cloth from the actual crime scene, she concluded.

One of the most dramatic visuals in the courtroom came when Sutton made a "rubbing" of the circular medallion that had been pried off the letter opener.

She then displayed an image of the rubbing on the SMART Board™, next to a small circular bloodstain that was on the altar cloth.

Sutton took an image from the rubbing of the medallion and an image of the circular bloodstain on the altar cloth, magnified them equally, and then superimposed one image on top of the other. She showed the jury that there were six points where the U.S. Capitol on the medallion aligned perfectly with the geometric bloodstains on the altar cloth.

Thebes, in cross-examining Sutton, questioned the reliability of bloodstain-pattern transfer analysis, saying that unlike DNA science, which is quantifiable and consistent from one expert to the next, bloodstain-pattern analysis is a subjective field in which bloodstains and weapons are measured, but then conclusions ultimately are based on a person's judgment and opinion.

"We are not going to get an absolute answer with bloodstain-pattern transfer analysis," Thebes said.

Doctor Steven Symes, a forensic anthropologist from Mercyhurst College specializing in sharp-force trauma, followed Sutton by telling jurors how he made casts and molds of the letter opener and the defect in Sister Margaret Ann's jawbone.

He tested the models to see how they fit and concluded that the wound was made by an instrument consistent with Father Robinson's letter opener.

World-renowned forensic investigator Dr. Henry Lee testified on April 27, the fifth day of the murder trial, and corroborated in his unique, charismatic style the conclusions that Paulette Sutton had reached independently.

Doctor Lee displayed images of the altar cloth's bloodstains on the SMART Board™, and illustrated the similarities between the details in the bloodstains and physical characteristics of the letter opener, including its ribbed handle, the curved blade and knuckle guard, and an acorn-shaped knob on the handle.

Wearing a dark blue suit and a pale yellow tie, Dr. Lee flashed an occasional smile and explained his analyses to the jury with the patience and thoroughness of a college professor.

The Taiwan-born investigator, who had investigated more than six thousand cases over forty years, joked that when members of the Toledo cold-case squad first approached him to ask if he would review the evidence, one of the men was Gary Cook, then an assistant prosecutor, but he could not remember who the other man was because "all Caucasians look alike."

Robert Wodarski, a night-shift security officer at Mercy, said he was making his last round through the hospital when he walked past the chapel around 6:50 or 6:55 a.m. and noticed that the doors were open and the lights were on.

Wardell Langston Jr., a maintenance worker, was cleaning the lobby floor when he heard loud footsteps on the open balcony overhead, coming from the direction of the chapel and running down the hallway where Father Robinson lived. The footsteps were so rapid and loud that he felt fearful, he said.

Under cross-examination by defense attorney Alan Konop, Langston said he wasn't sure if the footsteps went all the way to the end of the hallway, by the priest's apartment door, or if they had stopped much earlier.

Shirley Ann Lucas, the housekeeper who cleaned the nuns' convent three times a week, testified that Sister Margaret Ann Pahl was visibly upset after Good Friday services.

The nun left a note on the convent door asking the housekeeper to come down to the chapel. Sister Margaret Ann then pinned a key to the convent door in Lucas's pocket, "so I wouldn't lose it," she said.

It was the only time the nun did not personally open the door to let Lucas into the convent.

"She took my hand and wished me and my two daughters an Easter blessing and peace," Lucas testified. Then, fighting back tears, Sister Margaret Ann squeezed the housekeeper's hand tightly and said, "Why do they cheat God from what belongs to Him?"

Father Jeffrey Grob, a Roman Catholic priest and ritual expert from Chicago, testified that he saw numerous significant religious symbols and imagery at the murder scene indicating a ritual killing. He cited the timing of the slaying on Holy Saturday and the stabbing in the shape of an inverted cross as evidence that Sister Margaret Ann was killed as part of a ritual.

Jurors then watched a ninety-minute video of Father Robinson being interrogated by Investigator Tom Ross on the day of the priest's arrest, April 23, 2004. During the interrogation, the priest paused awkwardly several times before responding to simple questions about whether he had a key to the sacristy and whether he locked his residence. Father Robinson contradicted himself a number of times during the interrogation.

At the end of the video, Investigator Ross left the room momentarily. Father Robinson buried his face in his hands and sighed. Unaware the camera was rolling, he whispered loudly, "Oh my Jesus!" Then he uttered a few sentences that were not very clear.

On Thursday, May 4, the prosecution called eight witnesses to the stand to wrap up its case.

Three witnesses who had been working at Mercy Hospital at the time of the murder testified that they saw Father Robinson near the chapel around the time of the murder.

Doctor Jack Baron, lab worker Grace Jones, and EKG technician Leslie Ann Kerner all spoke confidently and in detail of seeing Father Robinson that fateful morning. Their testimony directly and dramatically contradicted Father Robinson's assertions to police in 1980 and again in 2004 that he had been in his residence at Mercy Hospital the entire morning, not leaving until Sister Phyllis Ann called to tell him about the slaying.

Jones, an African-American woman in a wheelchair, with a Southern accent and a speech impediment, said she had tried to tell police in 1980 about seeing Father Robinson walk out of the chapel carrying a duffel bag, but no one would listen. When she heard in April 2004 that the priest had been arrested for murder, she testified that her response was, "Thank you, Jesus!"

Doctor Baron said that when he told detectives during the original investigation that he had seen a priest near the chapel, "they seemed to jump right to the next question. I figured they already knew about it. But it always kind of bothered me."

Kerner, under cross-examination by Konop, had no good explanation for why she waited eighteen months to call the prosecutor's office after seeing Father Robinson's arrest reported on *Good Morning America* in April 2004.

Investigator Tom Ross of the Lucas County cold-case team explained how he and Sergeant Forrester first reopened the case in December 2003, making some preliminary connections between the bloodstained altar cloth and the letter opener, after which they sought the advice of a number of experts.

All of the experts said they found consistencies between the priest's letter opener and the stains on the altar cloth, Detective Ross testified.

On April 23, 2004, when Detective Ross interviewed Father Robinson at the priest's home, and then at the police station, the veteran investigator said there were a number of "internal inconsistencies" in the priest's responses—including what he was doing when he got the phone call saying that Sister Margaret Ann Pahl had been killed, whether he ran or walked to the sacristy, and whether or not he had a key to his residence.

After investigating Father Robinson for five months and finding every lead pointing to him as the murderer, the priest said nothing during the interview to change the detectives' minds.

Under cross-examination, Konop used a VCR to replay the part of the interview where Father Robinson was left alone in the interrogation room and began whispering.

The defense team had hired an audio expert to enhance a brief section of the tape. After fumbling to hit the right buttons, the audiotape began playing. Jurors leaned forward, listening attentively, as Father Robinson whispered "Sister . . ."

The rest of the priest's words were indistinct. Thebes said afterward that he believed Father Robinson had said: "Sister, please come back and tell them I didn't do it." But the only ones who thought they heard those words were Father Robinson's defense attorneys. To the rest of the courtroom, even the enhanced audio was only a vague mumble.

Chapter 58

While the prosecution called thirty witnesses to the stand over eight days of testimony, the defense attorneys called a dozen people in two days.

On the first day, the defense called five detectives, starting with Sergeant Steve Forrester of the Toledo police department and the county cold-case unit.

Konop, peering through glasses perched on the edge of his nose, zeroed in on a number of inconsistencies and omissions from the voluminous 1980 and 2003 police reports.

In the 1980 police interviews with Dr. Baron, for example, Konop pointed out to Sergeant Forrester that there was no mention of the medical intern making a wrong turn. The sergeant acknowledged that was true, and also that there was nothing in the 1980 report about the priest giving the doctor a "stare" when they passed in the hallway, as Dr. Baron had testified in court.

Konop also questioned the time frame around Grace Jones's testimony, saying that the witness said she went to get the newspaper sometime after 7:00 a.m. and afterward saw Father Robinson walk out of the chapel. But she gave widely varying times to different officers about when she saw the priest, ranging from 7:15 to 8:15.

Konop also grilled Sergeant Forrester on Jones's uncertainty over whether Father Robinson had walked through the exit doors or turned the corner and walked down a different hallway.

"Initially, she said he'd gone out the Madison Street door!" Konop said, his voice raised angrily. "Initially, that's what she said!"

Konop continued: "Father Robinson is charged with murder, is that correct? Isn't it vitally important to be as accurate as possible?"

"You've asked me that question a lot," Sergeant Forrester said. "And I've answered it a lot. I try to be as accurate as I can."

"Leslie Sue Kerner," Konop said. "She said she contacted you in the spring of '04. Any problem with that?"

"I don't think you'd lie to me," the sergeant replied, straight-faced but causing chuckles among some jurors.

209

Sergeant Forrester was excused after fifty minutes on the stand and Konop continued similar lines of questioning with retired detectives Dan Foster and Dave Weinbrecht, hammering away at any inconsistencies or discrepancies in the police reports from twenty-six years ago.

Detective Weinbrecht was asked about a pair of scissors that were reported missing from the sacristy after the murder, and how Dr. Renate Fazekas, the deputy coroner at the time, said some of the wounds in Sister Margaret Ann Pahl's body could have been made by scissors.

Detective Weinbrecht pointed out, however, that Dr. Fazekas also wrote in the autopsy that the wounds in the victim's face had to have been made by a weapon sharper than scissors.

He said he did not interview Father Robinson in 1980, but that by all accounts the priest appeared to be "a meek and mild type of individual" who hardly spoke except when directly asked a question.

Detective Weinbrecht said he conducted a second search of Father Robinson's hospital apartment, three days after detectives Arthur Marx and William Kina had seized the letter opener.

He testified that he confiscated a pair of shoes with rubber soles, a bottle of Valium issued by the hospital pharmacy on the day of the murder, and a priest's cassock with a stain that, after testing, turned out to be gravy.

Konop challenged the detective over the results of a "footsteps test" he had conducted in 1980, seeking to determine if the shoes that were seized from the priest's residence could have been the ones that made the "frantic footsteps" two hospital workers had heard the morning of the murder.

For the test, Detective Weinbrecht had two detectives, one wearing shoes with hard leather soles and the other with soft rubber soles, run along the path, and had the two employees determine which shoes sounded like the footsteps they had heard on April 5. The results were inconclusive.

Arthur Marx, the detective in charge of the 1980 investigation, was on the witness stand for two and a half hours under questioning by Konop and cross-examination by prosecutors.

Konop asked Detective Marx about the missing police reports from his two interrogations of Father Robinson in 1980. He testified that he is certain he took notes, but he does not know what happened to them.

"I have no idea, I can't tell you," Marx said. "It's been twenty-six years."

"And you said you wrote a report?"

"I know I did," Marx replied.

Under questioning by Konop, Detective Marx said he does not recall any of the details of the interview except for one statement by Father Robinson—that another person had confessed to him that he killed the nun.

"Out of all those hours, just that one little statement?" Konop asked.

Under cross-examination by assistant prosecutor Dean Mandros, Detective Marx said that Father Robinson told him on April 18, 1980, that, two days previously, someone had confessed to him that he had killed Sister Margaret Ann Pahl.

"How did you answer?" Mandros asked.

"I was shocked," Detective Marx said. "I told him I was a Catholic, I was raised Catholic, and I did not believe that. That's something [a priest] would never share, that he would take to the grave."

Konop blasted the retired detective for not looking for trace evidence—hairs, fibers, fingerprints, or blood—in the priest's apartment, the doors of the sacristy, furniture in the sacristy, the window ledge in the room, or the hallway where the footsteps had been heard.

The defense attorney also asked Detective Marx why he did not call the police crime lab and have technicians come to the murder scene and look for clues using chemicals.

"I don't even know if we had chemicals in 1980," Detective Marx said.

"This is an important case. Call someone up!" Konop shouted. "You did have telephones in 1980, didn't you?"

On Monday, May 8, the final day of testimony, defense attorneys called seven witnesses—three former police officers, two DNA experts, a sound engineer, and nationally known forensic anthropologist and best-selling *Bones* author Dr. Kathleen Reichs.

Ray Vetter, the 82-year-old former deputy police chief, testified that he never let his Catholic faith interfere with police work despite persistent rumors and allegations that he had helped cover up for Father Robinson in 1980.

"My job came first," he said on the witness stand.

He testified that he asked his friend, the cleric and Toledo power broker Monsignor Schmit, for a favor by asking him to talk to Father Robinson and see what he could find out, then report back to him.

Deputy Chief Vetter said he didn't recall interrupting a police interrogation of the priest on April 19, 1980, as several police officers had testified.

During the initial investigation, he said, it didn't take long before police zeroed in on Father Robinson as the only suspect in Sister Margaret Ann's murder. But after consulting with the prosecutor's office, officials concluded that there was insufficient evidence to convict the priest. And without enough evidence for a conviction, there was no point in arresting him, Vetter said.

The deputy chief said it was standard procedure not to mention anything about suspects to the media, and that the department was not covering up the fact that Father Robinson was the prime suspect.

"We never discuss suspicions with the news media, only facts," he said.

If news got out that someone was a suspect, it could tip the person off and he or she could flee the state or destroy evidence, Deputy Chief Vetter told the *Blade* before the trial.

During cross-examination, the state produced a letter that Father Ray Fisher had written to Bishop John Donovan—a letter that was among the 148 documents investigators seized from the Catholic Center's archives after executing a search warrant.

Portions of Father Fisher's letter that were read in court stated that Deputy

Chief Vetter had assured Father Fisher that no one in the police department was talking about Father Robinson as a suspect in the nun's murder. But he wrote that Father Swiatecki apparently was talking about Father Robinson to hospital personnel.

Konop questioned the deputy chief about the letter.

"Did you do anything to try to protect Father Robinson?" Konop asked.

"No," Vetter replied.

The deputy chief said he did not recall saying anything about Father Swiatecki telling hospital personnel that Father Robinson was a suspect. He also asserted that he did not recall interrupting a police interrogation of Father Robinson.

"As I said, it was twenty-six years ago," Vetter said.

"It wasn't a Catholic investigation?" Konop asked.

"It was a police investigation of a murder," Vetter replied.

Daniel Davison, a forensic investigator with the Ohio Bureau of Criminal Investigation and Identification, testified that he examined a hair found the day of the murder by police technician Ed Marok on a door in a hallway around the corner from the chapel.

Davison said the hair in question could not have come from Father Robinson because it was a blonde pubic hair.

Meghan Clement, technical director of North Carolina-based LabCorp, testified that she had conducted DNA tests on clippings from Sister Margaret Ann Pahl's fingernails. She said the only DNA found in those tests was from a male, and that it could not have been from Father Robinson.

Under cross-examination, assistant prosecutor Chris Anderson questioned Clement about how DNA can be transferred through casual contact—that someone's DNA could be transferred to another person through a handshake or a sneeze. He questioned whether the DNA on the nun's fingernails could have been deposited by any number of people, from medical personnel to coroner's office officials.

Doctor Kathleen Reichs, the businesslike forensic anthropologist best known for writing crime novels that inspired the Fox TV show *Bones*, took the stand wearing a yellow suit that was just a shade paler than her shoulder-length blonde hair.

Doctor Reichs said there were sixty-five board-certified forensic anthropologists in the world, and that setting standards had become a necessity because of the popularity of the *CSI* television programs and other dramas, books, and movies about forensics.

"Who's really an expert?" she said. "Because we're very popular now. We're really hot. We're on all the airwaves, TV, radio, and books. And a lot of people are calling themselves forensic anthropologists. By establishing board certification, we are policing ourselves, setting standards."

Doctor Reichs, who earned her Ph.D. in physical anthropology from Northwestern University, said she examined photographs and reports from 1980 and 2004 that were provided by the prosecutor's office and by forensic anthropologist Dr. Steven Symes.

She disputed the coroner's office's contention that it had conducted a "fit test" with the letter opener and the nun's mandible only on June 7—after the nun's bones had been cleaned of soft tissue.

Photographs clearly showed tests being conducted on uncleaned bone, Dr. Reichs testified.

"What is the effect of inserting an object into a defect before it was cleaned?" defense attorney John Thebes asked her.

"I would never do that," Dr. Reichs replied, "because of the potential for damage to the defect. There could be modification of the edges of the defect."

In particular, she said, the risk of contaminating such evidence was greater with bones that have become fragile with age. Sister Margaret Ann Pahl was killed a day before her seventy-second birthday.

Chris Anderson, cross-examining Dr. Reichs, asked whether it was unusual for her to testify in court based on reviews of photographs and reports, and not on direct examination of the physical evidence. She acknowledged that it was the first time she had done so.

The final witness that day was retired Toledo Police Lieutenant William Kina, who was called as a rebuttal witness.

Lieutenant Kina said that during the 1980 investigation, Deputy Chief Ray Vetter ordered all three copies of police reports about the nun's murder to be sent to his office.

The lieutenant said he had worked for Vetter for sixteen years and that the deputy chief kept a locked cabinet in his office that contained sensitive police files.

"He would lock all three copies in there to keep down the rumor mill," Kina testified.

Years later, Lieutenant Kina said, he met up with Vetter at a fiftieth wedding anniversary of a retired policeman.

"[Vetter] asked me what the nun's name was. He said he could never remember her name," Lieutenant Kina testified. "He said it was 'the biggest mistake of my life.' Then he turned and walked away."

After Lieutenant Kina was excused, Judge Osowik told jurors that "we are done with testimony."

He said the prosecution may present a rebuttal witness, but it would be "extraordinarily brief."

The closing arguments were scheduled for Wednesday, May 10, after which the jurors would begin deliberating on a verdict.

Chapter 59

The trial in Judge Osowik's courtroom resumed the morning of Wednesday, May 10, with the state calling two rebuttal witnesses, Dr. Diane Barnett and Julie Saul.

The prosecution's questioning of Dr. Barnett and Saul was aimed at challenging the testimony of Dr. Kathleen Reichs, the defense's expert witness who had asserted that coroner's officials could have contaminated the evidence when they inserted the letter opener into a defect in the nun's jawbone.

Doctor Barnett, who had been deputy Lucas County coroner for twenty-one years, said the victim's jawbone was "so hard, I could not remove it without a power saw. . . . This is not a fragile bone."

She conducted fit tests "fifty or sixty times" previously in her career, she said, and she was certain that the test on Sister Margaret Ann Pahl's mandible "in no way" altered the defect.

"In my way of thinking, Dr. Reichs presumed that I may have altered the defect. Scientists don't presume. They test," Dr. Barnett said crisply.

Chris Anderson, assistant county prosecutor, also asked Dr. Barnett if the wounds in Sister Margaret Ann's body could have been caused by scissors.

Doctor Barnett said she was certain that scissors could not have caused the wounds. The "wound pattern" of scissors was different than that of the letter opener belonging to Father Robinson, she said.

She then took two containers of modeling clay, one green and one yellow, and demonstrated the different patterns the instruments made by inserting the tip of the scissors into one container, and the tip of the letter opener into the other. She then passed the containers around to jurors, as close-ups of the actual wounds in Sister Margaret Ann's body were displayed on the SMART Board™.

When Saul took the stand, she also asserted that the mandible was a "very dense" bone that could not have been damaged by the carefully conducted fit test.

Anderson asked Saul if a forensic anthropologist could reach an authoritative conclusion by examining photographs and reports, but not examining the bones themselves.

"How important is it for a forensic anthropologist to review the bone?" Anderson asked.

"Very important," Saul replied. "Bones are three-dimensional. You have to study them from all different angles. It's very, very important to do this in person." She acknowledged that she had made a mistake in her previous testimony by not specifying which bones she had cleaned and how she had cleaned them. She said the nun's mandible was cleaned by rubbing away the soft tissue, and that the victim's neck vertebrae were cleaned by using a chemical.

After less than an hour of testimony from the rebuttal witnesses, Judge Osowik ordered a short recess before closing arguments.

As on the opening day of the murder trial, the courtroom was completely packed. All forty-five seats in the gallery were filled by members of the media, local attorneys and judges, relatives of the defense and prosecuting attorneys, friends and relatives of Father Robinson, representatives from the Sisters of Mercy, and a few seats for the general public. The bench behind the attorneys' tables was jammed with court officials, judges, attorneys, and local law-enforcement officials.

The bailiff gave her familiar shouts of "all rise," first for Judge Thomas Osowik and then for the jury.

The crowded courtroom turned silent as Dean Mandros, in a dark suit and striped tie, strode to a spot in front of the jury and began a carefully rehearsed closing argument that lasted nearly an hour—fifty-nine minutes, to be exact.

"This is not a case that can be tried without talking about God and religion," Mandros said. "After all, we have a Roman Catholic priest as the defendant, and a Roman Catholic nun is the victim. So whether you believe in God or providence or destiny or fate, it may be that this is a case that had to wait twenty-six years before it could be fairly tried.

"It's doubtful that in 1980 we could have gotten twelve people such as your-self who would sit here and say, 'Yes, I believe that a Roman Catholic [priest] could kill someone.'

"So whether you call it fate, or what have you, it just may be that we had to wait until 2006 for you to decide this case," Mandros said.

Although twenty-six years had passed, and some memories had faded, people remember important moments, like their first car or their senior prom, he said.

"Would you remember the day a nun was killed in your workplace? Maybe not every detail, but you'd remember the significant ones," Mandros said.

Although the state was not obligated to prove a motive, Mandros said he was going to describe one possible explanation for why the priest committed the mur-der. If the jurors agreed with the possible motive, it might prove helpful in their deliberations, he said. If they did not find it plausible, they were free to ignore it.

Father Jeffrey Grob, a Catholic priest with expertise in rituals, had testified that he found multiple signs that Sister Margaret Ann had been the victim of a satanic ritual slaying, but Mandros said he did not believe the nun was killed in a Black Mass or an occult slaying.

It was a much more ordinary motive, he said.

"This case is about perhaps the most common scenario there is for a homicide: A man got very angry at a woman, and the woman died. The only thing different is that the man wore a white collar and the woman wore a habit."

He said Father Robinson was an angry man—mad at God and mad at the church and mad at the world. He had problems with Sister Margaret Ann, whom he had described to police as a "dominant" woman. Priests were supposed to be higher up the ladder when it came to rank and power, but at Mercy Hospital, the relationship was reversed, and Father Robinson resented it.

Mandros quoted a comment by Father Robinson from a 2004 interrogation that had been shown in court: "It was their hospital," he said, referring to the nuns. "I just worked there."

He said the priest was tired of working at a hospital and having to deal with sick patients and worried families and giving last rites on a regular basis.

Father Robinson had confided to a colleague that he wanted to work as a military chaplain, but that request had been denied.

Sister Margaret Ann, meanwhile, had been upset to the point of tears over the way that Good Friday services had been cut short, Mandros said, and "less than 18 hours later, she was found butchered on the sacristy floor. He had had enough. He had taken a lot, but he wasn't going to take any more."

The assistant prosecutor then carefully reviewed the weeks of courtroom testimony, piecing together the pieces of the puzzle that the state said would show that Father Robinson was the killer.

"Now, if you don't think he's the murderer, then you believe an amazing series of coincidences," Mandros told the jurors.

For one example, he said, could it have been a coincidence that the bloodstains on the altar cloth just happened to match the shape and size of the priest's letter opener, according to testimony from two of the five experts in bloodstain-pattern transfer analysis?

And if the letter opener was the murder weapon, could someone else have used it to frame Father Robinson, Mandros asked. If that was the case, why would they wipe it clean and return it to the priest's residence, rather than taking off rubber gloves and leaving it, soaked in blood, at the crime scene?

Were the three witnesses who testified that they had seen the priest by the chapel around the time of the murder telling the truth, or were they all having the same hallucination, Mandros asked.

Or maybe they flew in from Texas and Missouri to frame the priest because "they had nothing better to do," he said.

"If you believe what they say, you know who went into that chapel. You know who killed Sister Margaret Ann Pahl," Mandros told the jurors.

He said Father Robinson was not satisfied by just murdering his victim, he wanted to humiliate and mock her as well.

That's why, after strangling her to the verge of death, he stabbed her with his saber-shaped letter opener nine times over the heart, in the shape of an upside down cross.

And that's why he killed her in the sacristy on one of only two days a year when the Blessed Sacrament—the body of Christ—was kept in that room.

He said the priest stabbed the nun another twenty-two times because he wanted to draw enough blood to soak his dagger and "anoint" his victim's forehead.

According to the 1980 autopsy, Father Robinson's final act of defilement was to pull Sister Margaret Ann's underwear down around her ankles and then penetrate the virginal nun with his letter opener, a crucifix, or a finger, Mandros said.

"Then he stands up and looks at his work," he said. "What is it that he's left on the floor? He's left a message. A message to Sister Margaret Ann Pahl? To be sure. Maybe to the church. Maybe to God himself: 'See how angry I am? See what you made me do? This is how angry I am.' He left a message for everyone to see."

The eerie silence in the courtroom was broken when Alan Konop stood to begin the defense's closing arguments. But after thanking the jury, in a raspy voice, for their time and attention, Konop's voice was too weak and he was forced to turn things over to Thebes.

"Father Robinson is not guilty. He's not guilty," said Thebes, speaking slowly and passionately, "because the state of Ohio has not proven to you beyond a reasonable doubt that this letter opener is the murder weapon.

"Their whole prosecution is premised on that fact. They need to show to you beyond a reasonable doubt that that's the murder weapon. If they cannot do it, ladies and gentlemen, the ballgame's over."

In his forty-five-minute closing, Thebes asserted that cold-case investigators were never interested in pursuing justice, they were only interested in arresting Father Robinson.

He then focused on a number of points raised during testimony that the defense felt were sufficient to raise reasonable doubt.

The missing pair of scissors, he said, fit the pattern of the wounds in the nun's body.

The circular bloodstain that Dr. Henry Lee and Paulette Sutton said was made by the U.S. Capitol on the letter opener's medallion could have been made by a nickel, Thebes said.

He questioned whether Dr. Diane Barnett and Julie Saul, both witnesses for the prosecution, were qualified to speak on the trauma to Sister Margaret Ann Pahl's bones, since neither of them was a board-certified forensic anthropologist, as was the defense's expert witness, Dr. Kathleen Reichs.

Thebes, pacing slowly around the courtroom as he spoke, described the field of blood-transfer pattern analysis as a "subjective" science that hinges on an individual's judgment, not on objective, quantifiable data. And he pointed out that DNA evidence in this case—taken from the nun's fingernails and underwear—excluded Father Robinson as a possible contributor.

If he were guilty, the prosecutors would have found Father Robinson's DNA at the crime scene.

"That's what killers do, they leave their DNA," Thebes said.

After the judge ordered a recess for lunch, Chris Anderson resumed the state's closing arguments by reviewing in depth the DNA and scientific evidence that had been presented in courtroom testimony.

He downplayed the significance of DNA results from the 1980 murder, saying that it proved nothing because police in that era did not take steps to protect the evidence from contamination.

With a sly smile, Anderson, an avid coin collector, told jurors that they should think twice about accepting any nickels from Mr. Thebes, because the building on the back of that coin is Thomas Jefferson's home at Monticello, not the U.S. Capitol. His warning brought a rare burst of laughter from jurors and the gallery on an otherwise somber day in court.

With a 1980 photograph of Father Robinson displayed on the SMART Board™, Anderson told jurors that "the state of Ohio is not asking you to convict a 68-year-old man, it is asking you to convict a 42-year-old man, 26 years later."

There are laws of man, and there are laws of God, he said.

"Based upon the laws of God, Robinson may be judged at a later date," Anderson said. "Based upon man's laws, the State of Ohio has proved this case beyond a reasonable doubt."

Chapter 60

Judge Thomas Osowik, after nearly three hours of closing arguments, moved straight to the jury instructions. The lengthy document included a detailed explanation of one of the most important elements of the trial: how the court defines "reasonable doubt."

"Members of the jury, you have heard the evidence and the arguments of counsel," he said.

The jurors' function, he told them, was "to decide the disputed facts."

The defendant pleaded not guilty and is "presumed innocent until his guilt is established beyond a reasonable doubt," the judge said.

Reasonable doubt is present "when, after you have carefully considered and compared all the evidence, you cannot say you are firmly convinced of the truth of the charge. Reasonable doubt is a doubt based on reason and common sense. Reasonable doubt is not mere possible doubt, because everything relating to human affairs or depending on moral evidence is open to some possible or imaginary doubt. Proof beyond a reasonable doubt is proof of such character that an ordinary person would be willing to rely and act upon it in the most important of his or her own affairs."

The judge also explained the difference between direct and circumstantial evidence.

"Direct evidence is the testimony given by a witness who has seen or heard the facts to which he or she testifies and includes exhibits admitted into evidence," Judge Osowik said. "Circumstantial evidence is the proof of facts or circumstances by direct evidence from which you may reasonably infer other related or connected facts which naturally and logically follow, according to the common experience of mankind."

He pointed out that in a court of law, "direct evidence and circumstantial evidence are of equal weight."

Judge Osowik, speaking swiftly and clearly, explained that jurors were not obligated to believe every witness who testifies under oath, but that they should rely on their own judgment in determining the person's credibility.

He also told them that Father Robinson, as with all defendants in criminal court, had a constitutional right not to testify.

"It is not necessary that the defendant take the witness stand in his own defense. . . . The fact that he, the defendant, did not testify must not be considered for any purpose," Judge Osowik said.

He reminded them that proof of motive is not required for a conviction, and he also reminded the jurors that they were not to consider the punishment in the case, only whether they believed the priest was guilty or not guilty.

The more than two hundred items of evidence introduced in court would be available for their review during deliberations, the judge said.

He told the panelists to select a foreperson and, when all twelve jurors agreed upon a verdict, to notify the bailiff by knocking on the door.

At 3:37 p.m., the alternates were excused and the twelve jurors, stern-faced with the serious decision set before them, stepped down from the jury box, walked across the courtroom, past the prosecutors' and defense's tables, staring straight ahead all the while, and walked through the door into the jury room.

The jurors were given a short break for refreshments, taking an elevator to the basement of the courthouse to a small snack bar in the center of the floor, then returned to the jury room shortly before 4:00 p.m.

Within ten minutes, the jury sent a note to the judge requesting a list of all the witnesses who had testified during the three-week trial. A few hours later, they asked for a DVD player to play the video of the 2004 interrogation of Father Robinson that had been shown in court.

Father Robinson, meanwhile, hosted a gathering of friends and relatives in his west Toledo home that night.

A little before 8:00 p.m., the jurors filed back into a mostly empty courtroom, where Judge Osowik reminded them not to talk to anyone about the case, not to read the newspapers, watch TV, or check the Internet for news, and to be back in the courtroom at 9:00 the next morning to resume deliberations.

John Alleva, a Court TV producer and New York attorney, watched the jurors as they exited the courtroom. "They're close to a verdict," he told a reporter. "Just look at their faces. They're all so serious—like they have the weight of the world on them."

Chapter 61

On Thursday morning, May 11, the weeks of sunny, mild spring weather gave way to dark clouds and high temperatures dipping into the fifties.

A few days earlier, Jean Atkin, administrator of the Lucas County common pleas court, had met with media representatives to discuss procedures once the jury had reached its verdict.

Court bailiff Tanya Butler would be responsible for notifying Judge Osowik, the attorneys for the state and the defense, the court administrator, and court deputies.

Atkin would then notify the media by e-mail and phone.

All parties would have thirty minutes to get to the courtroom, where the judge would read the verdict and poll the jurors individually.

Around 11:00 a.m. Thursday, as lawyers and reporters who had been involved in the case went about their daily routines, keeping one eye on the courthouse, phones began to ring and Atkin sent an e-mail to the press at 11:02 a.m.

"The jury has reached a verdict in the matter of State of Ohio v. Gerald Robinson. The verdict will be announced at 11:30 a.m."

The announcement hit like a tornado. Virtually no one—aside from Court TV's Alleva—had expected such a quick decision. Lawyers, reporters, photographers, deputies—the entire courtroom community that had sprung up around the Father Robinson trial—dropped everything and raced to the courthouse.

Father Robinson, dressed as always in his clerical collar, walked briskly to the courthouse escorted by Alan Konop and John Thebes as TV crews and news photographers raced ahead of him, some running backwards as they pointed their cameras in his face.

The priest stopped briefly at the courthouse security entrance, putting his wallet and rosary beads in a tray and then walking through the metal detector.

Dean Mandros, striding up the stairs from his second-floor office, admitted to being slightly nervous about the fast verdict. "We either presented a very underwhelming case, or a very overwhelming one," he said.

Inside Courtroom 5, every seat was quickly filled and the room was smolder-ing with tension. Among those who had hurried to take their seats in the gallery were Father Robinson's brother Tom and sister-in-law Barbara, and the priest's closest friends, Father Bernard Boff and Gary and Kathy Glowski.

Missing was Lee Pahl, the 53-year-old nephew of Sister Margaret Ann Pahl who had been in the front row for most of the trial. But Lee lived in Edgerton, the nun's hometown, more than an hour's drive west of Toledo—too far to get to the courthouse for the surprisingly quick verdict.

A court deputy warned those in the audience to control themselves when the verdict was read—whichever way the jury decided—or they could be arrested for contempt of court.

Court bailiff Tanya Butler once again announced "all rise" for Judge Osowik, that court was now in session, and then ordered the courtroom to rise once again for the jury.

The jurors entered through the same door as usual, walking across the court-room to their seats in the jury box. Only this time, the first few jurors did not just look straight ahead as they walked past Father Robinson, they turned their heads away from the defendant, toward the judge.

The judge told everyone to be seated, then asked the bailiff for the verdict form.

"We, the jury—will the defendant rise," Judge Osowik said, "find the defen-dant guilty of murder."

A loud gasp rose from the gallery, followed by a brief and strained silence. The world seemed to freeze in place, like a missed heartbeat.

Father Robinson's four attorneys dropped their heads forward, ever so slightly, as the priest stood still, staring straight ahead, blinking a few times but showing no emotion.

"I'm going to poll the jury now," Judge Osowik announced, and then called each juror by name, individually.

"Is this your signature and does this reflect your verdict?"

All twelve replied yes, and yes.

"Anything from counsel? Does the defendant wish to say anything?"

A quiet, "No, your honor."

Barbara Robinson, the priest's sister-in-law, was trying to stifle her sobs, her chest heaving, the tears flowing down her cheeks.

Judge Osowik continued to methodically and efficiently follow procedure. He recited the relevant Ohio Revised Code and immediately sentenced Father Robinson to fifteen years to life in prison.

Court deputy Bob Dietrich, meanwhile, had walked around the table and stood behind the priest. He quietly slipped a pair of handcuffs over the cleric's wrists.

"All right," Judge Osowik said, "anything further from defense?"

"No, your honor."

"Anything further from the state?"

"No, judge."

Father Robinson, hands cuffed behind his back, was escorted past the gallery, through the courtroom's wood-and-frosted-glass doors, and into a waiting elevator. Deputies rode with him to the sub-basement, where an underground tunnel connects to the Lucas County jail.

The courtroom felt as if all the air had been suddenly sucked out of it. Everything happened so fast.

Sister Margaret Ann's murder, after going unsolved for twenty-six years, was now case closed. In an instant, her killer was convicted, sentenced, handcuffed, and taken to jail. From the time Judge Osowik was handed the verdict form to the moment the elevator doors closed on Father Robinson, a total of four minutes had elapsed.

As the courtroom began emptying out, with a mix of people carefully controlling their extreme feelings of joy or despair, Atkin announced that a press conference would be held in the first-floor jury assembly room.

The three assistant county prosecutors who tried the case—Kiroff, Anderson and Mandros—walked out of the courtroom and into the lobby, where a small crowd of students burst into applause. Mandros shook his head sternly and waved a hand, bringing the clapping to an immediate halt.

Later, he told a reporter that the applause was inappropriate.

"I don't see it as a reason to celebrate," he said. "We're dealing with a homicide case. We're trying to hold the person responsible accountable. We didn't go back in the office and high-five each other."

Barbara Robinson, the priest's sister-in-law, sidled out of the gallery's second row and paused in front of Claudia Vercellotti, the SNAP leader. "I hope you rot in hell," Mrs. Robinson said through clenched teeth. Vercellotti, stunned, did not say a word but wiped a tear from her eye.

In her emotional distress, the priest's sister-in-law apparently blamed Father Robinson's conviction on Vercellotti who, along with psychologist Dr. Robert Cooley, had taken Sister Mary Curtiss's allegations to the Ohio attorney general's office in 2003. Contacted at home later that day, Mrs. Robinson declined to comment on the verdict or on her statement to Vercellotti.

Chapter 62

Moments after Father Robinson was swept out of the courtroom, the jury was dismissed and left quickly, guarded by court deputies.

None of the jurors chose to speak to the media at the press conference downstairs.

The priest's brother Thomas and the rest of the supporters who had faithfully attended every day of the trial also shunned the press. The killer's close friend and colleague, Father Bernard Boff, said curtly, "No comment. Obviously, I have feelings. But no comment."

Lee Pahl, the victim's nephew, sped to Toledo from his hometown of Edgerton, near the Indiana border, arriving an hour after the verdict was announced.

"I'm just glad the long ordeal is finally over," he said with a grin.

Reporters for CNN, Court TV, and every Toledo-area television station raced to their vans, trailers and tents along Michigan Avenue to report on the verdict. Some stood on the lawn, microphones in hand, interviewing passersby, attorneys, or reporters who could spare a few minutes.

After announcing the stunning verdict, the media began gathering in the jury assembly room for the press conference.

Lucas County prosecutor Julia Bates took the first turn in the spotlight as members of the prosecution and cold-case teams lined up behind her. They were all reserved, but clearly elated that the case was over and the defendant behind bars.

"This was an extremely long and involved investigation," Bates said, "and I'm extremely proud of the very professional and very tactful performance displayed by the members of the prosecutor's office—Dean Mandros, Chris Anderson, Larry Kiroff, our newest assistant prosecutor Brad Smith, and investigators Steve Forrester, Tom Ross, and Tom Staff."

The prosecutor made a few more brief comments, then invited questions from the press.

What is the earliest that Father Robinson would be eligible for parole?

"It's a fifteen-years-to-life sentence and it would be up to the state parole board to determine when and if he would be released on parole," she said. "The earliest that that could occur would probably be at least ten and a half years."

How much did the trial cost?

"We've been expecting that question," she said with a smile. "The cost, to date, has been approximately $38,000. I guess I'd put it to you this way: 'What is the cost of a life?' I really do believe that $38,000 is really a small price to pay for justice in a twenty-six-year-old case."

What does the verdict mean to the community?

"What I hope it means is that we really do care about all of the victims, not just this victim because this case has generated so much publicity."

Were you confident that the jury would convict Father Robinson?

"We never know," Bates said. "We don't know. We can't know."

It was then Mandros's turn to face the media.

"We full well understand the fascination with the facts of this case and why all of you are here, and we understand it's an unlikely factual situation that will ever be repeated," he said. "But I think it's important to also recognize that, ultimately, this was just a murder case where a woman met a very horrific and undeserved death. And that's something important to keep in mind.

"We worked on this case for years, literally, and no one could really understand the amount of hours that have been put into this prosecution. It started really with the cold-case investigators Steve Forrester and Tom Ross. When they first started discussing the case with us, we weren't initially any more excited than the prosecutors were back in 1980. But between their work effort and their investigation and their willingness to keep moving forward, they produced enough evidence to where we felt it certainly was our obligation to go forward."

He also credited prosecutor Bates.

"Mrs. Bates had a lot of courage. The Catholic Church is an institution, it's something that you're not anxious to necessarily be on the other side of," Mandros said.

How do you feel about the verdict?

"We're very satisfied with the verdict, obviously. The case presented obvious hurdles in terms of what we needed to overcome. The age of the case was a factor that had to be dealt with. The fact that the defendant was a priest was a factor that we had to deal with. However, I will tell you that we always believed in the arguments that we were making. We always believed we were prosecuting the right individual. We always believed that the letter opener was clearly the murder weapon. We always believed that he lied to the police about his whereabouts, and that there wouldn't be any reason for him to make the lies he made unless he was trying to protect himself."

Did the priest's not taking the stand hurt his defense?

"Well, I don't know what to do about him not testifying. I mean, you can draw your own inferences from that."

What about his demeanor during the trial—just staring blankly ahead most of the time?

"Regarding his demeanor, I don't know what to make of that, either," Mandros said. "If you were in the courtroom during break, you saw a different side of the person. He was up and active and laughing and interacting with people. And when he sat at counsel table, he had another demeanor entirely. He was able to take himself someplace else."

Bates was then asked about the prosecutor's office crediting the Toledo Catholic diocese for its cooperation. When the question was asked, Mandros and Chris Anderson, standing off to the side of the podium, looked at one another with raised eyebrows.

"Well, this case wasn't about that," Bates said. "Dean was absolutely right, this case was about anger and about the death of a virginal servant of the Lord. So whatever involvement there was with us getting information and cooperation, it's really not about that and I really don't want to go into that."

Where is Father Robinson now?

"Well, he's probably in the Lucas County jail," Bates said, "and they will be transporting him to the [Northwest Ohio] Corrections Center, where they will do a classification, and an intake report, just like on any other prisoner. And it would be the Ohio Department of Rehabilitation and Correction that would ultimately decide where he would be located."

After the prosecutor's office was finished, defense attorneys Thebes, Konop and Khoury—Callahan did not join them—entered the media room looking exhausted and, understandably, dejected.

"Obviously, we are extremely disappointed with the outcome," Thebes said, his eyes red and watery. "Today is difficult. But the jury has spoken and, unfortunately, that's the way it is."

He said he thought the low point of his professional career had been the day he first met with Father Robinson in jail after the priest's arrest in April 2004. "Today," he said, "is much worse."

Konop was asked what the defense might have done differently, in retrospect, but he cut the question short with a wave of his hand.

"What was done was done. The verdict was rendered. We respect the verdict, and there will be an appeal and we do think there are some appealable issues."

He said he was worried about Father Robinson's health.

"He's not well. He's not very well," Konop said, refusing to elaborate. "That's a real, real serious concern."

Prison life will not be easy for the frail, elderly priest, he said.

"Well, he'll be in an environment that's a pretty rough environment," Konop said. "It can be very, very difficult for him."

At the former Mercy Hospital where the 1980 murder took place, the president of the Sisters of Mercy religious order, Sister Marjorie Rudemiller, held a press conference later that day.

"We have prayed for truth to prevail and for a fair and just trial. The jury has spoken, and we respect their decision," Sister Marjorie said. "God's grace enables us to forgive the person who caused her death."

Bishop Leonard Blair did not meet with the media in person, but instead issued a statement.

"This is a sad day for the Diocese of Toledo. In the matter of the State of Ohio versus Gerald Robinson, a jury of his peers has convicted him of the 1980 murder of Sister Margaret Ann Pahl," the bishop said.

"I ask for prayers for all of those involved—Sister Margaret Ann, her family, and the Sisters of Mercy, as well as those witnesses who testified at the trial, the jury, the judge and the attorneys who participated, and for Father Robinson.

"Let us hope that the conclusion of the trial will bring some measure of healing for all those affected by the case as well as for our local church."

Meanwhile, Gerald John Robinson was behind bars in a stark concrete room in the county jail, where he was patted down, fingerprinted, and photographed like every new incoming inmate.

Some of the other prisoners recognized him and shouted through their cell bars at the slump-shouldered cleric. "Father, did you do it? Did you kill the nun?"

Listed as five feet seven, 180 pounds, the priest stripped off his black jacket, his clerical collar, and other clothing and exchanged them for a faded brown prison jumpsuit.

Sheriff's deputies took an inventory of his possessions, which they placed in Bin No. 182: a set of keys, a set of rosary beads, a Saint Christopher medal, a white handkerchief, and a wallet containing a hundred dollar bill, a fifty dollar bill, and four one-dollar bills.

Robinson was then taken to Cell No. 9, on the second floor, a six-foot-by-eight-foot room with concrete walls, a built-in cot, a toilet, and a sink. There was a steel door with a window and a food slot, and an opaque window lined with metal slats.

Jail officials placed the priest on "Strict Code 1"—suicide precaution—which was standard procedure for all new inmates. They checked on him every ten minutes and barred him from having linens, towels, or shoestrings.

On May 18, a week after the verdict, the retired priest was taken by transport van to the Correctional Reception Center southwest of Columbus to undergo screenings and assessments. A few days later, he was transferred to Warren Correctional Institution in Lebanon, Ohio, a high-security prison with more than a thousand hard-core inmates.

Survivor Doe, the anonymous Toledo woman who sued Father Robinson alleging he abused her and tortured her in satanic rituals when she was a child, said she watched the trial all the way through on television.

"I watched and I prayed and I prayed. The minute they read the verdict, I hit the floor," she said. "Everything was released. I had the sense of peace I've been searching for."

On June 26, John Donahue, a local attorney and former assistant Wood County prosecutor, notified the Ohio Sixth District Court of Appeals that he would represent Father Robinson in appealing his murder conviction.

Several weeks later, Mandros sat in his courthouse office and reflected on the unique case that had consumed so much of his life for the last two years.

He said he firmly believed everything he said in his closing arguments, including his theory that the priest killed Sister Margaret Ann Pahl in a fit of anger.

He acknowledged that several experts in church ritual and the occult were convinced that the murder was a satanic ritual killing—one of the most classic cases they had ever seen.

Mandros said he believed he could convince a majority of jurors of that scenario, but not all twelve of them. And the verdict had to be unanimous.

"It's hard enough to get them to believe that a priest did this. Let alone that a priest did this as part of a satanic ritual. It's just too far out of the normal range of experience for people to buy into," he said.

Although the assistant prosecutor is convinced that Father Robinson killed Sister Margaret Ann Pahl in a fit of rage, there is one man who could change his mind.

"Only one person really knows what happened in that sacristy," Mandros said. "And he's sitting in a prison cell right now. Maybe someday he'll talk."